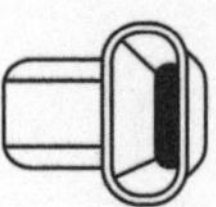

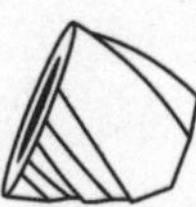

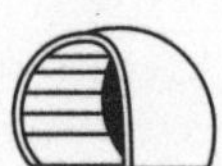

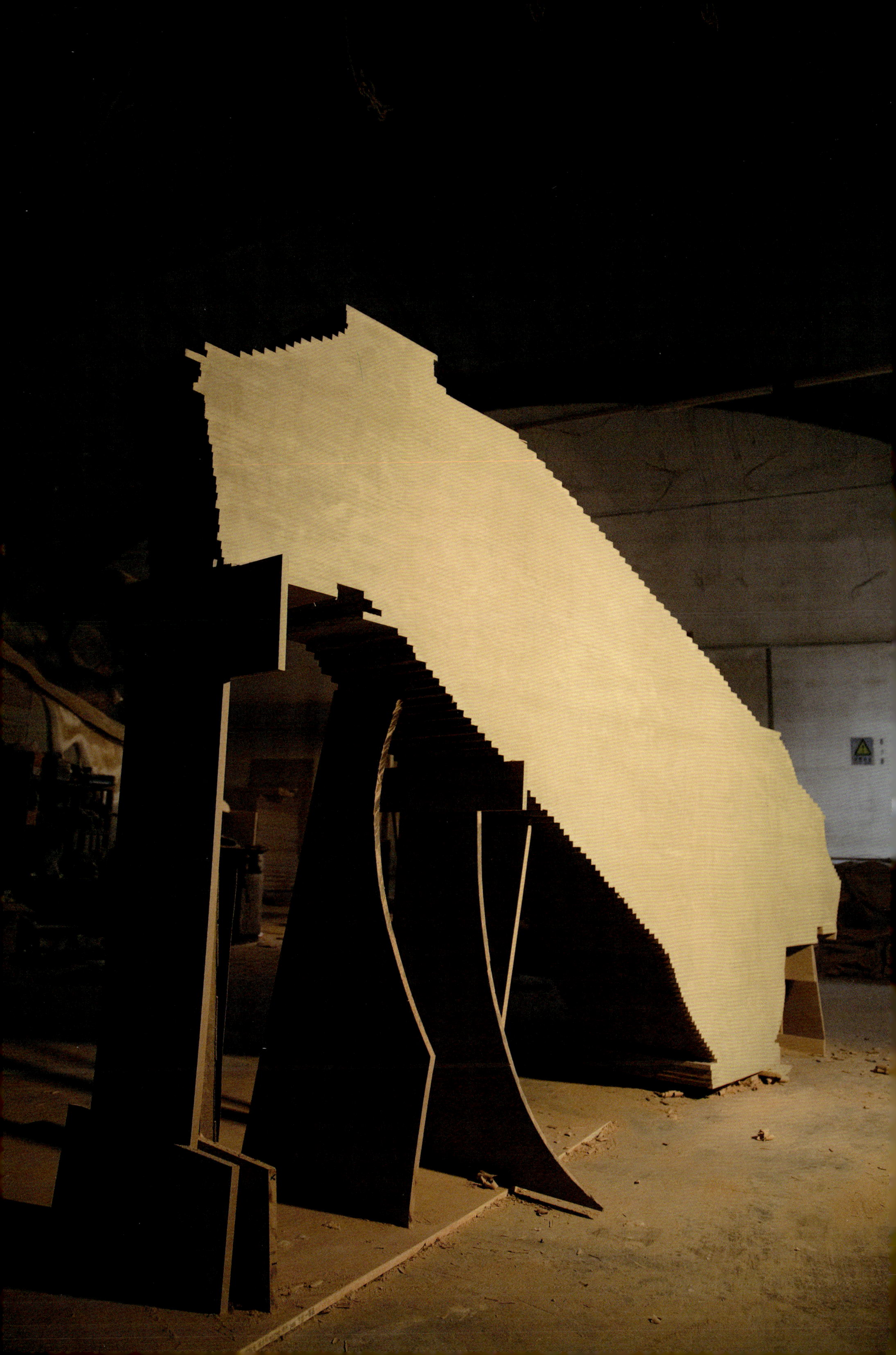

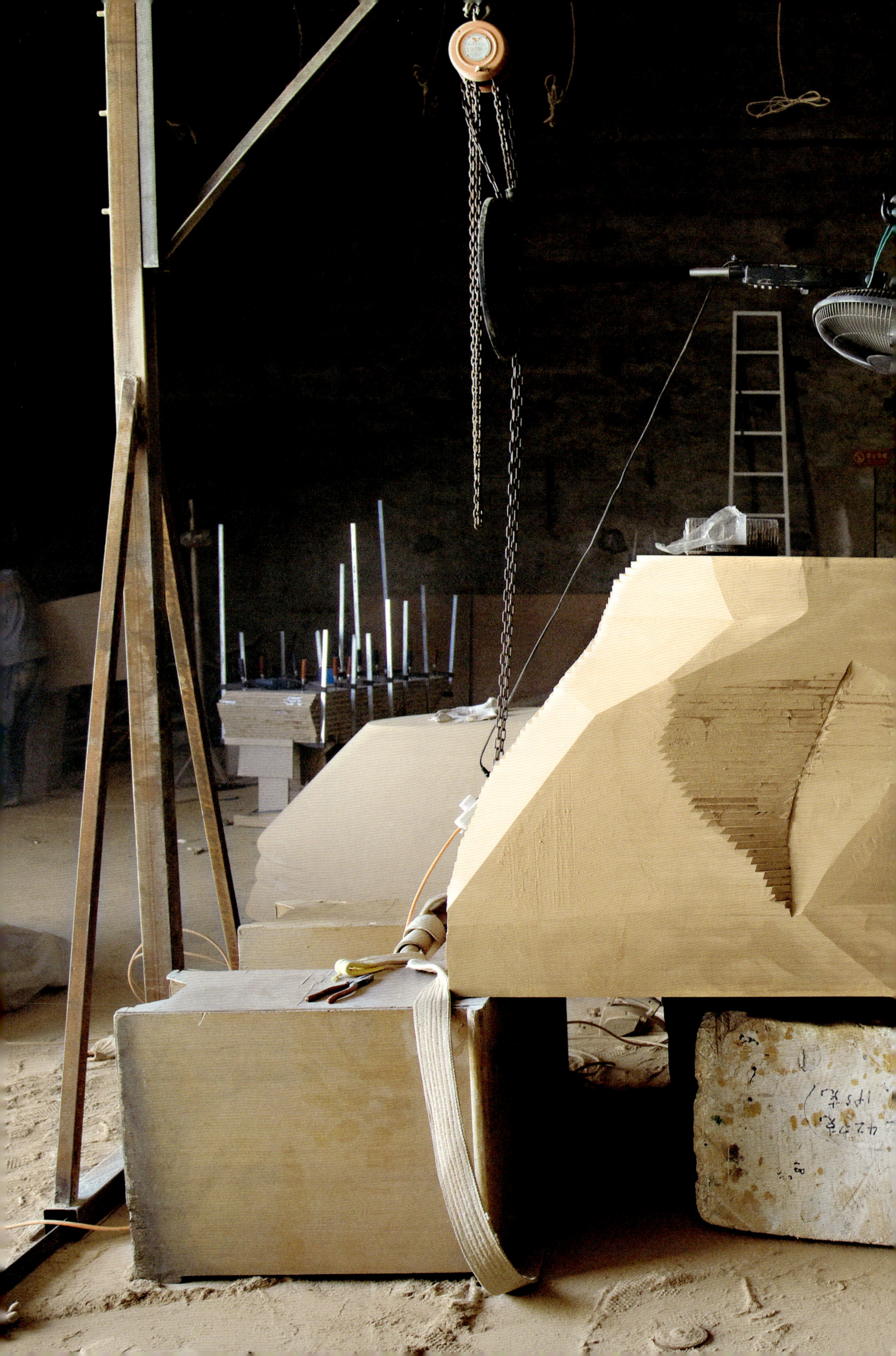

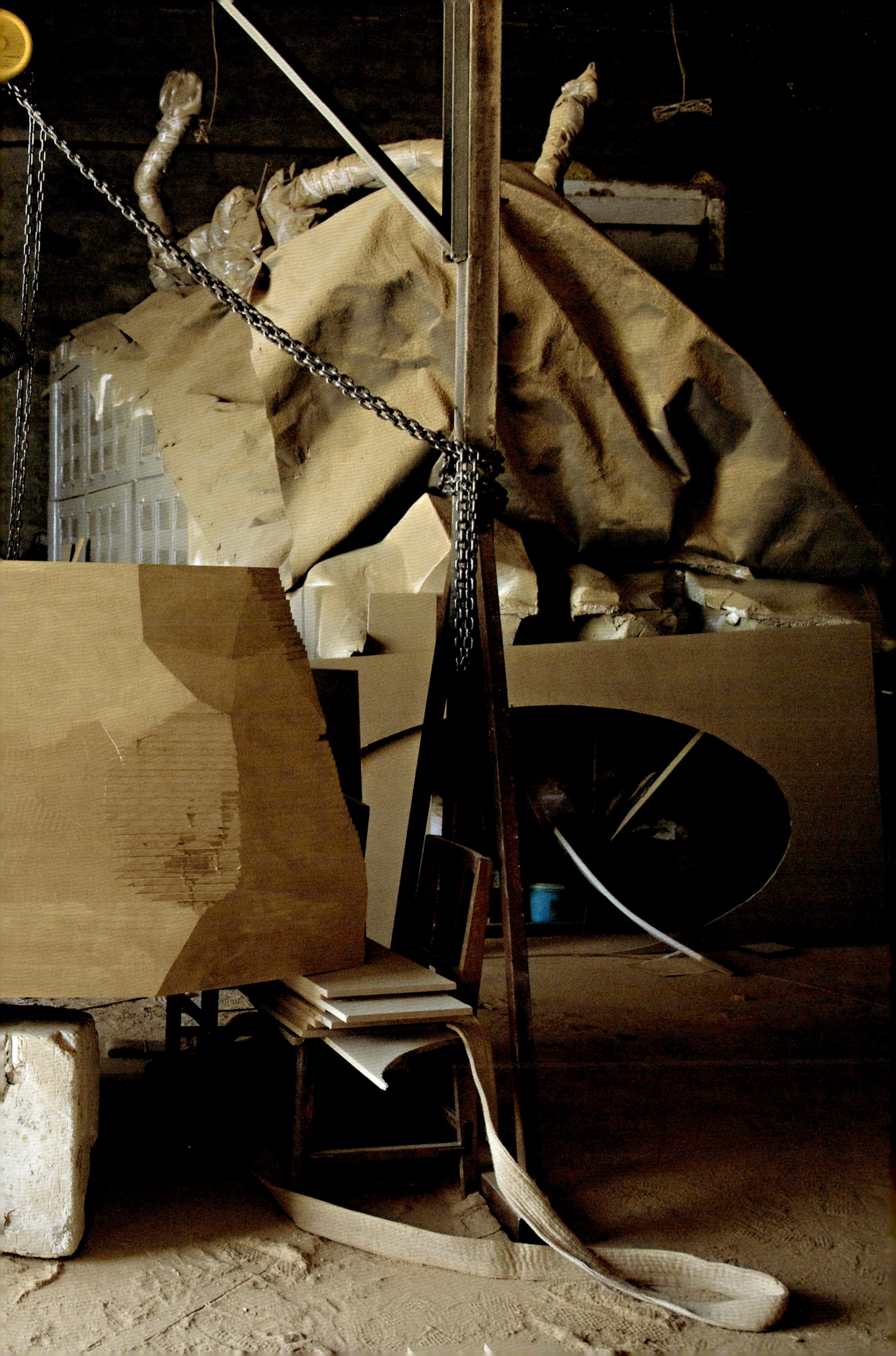

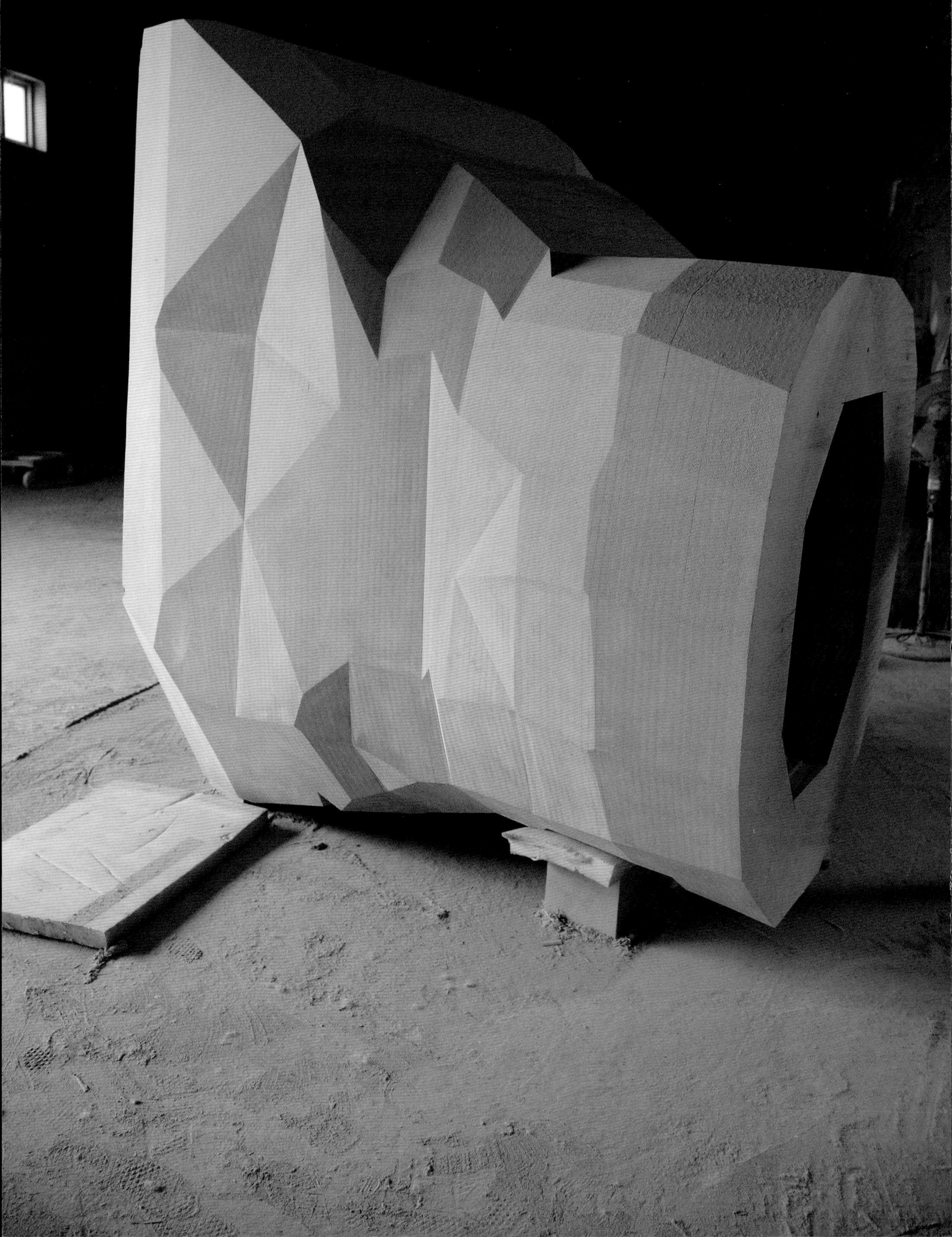

wang jianwei time temple

汪建偉：時間寺

GUGGENHEIM

Published on the occasion of the exhibition

Wang Jianwei: Time Temple
This exhibition is made possible by The Robert H. N. Ho Family Foundation.

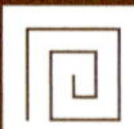
何鴻毅家族基金
THE ROBERT H. N. HO FAMILY FOUNDATION

Solomon R. Guggenheim Museum, New York
October 31, 2014–February 16, 2015

ISBN: 978-0-89207-516-4

Guggenheim Museum Publications
1071 Fifth Avenue, New York, New York 10128
guggenheim.org

Available through
ARTBOOK | D.A.P.
155 Sixth Avenue, 2nd Floor, New York, New York 10013
artbook.com

Distributed outside the United States and Canada by
Thames & Hudson, Ltd.
181A High Holborn Road, London WC1V 7QX, United Kingdom
thamesandhudson.com

Design: Sarah Gephart and Federico Pérez Villoro, MGMT. Design
Editorial: Elizabeth Franzen and Katherine Atkins
Production: Minjee Cho
Chinese to English Translation: Lee Ambrozy, Rebecca Karl, and Jenny Lee
English to Chinese Translation: Shu-Wen Lin
Printed in Italy by Trifolio

Cover: Wang Jianwei, *Time Temple*, 2014 (detail, pp. 54–55)
Back cover: The three icons are graphic representations by Wang Jianwei and were created during the artist's proposal for the commission *Time Temple*. These icons represent the three spaces in the Guggenheim Museum where the artist's work would reside during the exhibition, and which include (from top to bottom): Annex Level 2, the rotunda, and the Peter B. Lewis Theater.

《汪建偉：時間寺》出版於展覽之際
此展覽由何鴻毅家族基金支持贊助

所羅門．R．古根海姆美術館
2014年10月31日－2015年2月16日

ISBN: 978-0-89207-516-4

古根海姆美術館出版品
紐約州紐約市第五大道1071號，10128

發行
ARTBOOK | D.A.P.
紐約州紐約市第六大道155號2樓，10013

美國及加拿大以外地區經銷發行
Thames & Hudson, Ltd.
英國倫敦High Holborn路181A號，WC1V 7QX

設計：Sarah Gephart及Federico Pérez Villoro，MGMT. Design
編輯：Elizabeth Franzen及Katherine Atkins
製作： Minjee Cho
中譯英：安靜、柯瑞佳及李晉美
英譯中：林淑雯
印刷：義大利Trifolio

封面：汪建偉，《時間寺》，2014年（作品局部，第56頁）
封底：這三個圖示是汪建偉的藝術家作品示意圖，創作於委約計劃《時間寺》的提案期間；這三個圖像重現藝術家作品在古根海姆展覽期間，所使用的三個空間，從上到下分別是：二號塔樓、圓形大廳以及Peter B. Lewis劇院。

Contents

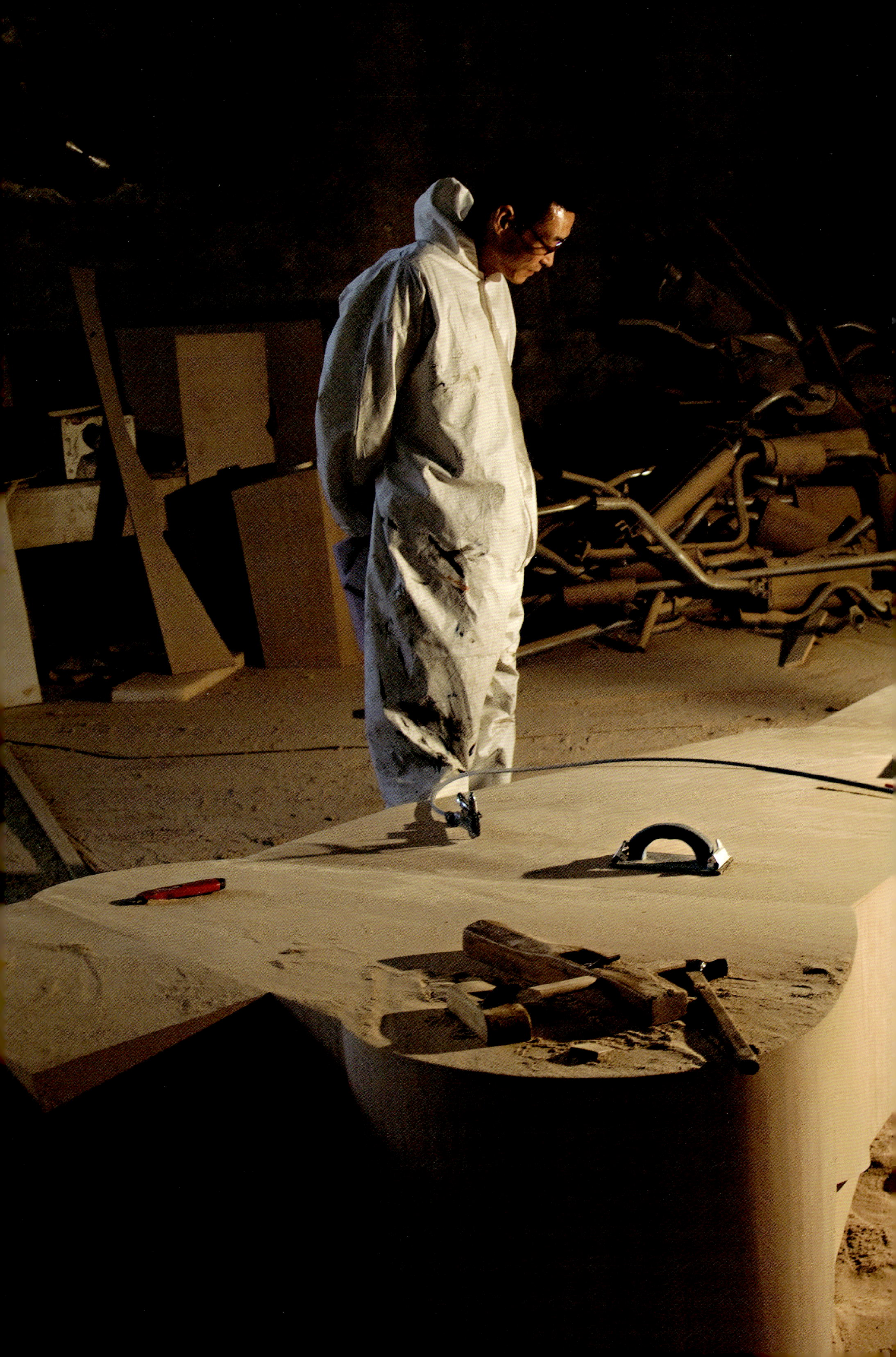

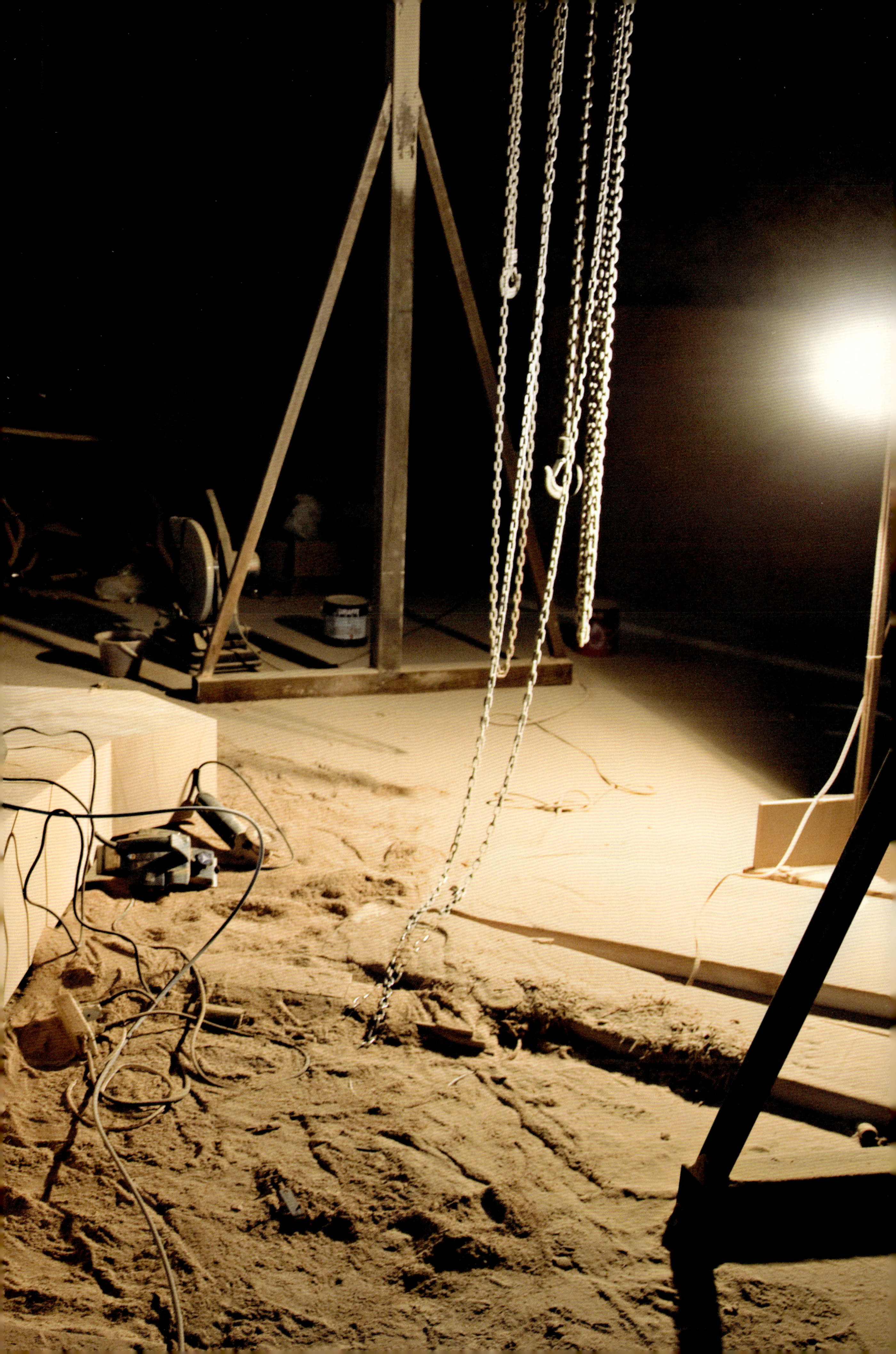

THE SOLOMON R. GUGGENHEIM FOUNDATION

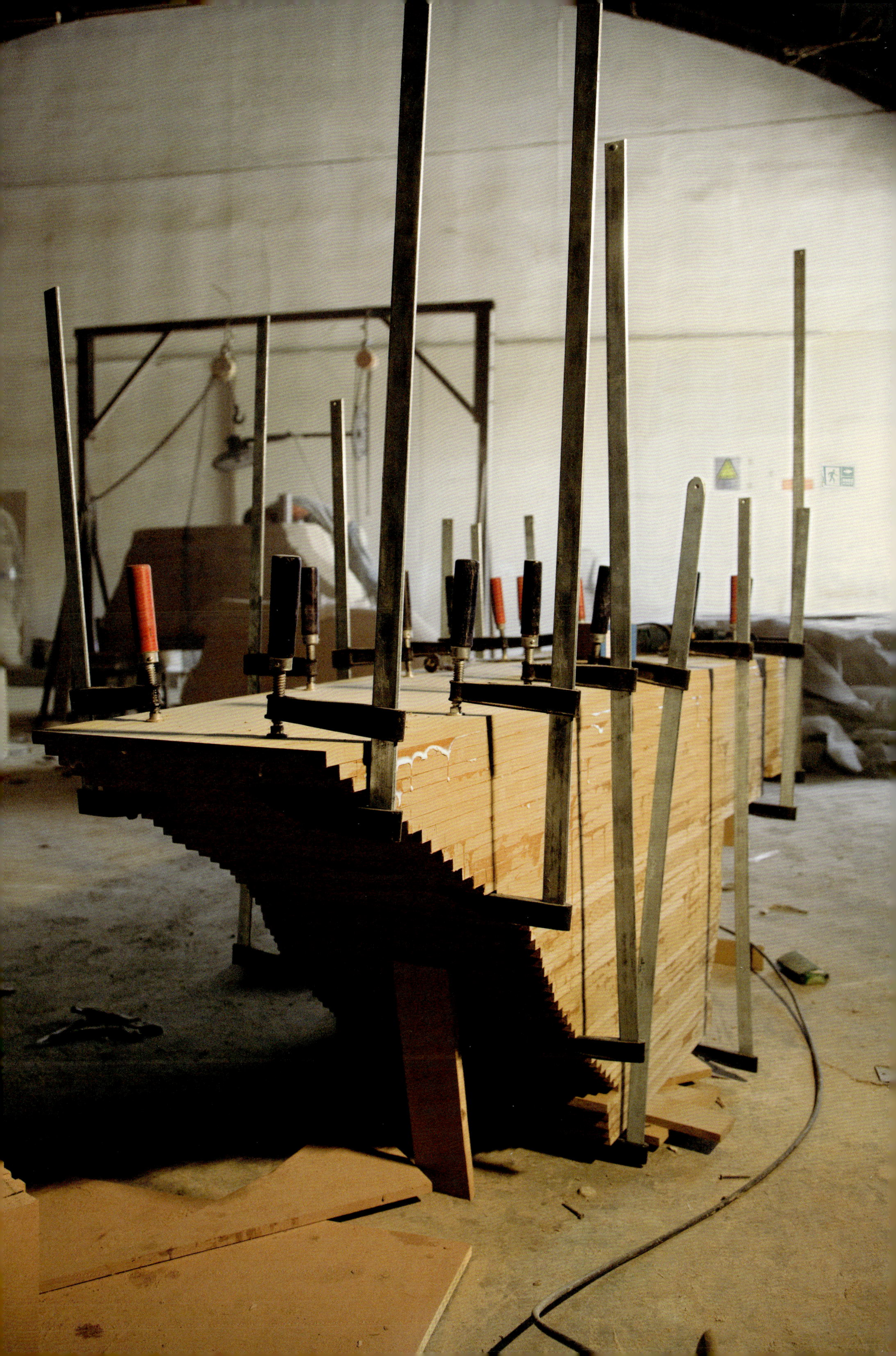

Statement

Robert Yau Chung Ho

Chairman, The Robert H. N. Ho Family Foundation

Almost a decade ago, my father Robert H. N. Ho established our family foundation focusing on two important themes: Chinese arts and culture, and Buddhism. We approach Chinese culture broadly, supporting projects that highlight its history and heritage, as well as encourage the expansion of contemporary artistic culture.

The Robert H. N. Ho Family Foundation and the Solomon R. Guggenheim Foundation have worked together on several projects in recent years. Our collaboration is based on a shared strategic vision to advance the field of contemporary art, without which modern Chinese society and culture would not be complete. We are proud to support The Robert H. N. Ho Family Foundation Chinese Art Initiative, as it not only contributes to the realization of this vision but it will also provide additional impetus for the current globalization of Chinese culture in which contemporary art is one of the most visible elements. Furthermore, we believe this initiative, under the expert stewardship of the Guggenheim, will strengthen the discourse, scholarship, and thinking around contemporary Chinese art, while fortifying creativity and integrity in the field.

Wang Jianwei is an artist who has been deeply involved within the Chinese art community since the 1980s. He is recognized for his exceptional work in a variety of artistic mediums and admired for his intelligent and thought-provoking observations of contemporary Chinese art and society. It is fully deserved that such a wide-ranging and influential artist has been chosen to create a body of work for the first commission of The Robert H. N. Ho Family Foundation Chinese Art Initiative. We welcome *Time Temple* with great excitement and we sincerely hope that those who experience the exhibition, and the associated outreach and educational programs, will gain a deeper insight into China's visual culture, both past and present.

Finally, we would like to express our heartfelt gratitude to the entire Guggenheim staff under director Richard Armstrong's leadership for their vision and professionalism in the development and realization of this project.

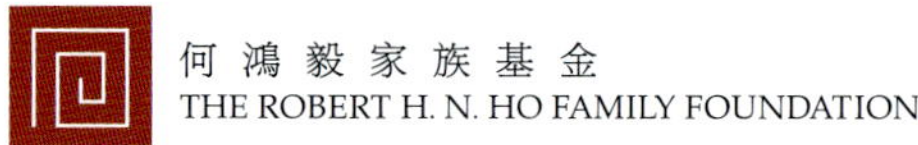

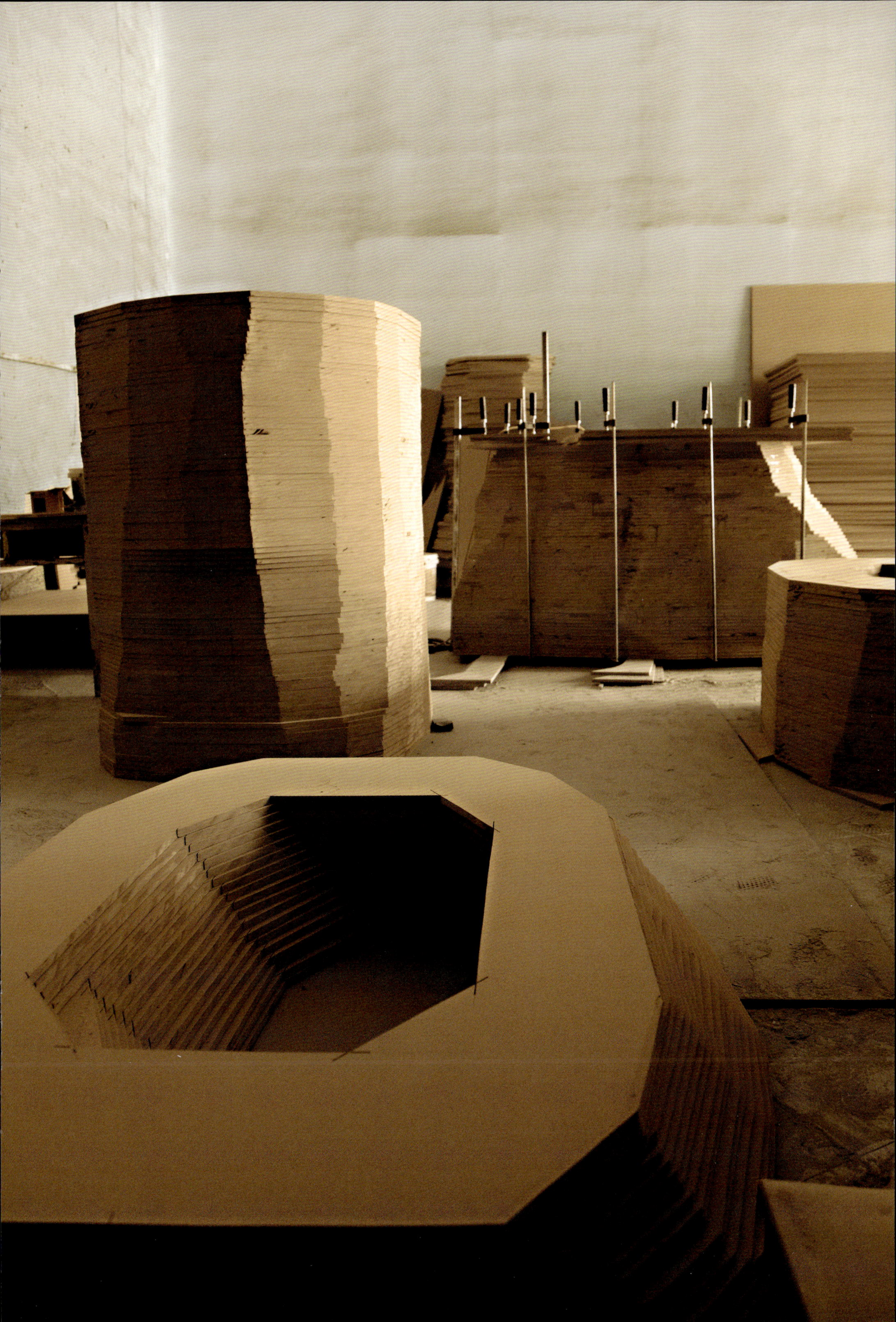

Foreword

Richard Armstrong

Director, Solomon R. Guggenheim Museum and Foundation

The Solomon R. Guggenheim Museum has long upheld the visionary and often provocative work of living artists, from Vasily Kandinsky to Tino Sehgal, Louise Bourgeois to Anish Kapoor. More recently, the museum has strengthened its curatorial and educational programs to present global perspectives on modern and contemporary art. These rich, diverse points of view should expand the public's thinking as well as the Guggenheim Museum's abiding engagement with the art of our time. The selection of Wang Jianwei as the Guggenheim Museum's first commissioned artist for The Robert H. N. Ho Family Foundation Chinese Art Initiative at the Guggenheim furthers the museum's dedication to exploring less examined trajectories of contemporary art with the potential to inspire contemporary modes of creative expression, critical thinking, and cultural understanding.

Wang Jianwei: Time Temple is the first North American museum exhibition devoted to the influential Beijing-based artist and thinker Wang Jianwei. With a career that spans three decades, Wang is a pioneering artist whose work reconciles classical Chinese thought, postmodern philosophy, and contemporary visual culture. The Guggenheim is proud to present Wang's ambitious exhibition illustrating the full scope of his creativity in sculpture, painting, film, and theater.

The exhibition was developed under the auspices of The Robert H. N. Ho Family Foundation Chinese Art Initiative and made possible by a major grant from the Foundation that includes the creation of a new curatorial position specializing in Chinese art, and the commissioning of major artworks by three artists or groups of artists from mainland China, Taiwan, Hong Kong, or Macao over a five-year period. The newly commissioned works will enter the Guggenheim's permanent collection as The Robert H. N. Ho Family Foundation Collection. Each commission will be exhibited at the museum in New York between 2014 and 2017, and each will be accompanied by a robust offering of publications, lecture series, and educational programs.

We deeply value our long-term relationship with The Robert H. N. Ho Family Foundation and are grateful to collaborate on a program that fosters creativity and enhances the international discourse on contemporary Chinese art. We offer our sincerest thanks to Robert H. N. Ho, Founder, and Robert Y. C. Ho, Chairman, who have championed this project from the outset and recognized the significance of commissioning Chinese artists and presenting their work within the context of the Guggenheim's international collections and programs. Ted Lipman,

Chief Executive Officer, and Jean Miao, Director of Operations, have facilitated our good work with the Foundation; this project would not be possible without their keen support and advice.

Wang Jianwei: Time Temple is organized by Thomas J. Berghuis, who joined the Guggenheim as The Robert H. N. Ho Family Foundation Curator of Chinese Art in 2013. His close work with Wang and the artist's studio on the initiative's first commission reflects his extensive knowledge and experience and ensures the lasting impact of this project. Thomas's deep investment in the Asian art community has also strengthened the museum's collegial network, furthering relationships for future projects.

Under the leadership of Alexandra Munroe, Samsung Senior Curator of Asian Art, the Asian Art Initiative, now in its eighth year, continues to advance and disseminate the achievements of modern and contemporary Asian art and enlarge the institution's related global arts programs. Through the acquisition of works into the collection, international exhibitions, and educational outreach for scholars and the public, we mean to prove our global commitment.

The Guggenheim's international arts initiatives enjoy the unfailing support of the Solomon R. Guggenheim Foundation Board of Trustees. We offer special thanks to Jennifer Blei Stockman, President, for her encouragement, and to John S. Wadsworth Jr., Trustee Emeritus, and his wife, Susy, for their extraordinary philanthropic focus on contemporary Asian art.

On behalf of the trustees, I offer deepest thanks to Wang Jianwei for his commitment to The Robert H. N. Ho Chinese Art Initiative and for the extraordinary art he has produced for the commission. His works will carry institutional history and stimulate greater understanding and appreciation of art from China today.

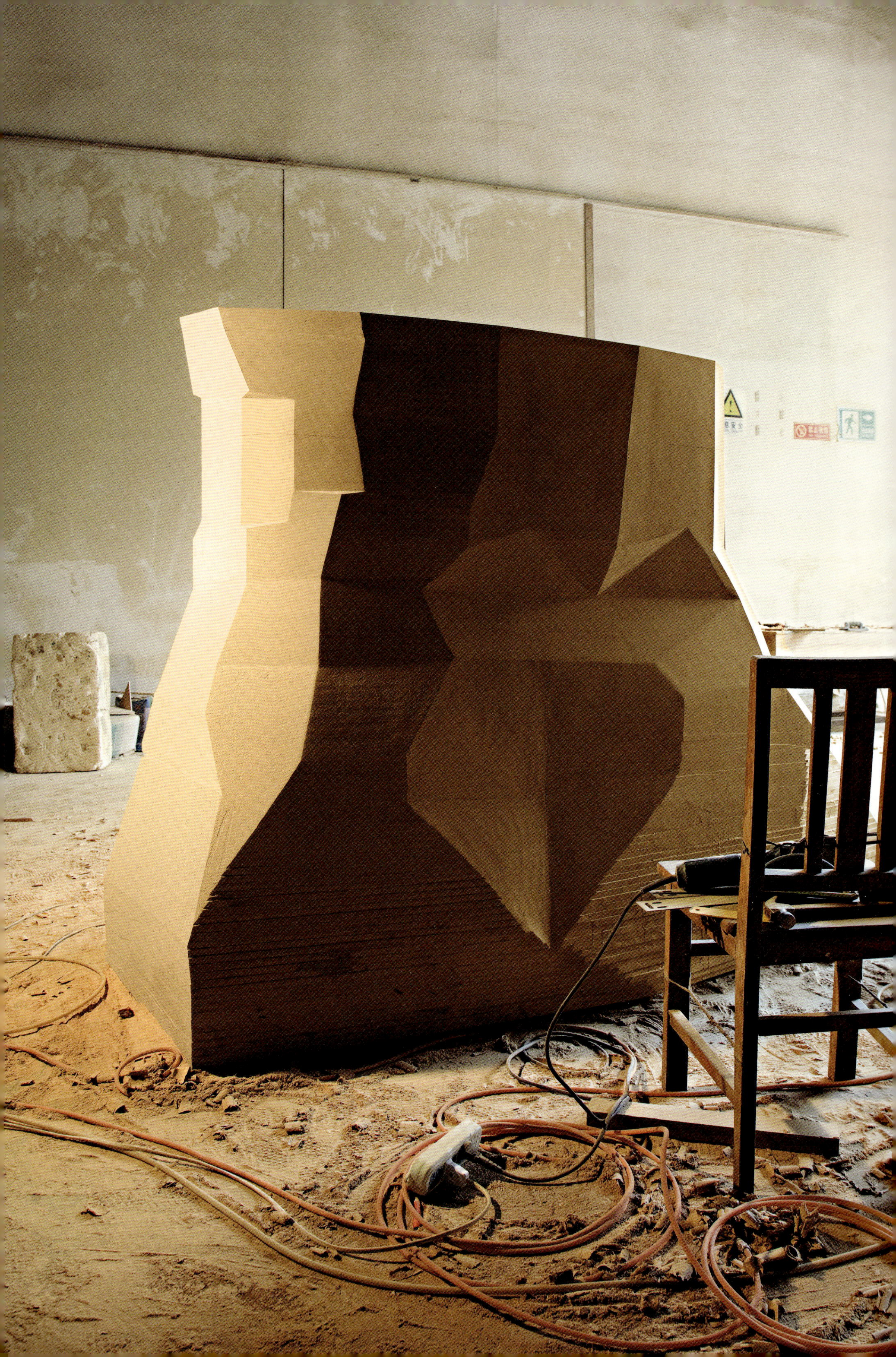

Acknowledgments

Thomas J. Berghuis

The Robert H. N. Ho Family Foundation Curator of Chinese Art

Wang Jianwei: Time Temple is both a timely acknowledgment of the highly innovative work of the Beijing-based artist Wang Jianwei and the first in a series of three exhibitions of commissions by Chinese artists that will enter the Solomon R. Guggenheim Museum's collection as part of The Robert H. N. Ho Family Foundation Collection. Deepest thanks are due to Richard Armstrong, Director of the Solomon R. Guggenheim Museum and Foundation, under whose leadership the Guggenheim has continued to initiate incisive curatorial programs in an international context. Richard has given this project his full attention, passion, and support along with his always sage advice. I owe sincere gratitude to Nancy Spector, Deputy Director and Jennifer and David Stockman Chief Curator, Solomon R. Guggenheim Foundation, for her stewardship and support of innovative curatorial practice. Alexandra Munroe, Samsung Senior Curator of Asian Art, Solomon R. Guggenheim Museum, has been a true mentor and an inspiring colleague, driving this initiative to its full potential by instilling rigor and precision in this project's attempt to expand the discourse of contemporary Chinese art.

A pioneer of contemporary Chinese art, Wang Jianwei has created a body of work that merits further attention and study. Wang considers important new directions in contemporary art by incorporating time-based processes of painting, sculpture, installation, theater, performance, and film production into his practice. His work reflects the versatile context in which contemporary Chinese art is being produced today. I thank the artist for his great vision, depth of research, and profound engagement with the history and vision of the Guggenheim Museum by creating a "time temple" for contemporary art. Wang has also been one of the most kindhearted artists with whom I have worked. I would especially like to recognize his wife, Zhu Guangyan, for her invaluable support during the process of developing this new work and for being such a wonderful host during my many visits to Beijing.

At the Wang Jianwei Studio, the artist and Studio Manager Xu Boxin; Studio Coordinator Wu Fei (Flora); and the studio team deserve sincere acknowledgment for their dedication throughout this endeavor. At the Long March Space, Beijing, I thank Lu Jie, Founder; David Tung, Gallery Director; Theresa Liang, Director, International Programs; and the entire team, whose support for Wang's work has been instrumental in planning this commission. At Chambers Fine Art, New York, Christophe Mao, Founder and Director, and John Tancock, Director, have provided long-term support for the artist's work and have facilitated widespread interest in contemporary Chinese art through their galleries in New York and Beijing.

This exhibition would not have been possible without The Robert H. N. Ho Family Foundation, under the direction of Robert H. N. Ho and Robert Y. C. Ho. Their long-standing philanthropy has furthered the understanding of Chinese art and culture worldwide. Robert H. N. Ho invests this project with great knowledge of Chinese culture. Robert Y. C. Ho has been someone with whom I have also shared many valuable conversations on contemporary art. Ted Lipman, Chief Executive Officer, The Robert H. N. Ho Family Foundation, has provided his strong vision and lent his in-depth knowledge of Chinese culture and art, and Meiyee Wong, Program Director, and Janet Tong, Public Relations and Communications Manager, have been instrumental in working with us on the initiative. I would like to especially thank Jean Miao, Director of Operations, for her wonderful character, great insight, and strong familiarity with contemporary Chinese art.

The Guggenheim's Asian Art Council was formed as a curatorial think tank in 2006 to advise on the critical issues emerging in Asian cultural studies, global art history, and artistic practice today. The council has contributed thoughtful guidance to this initiative, and I would like to acknowledge the 2014 membership: Apinan Poshyananda, acting Minister of Culture and Permanent Secretary of Ministry of Culture, Government of Thailand; Geremie Barmé, Director, Australian Centre on China in the World, and Professor of Chinese History, Australian National University, Canberra; Iftikhar Dadi, Chair and Associate Professor, Department of Art, Cornell University, Ithaca, New York; Jane DeBevoise, Chair, Board of Directors, Asia Art Archive, Hong Kong and New York; Okwui Enwezor, Director, Haus der Kunst, Munich; Patrick Flores, Curator, Jorge B. Vargas Museum and Filipiniana Research Center, and Professor, Department of Art Studies, University of the Philippines Diliman, Quezon City; Geeta Kapur, critic and curator, New Delhi; Mami Kataoka, Chief Curator, Mori Art Museum, Tokyo; Hongnam Kim, independent curator and former Director, National Museum of Korea, Seoul; Kian-Chow Kwok, Senior Advisor, National Gallery Singapore; Dinh Q. Lê, artist, Ho Chi Minh City; Qiu Zhijie, artist and Professor, School of Intermedia Art, China Academy of Art, Hangzhou; Enin Supriyanto, independent curator, Jakarta; Philip Tinari, Director, Ullens Center for Contemporary Art, Beijing; Wu Hung, Harrie A. Vanderstappen Distinguished Service Professor of Chinese Art History and Director, Center for the Art of East Asia, University of Chicago; and Zheng Shengtian, Managing Editor, *Yishu*, Vancouver.

At the Guggenheim Museum, words can never be enough to describe the tremendous work of The Robert H. N. Ho Family Foundation Chinese Art Initiative team of Stephanie Kwai, Assistant Curator, and Elissa Edgerton Black, Senior Project Manager. Stephanie worked closely with the Project Team and the artist's studio to support the implementation of this commission-based exhibition, catalogue, and related projects. Her rigorous scholarship, meticulous care, and consummate grace have assured the successful realization of *Time Temple*. Elissa expertly managed every aspect of this international project across all of the Guggenheim's departments, liaising with The Robert H. N. Ho Family Foundation in Hong Kong and with the artist's studio in Beijing to realize the project's ambitions. The Robert H. N. Ho Family Foundation Chinese Art Initiative is fundamentally dedicated to educational outreach, and we are grateful to work with Kim Kanatani, Deputy Director and Gail Engelberg Director of Education, and other colleagues listed as the Project Team. John L. Wielk, Deputy Director, Corporate and Institutional Development, and Kerri Schlottman-Bright, Director, Institutional Development, were crucial in uniting The Robert H. N. Ho Family Foundation with the Guggenheim for this collaboration.

The success of an initiative of such international scope will be measured by its impact. In this regard, we are fortunate for the leadership of Eleanor Goldhar, Deputy Director and Chief of Global Communications, and her expert team, including Betsy Ennis, former Director of Media and Public Relations, Renee Dumouchel, Associate Director, External Affairs, and Keri Murawski, Senior Publicist.

Special gratitude goes out to Elizabeth Levy, Managing Director, Publishing and Digital Media; Elizabeth Franzen, Associate Director, Editorial Affairs, and Project Manager for *Wang Jianwei: Time Temple*; Minjee Cho, Production Manager; and Katherine Atkins, Assistant Managing Editor, in the Publishing and Digital Media department for their unfailing dedication and support of the curatorial vision and for working with good humor and spirit through the complex editorial process to produce this catalogue. I would like to acknowledge the talented designers Sarah Gephart and Federico Pérez Villoro at MGMT.Design, who designed this book that reflects the artist's methodology so beautifully.

A project with this level of intellectual depth requires the input of many colleagues—artists, curators, writers, and critical thinkers. I would especially like to thank Gao Shiming, Director, School of Intermedia Art, China Academy of Art, for his thoughtful contribution to this volume. Artists Qiu Zhijie and Song Dong, as well as documentary filmmaker Wu Wenguang taught me early on about the value of art in contemporary China. Li Xianting, a Beijing-based independent curator and art critic, deserves special thanks for being an inspiration for my work in the field of Chinese art. John Clark, Emeritus Professor, Department of Art History and Film Studies, University of Sydney, shared his deep insight into Asian art history; Pi Li, Senior Curator and Uli Sigg Curator of Chinese Art, M+, Hong Kong, similarly proffered his invaluable knowledge of Chinese contemporary art.

At the Asia Art Archive, Hong Kong, Claire Hsu and the entire team encouraged our research. In New York, several pioneers of Asian art welcomed me to this city, including Melissa Chiu, Director, Hirshhorn Museum and Sculpture Garden, Washington, D.C., and former Director, Asia Society Museum; John Rajchman, Adjunct Professor, Department of Art History and Archaeology, Columbia University; Christopher Phillips, Curator, International Center for Photography; and Jane DeBevoise.

I am grateful to my family—my mother, Annette Fehrmann; my sister, Laura Fehrmann; and my late father, Jaap Berghuis—who have supported me from the Netherlands through all of my worldly adventures. Finally, I also extend my gratitude to my wife, Jenny Wong; daughter, Anouk Berghuis; and newborn son, Jakob Eli Berghuis, for being by my side. I would not be where I am today without their unconditional love and support.

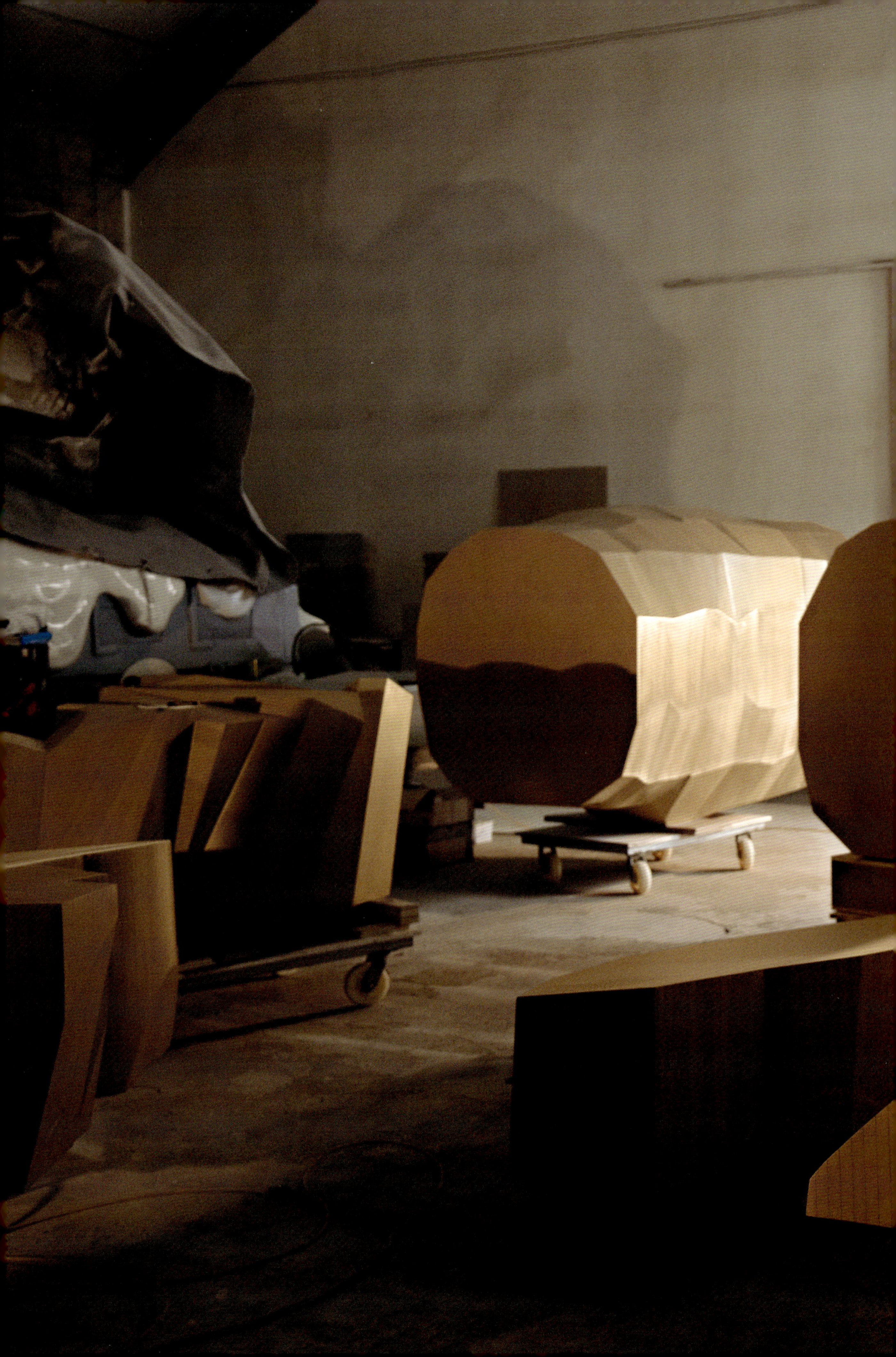

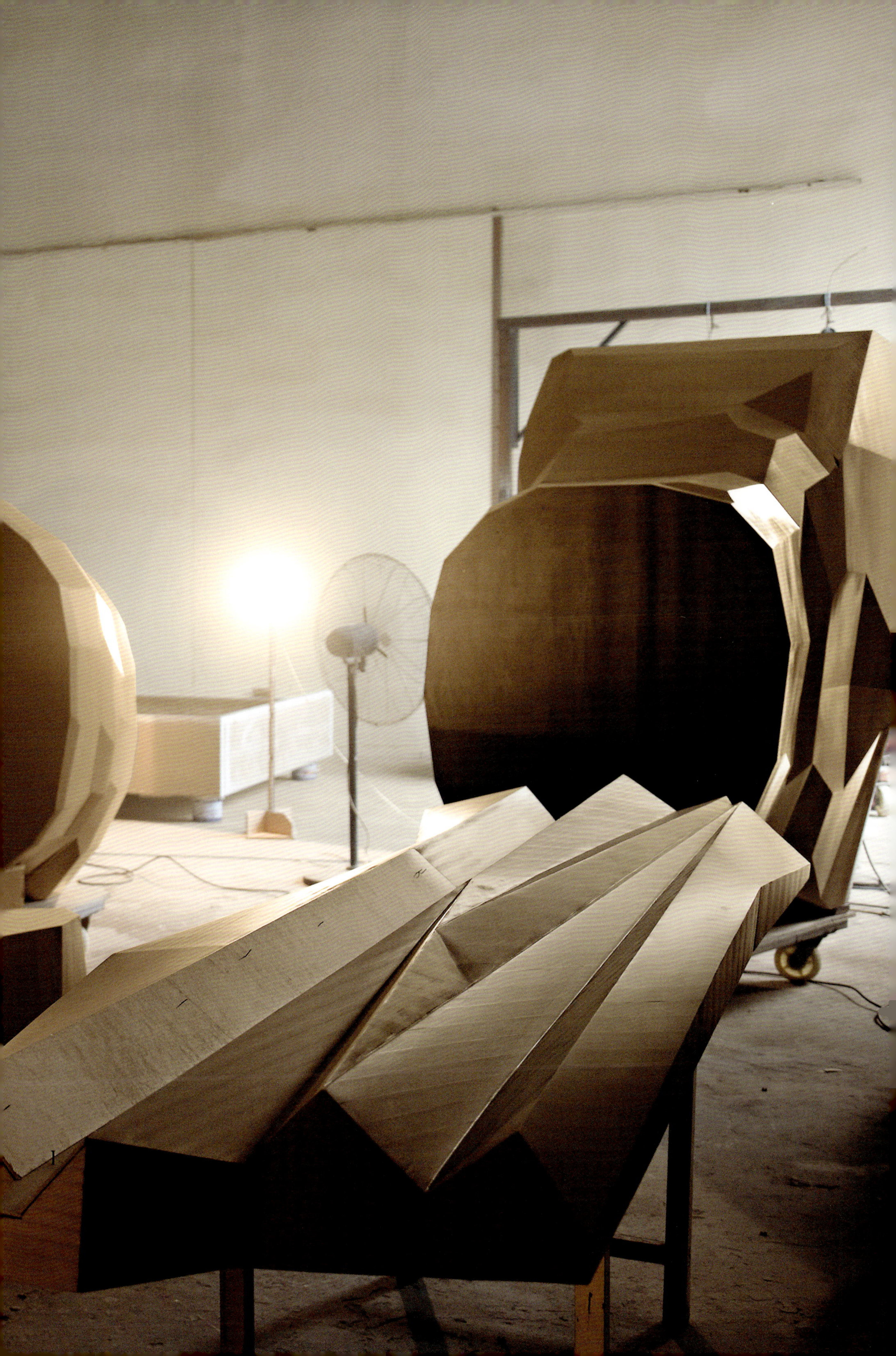

Project Team

ART SERVICES AND PREPARATION

David Bufano, *Director, Art Services and Preparation*

Barry Hylton, *Senior Manager, Exhibition Installations*

and the team

CONSERVATION

Julie Barten, *Senior Conservator, Collections and Exhibitions*

Joanna Phillips, *Conservator, Time-Based Media*

Esther Chao, *Associate Conservator, Objects*

CONSTRUCTION

Richard Burgess, *Head of Exhibition Construction*

and the team

CURATORIAL

Nancy Spector, *Deputy Director and Jennifer and David Stockman Chief Curator*

Alexandra Munroe, *Samsung Senior Curator, Asian Art*

Thomas J. Berghuis, *The Robert H. N. Ho Family Foundation Curator of Chinese Art*

Lauren Hinkson, *Assistant Curator, Collections*

Stephanie Kwai, *Assistant Curator, Asian Art*

Jeewon Kim, Siqiao Lu, Xiaorui Zhu, and Ying Zhu, *Asian Art Interns*

DEVELOPMENT

John L. Wielk, *Deputy Director, Corporate and Institutional Development*

Kerri Schlottman-Bright, *Director of Institutional Development*

Paola Zanzo-Sahl, *Director, Special Events*

Leah Moliterno, *Manager, Special Events*

EDUCATION

Kim Kanatani, *Deputy Director and Gail Engelberg Director of Education*

Sharon Vatsky, *Director of School and Family Programs*

Christina Yang, *Director of Public Programs*

Evelyn Peng, *Education Associate, Public Programs*

EXHIBITION DESIGN

Melanie Taylor, *Director, Exhibition Design*

Kelly Cullinan, *Exhibition Designer*

EXHIBITION MANAGEMENT

Jennifer Bose, *Director of Exhibition Management*

Elissa Edgerton Black, *Senior Project Manager, The Robert H. N. Ho Family Foundation Chinese Art Initiative*

Julia Zhang, *Project Coordinator, The Robert H. N. Ho Family Foundation Chinese Art Initiative*

EXTERNAL AFFAIRS

Eleanor Goldhar, *Deputy Director and Chief of Global Communications*

Renee Dumouchel, *Associate Director, External Affairs*

Kris Parker, *Senior Manager, Communications*

Alisha Levin, *Associate Manager of External Affairs, Special Initiatives*

FABRICATION

Peter Read, *Director, Fabrication*

Christopher George, *Chief Fabricator*

Doug Hollingsworth, *Chief Cabinetmaker*

Peter Mallo, *Chief Framemaker*

Rich Avery, *Technical and Production Specialist*

Chris Hanson, *Cabinetmaker/Fabricator*

Steven Ott, *Cabinetmaker*

FACILITIES

Peter Read, *Director of Facilities and Office Services*

Megan Chusid, *Associate Director of Facilities and Office Services*

Michael Zall, *Manager, Facilities Operations*

Ian Felmine, *Chief Engineer*

and the team

FINANCE

Lesley Lana, *Budget Manager*

Dafna Landau, *Senior Financial Analyst*

GRAPHIC DESIGN

Marcia Fardella, *Director, Graphic Design, and Chief Graphic Designer*

Janice I-Chiao Lee, *Design Manager, Graphic Design*

Peter Raphael Castro, *Production Manager, Graphic Design*

INTERACTIVE

Laura Kleger, *Director, Interactive*

Robert Duffy, *Interactive Project Manager*

Caitlin Dover, *Editor, Interactive*

LEGAL

Sarah Austrian, *Deputy Director, General Counsel, and Assistant Secretary*

Dana Wallach, *Associate General Counsel*

Yayoi Shionoiri, *Assistant General Counsel*

Kaleidoscopes

Thomas J. Berghuis

Rehearsal is the activity of latency, possibility, and continuity.
–Wang Jianwei

For Wang Jianwei, art making is a continuous rehearsal. He uses a process-based and iterative practice that incorporates theater and time-based performance into his paintings, installations, and films, challenging the boundaries of conventional mediums. Steeped in dense layers of history, reality, and memory, Wang's works are both conceptually driven and grounded in everyday life. He actively confronts the viewer with the ways in which Chinese society operates and with how individuals can find their own personal freedom. By doing so, he draws the viewer into manifold perspectives on social and political life in China, a kaleidoscope of reality, spectacle, and fiction. Wang thinks of his art as a strategy for human interaction, generating for the viewer new and creative engagements with culture, society, and daily life. Moreover, his examination of everyday reality in contemporary Chinese society informs his engagement with China as it relates to the rest of the world.

Like many in China, Wang and his family were sent down to the countryside during the Great Proletarian Cultural Revolution (1966–76).[1] Formal education was frowned upon, and most sources of learning were scarce. Wang recalls that in 1975, when he was seventeen, he came across a partial translation of the novel *Voskreseniye* (*Resurrection*, 1899) by Leo Tolstoy, whose literature and philosophy had influenced modern Chinese intellectuals since the early twentieth century. In this story, a man is tormented by the social injustices of his time and the consequences of his self-indulgences, and is thus forced to confront his own morality.[2] Wang's copy held only its middle section, leaving the missing first and final parts to his imagination. This vital need to fill in the lost parts of stories and the use of literature as inspiration became important driving forces for the artist.

During the 1980s, existentialist literature became popular in China as artists, writers, and intellectuals sought new humanistic values for the good of society. *Le Mythe de Sisyphe* (*The Myth of Sisyphus*, 1942) by Albert Camus was one particularly influential work. This essay about the absurd search for meaning in a world devoid of God, ideology, truth, and universal values befitted China's intellectual climate as it moved away from entrenched Maoist beliefs. Additionally, the 1980s witnessed a growing interest in Friedrich Nietzsche and his idea of the death of God, which compared closely to the death of Mao Zedong and Maoism.[3] Along with magical realism and absurdist fiction, these literary influences would shape Wang's concerted thinking on the conditions of human existence: while pursuing graduate studies at Zhejiang

Dodge, 2006

HD color video, with sound, 8 min., 23 sec.

RIGHT: video still

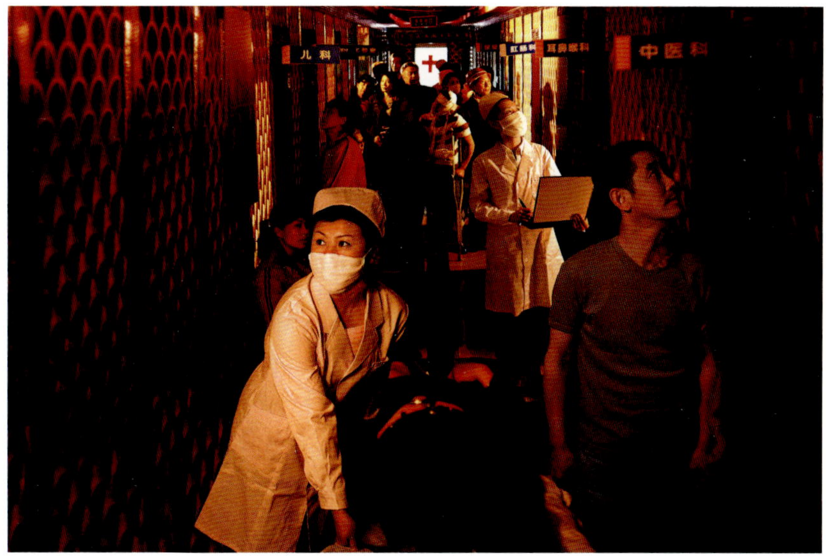

Academy of Fine Arts (now China Academy of Art) in Hangzhou from 1986 to 1988, Wang discovered the writings of Jorge Luis Borges, whose fanciful novels challenged the dominant notions of realism and naturalism. In his work, Borges poses reality as a series of uncertain relationships and focuses his stories on labyrinths, dreams, libraries, mirrors, and the concept of infinity. These motifs encouraged Wang to reflect further on the multiple layers of reality and fiction that can be invested in creating a work of art.

In further assessing Wang's inspiration and career, one must look to the New Measurement Group (Xin kedu). Founded in Beijing in 1988 by Gu Dexin, Wang Luyan, and Chen Shaoping, the New Measurement Group was instrumental in formulating a conceptual language for art. These artists would meet regularly to find common ground on every aspect of their work from types of material to working methods, thus creating a new rational and commonsensical art for China.[4] Wang also cites the influence of the Conceptual artist Joseph Kosuth, particularly the work *One and Three Chairs* (1965), which Wang saw in Paris in the late 1990s. The work features an object, an image, and text to represent the concept of a chair in three ways. According to Wang, it conveys "the idea that cognition occurs ahead of the arrival of physical objects."[5] These ideas inspired Wang to develop art forms that fundamentally question the social and political constructions of meaning, truth, and language.

Nowadays, Wang views his work as part of a "multimedia theater," a complex genre in which theater is the basis of all art forms, including painting, sculpture, installation, video, performance, and photography.[6] Moreover, his works realize the structures of contingency, process, and interaction, which more fully represent the dynamism of lived experience and one's sense of being in the world. His recent works move into direct contact with contemporary form and the formation of contemporary art through the concept of rehearsal. In his essay for this volume, Wang analyzes the rehearsal process as a particularly contemporary working method through its intimate bond with the time in which it occurs. As the artist stated further in his preparation for *Time Temple* (2014), the first commission for The Robert H. N. Ho Family Foundation Chinese Art Initiative at the Guggenheim Museum, "I have to convey the complexity of my thinking through form, not through language."[7] Part of this form is manifested in the rehearsal that links his practice to the art of theater.

Dodge, 2006

HD color video, with sound, 8 min., 23 sec.

RIGHT AND OVERLEAF: video still

Theater and the Art of Imaginary Realism

For Wang Jianwei, theater provides the stage on which to connect the push and pull of everyday reality, as layered through a kaleidoscope of perceptions. Wang often builds a social, political, and aesthetic model from which he stages an event, and whereby he creates work to advocate for social change. Theater is a form and a formation as well as "a place for exchanging information" in such a way that the viewer becomes an active participant in the work.[8]

In 2006, Wang produced *Dodge* (pp. 25, 27–28), whose video shows a carefully choreographed performance involving actors staging a multidimensional passage in which a karaoke bar, a train, the Chinese stock markets, and a hospital intersect in a dreamy Borgesian sequence.[9] In *Dodge*, the political realm is societal, mingling pleasure, disease, and the economy. The work captures the zeitgeist of contemporary life in urban China, a fusion of people's illusions and disillusions.

Many of Wang's works present elaborate social phenomena. *Hostage* (2008, pp. 29–31) examines how people in China, particularly throughout the twentieth century, have been held captive by history and ideology. Comprising an installation, a video, and eight photographs, *Hostage* was first conceived as an intricate theater production in front of a camera—carefully staged, choreographed, and directed in the artist's studio.[10] The video starts with a well-known image of a shepherd, a peasant girl, and a soldier: all key symbols of the Maoist revolutionary forces (p. 29). The video is set in a large, redbrick building where workers, peasants, and soldiers perform prescribed recreational activities and movements based on revolutionary Chinese culture. In the end, the redbrick structure collapses (p. 30), symbolically marking the meltdown of ideology and the end of twentieth-century China—its history,

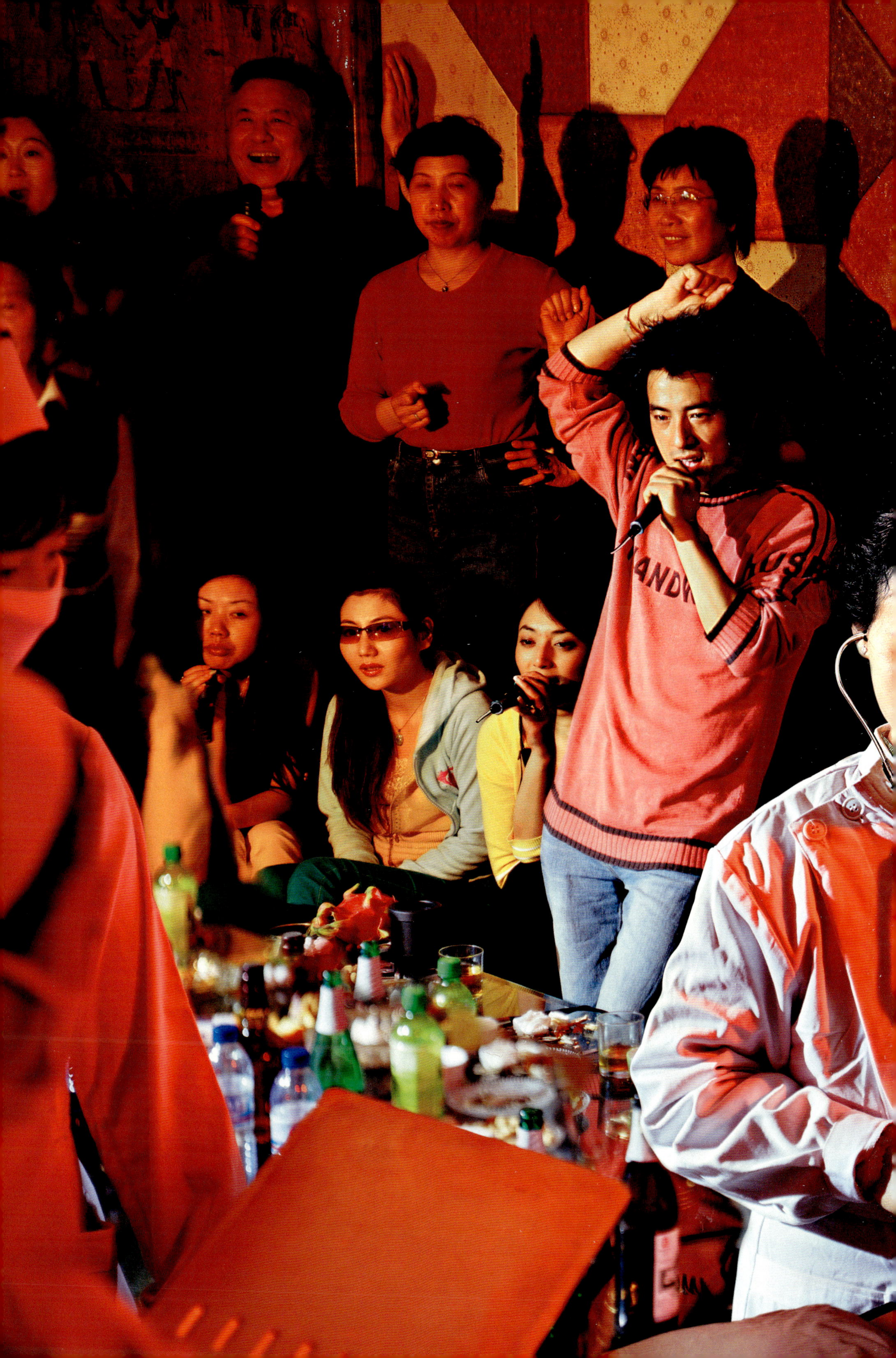

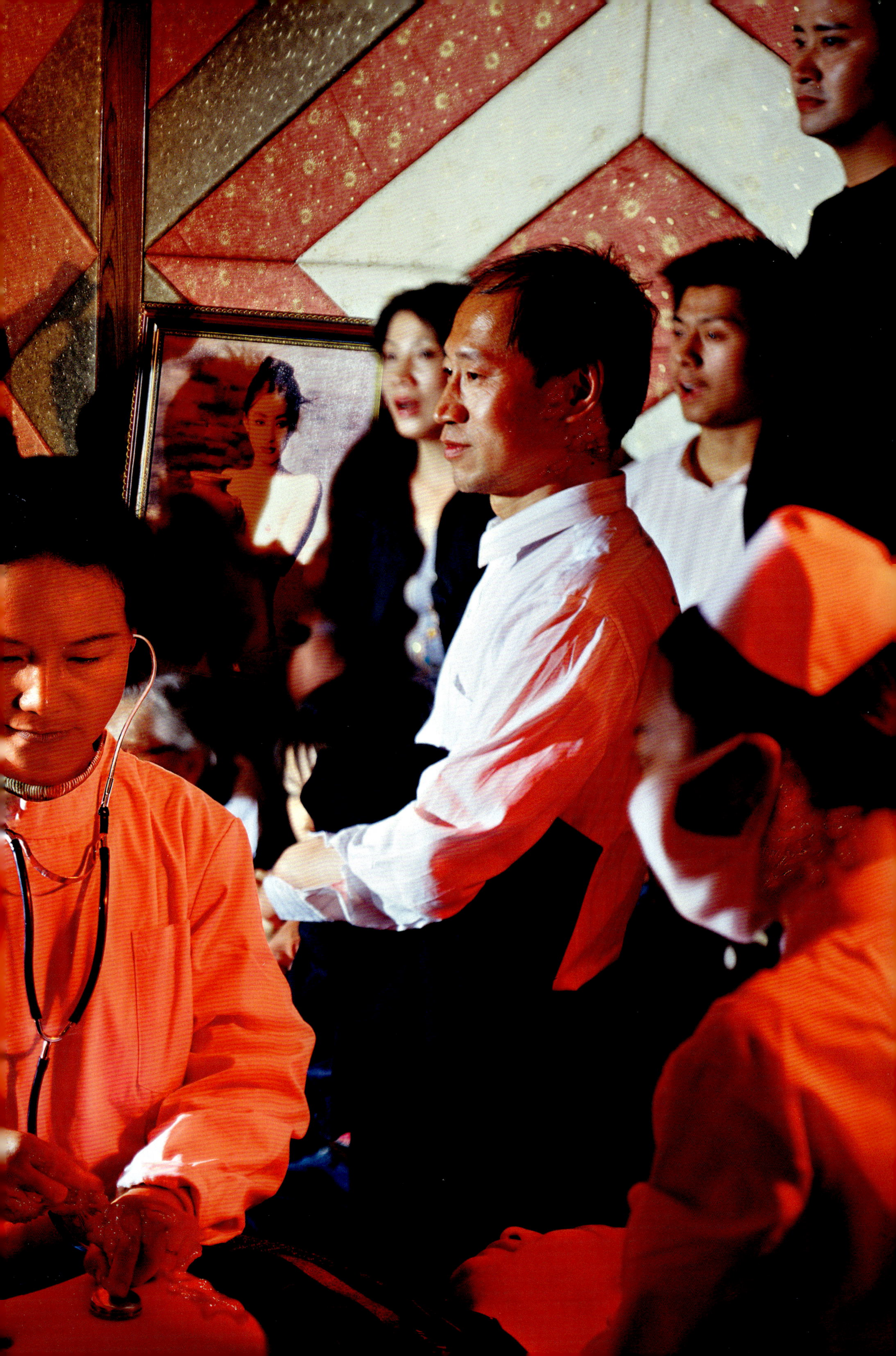

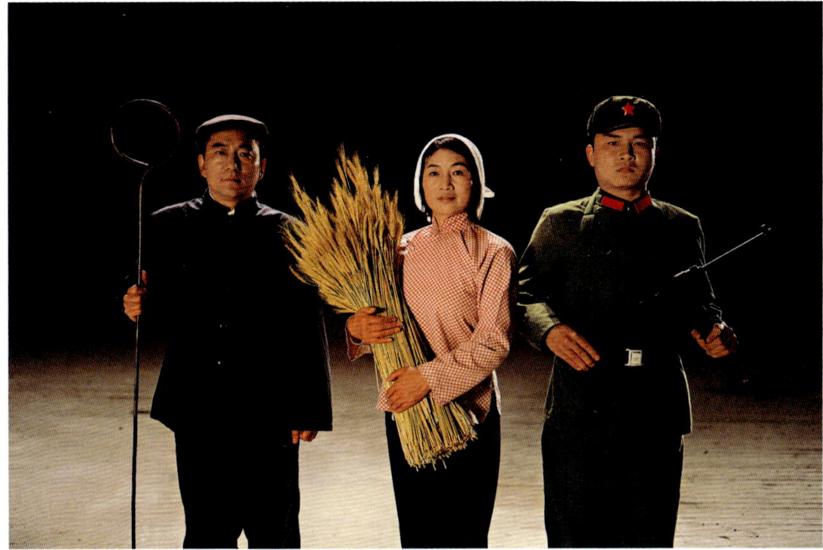

Hostage, 2008

HD color video, with sound, 32 min.; eight chromogenic prints; fiberglass; spray paint; metal pipes; generator; and curtain; installation: dimensions variable

RIGHT: video still

its industry, and the Cultural Revolution—as well as other social revolutions in China and worldwide. In reflecting on the idea of revolution in relation to his work, Wang has stated, "My own revolution coincided with the social revolution. I think revolution happens when you distrust anything in its current state, including yourself."[11]

Hostage features four large sculptures made from fiberglass and machinery, revolving around *General Report* (p. 31, top), a 9-meter-long object that resembles an industrial machine devoured in part by a dense white liquid or smoke pumping from the machinery. Against the background of *General Report* stands a red curtain that marks a stage and hangs over another piece of machinery, all lit by bright lights (p. 31, bottom); a rusted generator stands in front of the curtain. This part of the installation portrays the lost promise of industrialization and modernization and provides an important link between *General Report* and *A Closed System*, another main component, which features a partially melted space capsule with two astronauts inside, signaling China's entry into the global space race. While China is held hostage by this collective dream of progress and innovation, its people suffer in new and strange ways.

Welcome to the Desert of the Real (2010, pp. 32–35) was Wang's next attempt to capture the spirit of the tremendous changes in Chinese

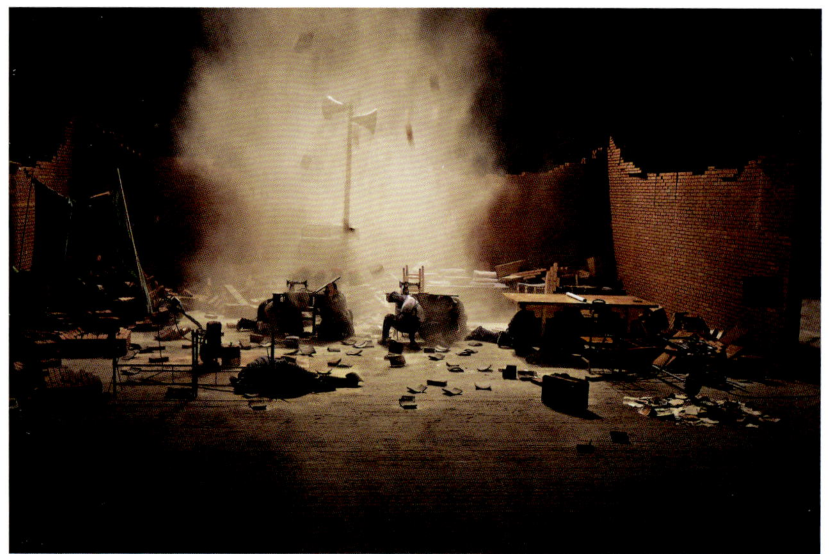

Hostage, 2008

HD color video, with sound, 32 min.; eight chromogenic prints; fiberglass; spray paint; metal pipes; generator; and curtain; installation: dimensions variable

Installation view: *Edge of Elsewhere*, Campbelltown Arts Centre, Australia, January 16–March 14, 2010

LEFT: video still

RIGHT, TOP TO BOTTOM: *General Report* (in foreground); *Closed System* (in background)

society as individuals try to pursue their dreams instead of seeing the reality of their daily lives. Created two years after the 2008 Olympic Games in Beijing, a showcase for China to contribute to the ideal of "one world, one dream,"[12] the work is a reaction to the "loss of identity" and feeling of "uncertainty" as the nation makes a place for itself on the world stage while negotiating domestic conflicts.[13] At its core is an account of a sixteen-year-old boy who has moved with his parents from the countryside to a provincial city. Despite having dreamed of the city since childhood, the boy once there loses any sense of self and becomes addicted to computer games (p. 32). As Wang relates, "Only the fictitious world could give him a true position as well as Internet games from where he could acquire his freedom."[14] In the end, the boy kills a man in the street in broad daylight with no explanation, except that he had lost any sense of reality beyond his virtual existence in computer games (pp. 33–34).[15]

The title *Welcome to the Desert of the Real* references a 2002 essay of the same name by Slavoj Žižek, which in turn derives from a line in the 1999 movie *The Matrix*. His Marxian and psychoanalytic analyses of the political responses to the 9/11 attacks offer a critique of global capitalist and fundamentalist, totalitarian ideologies, which produce

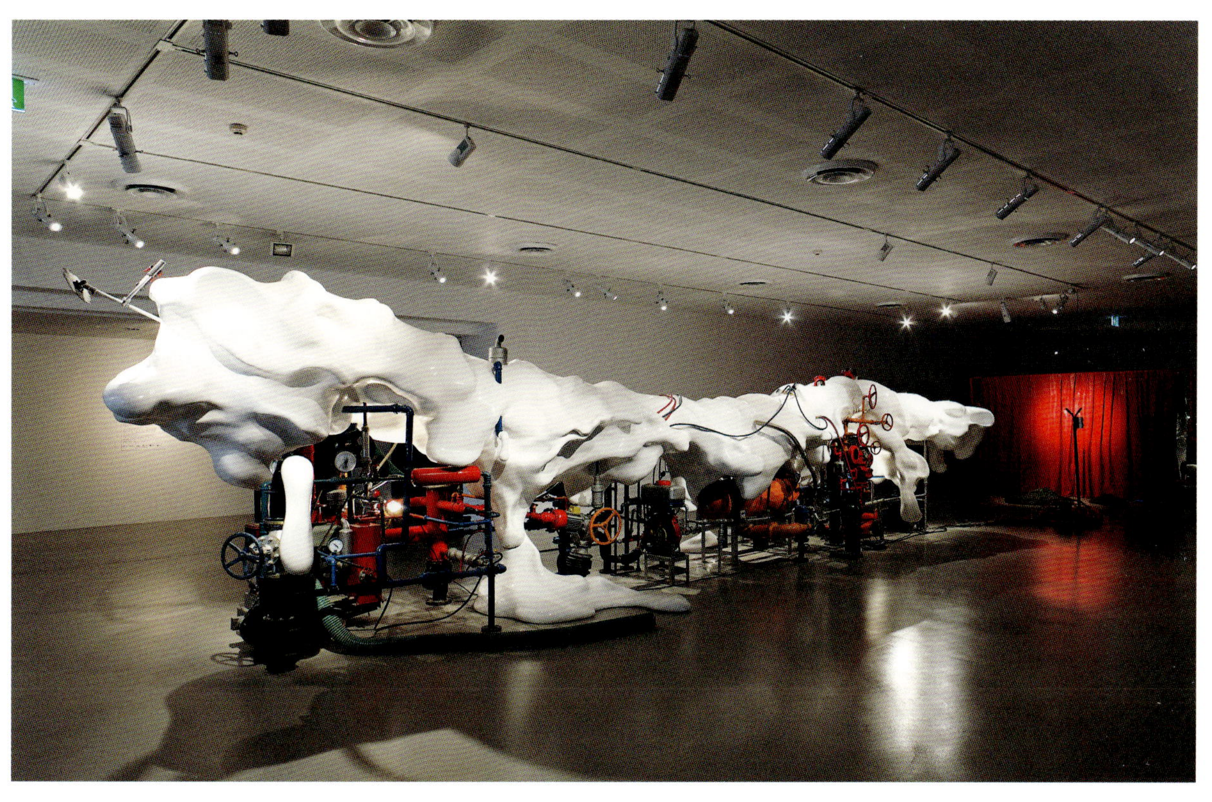

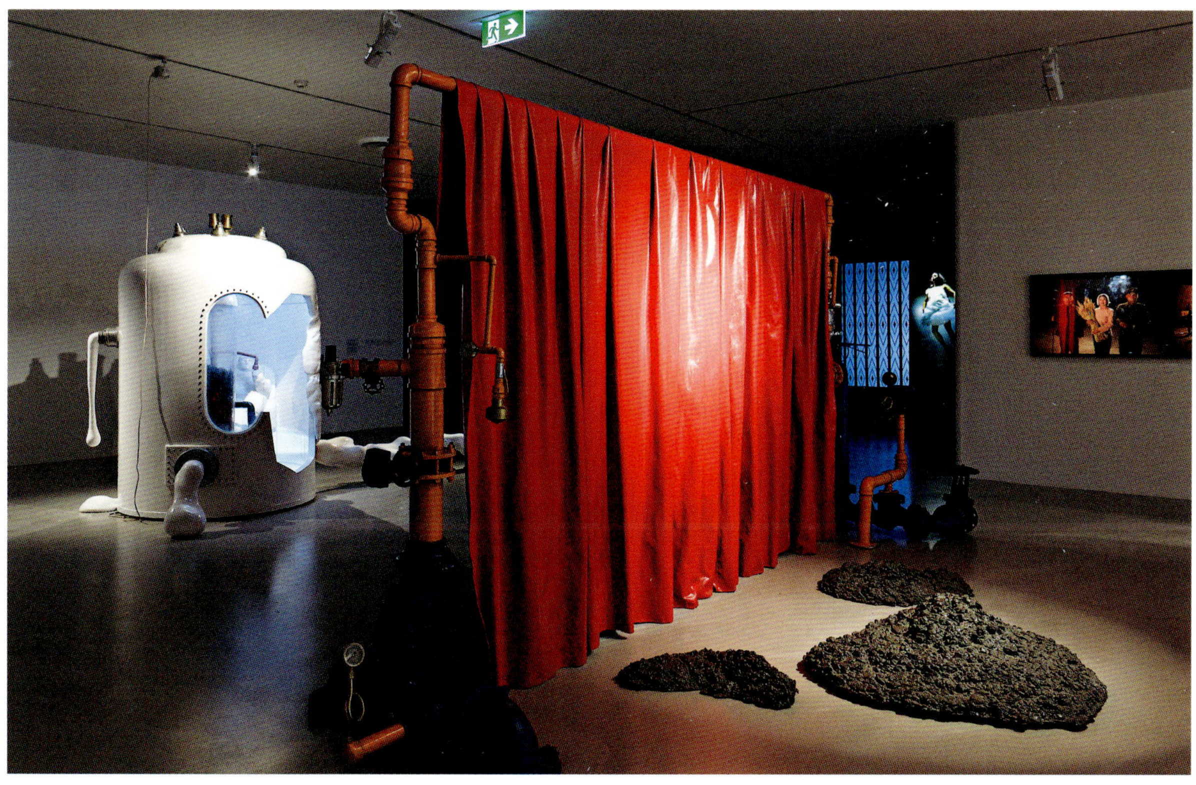

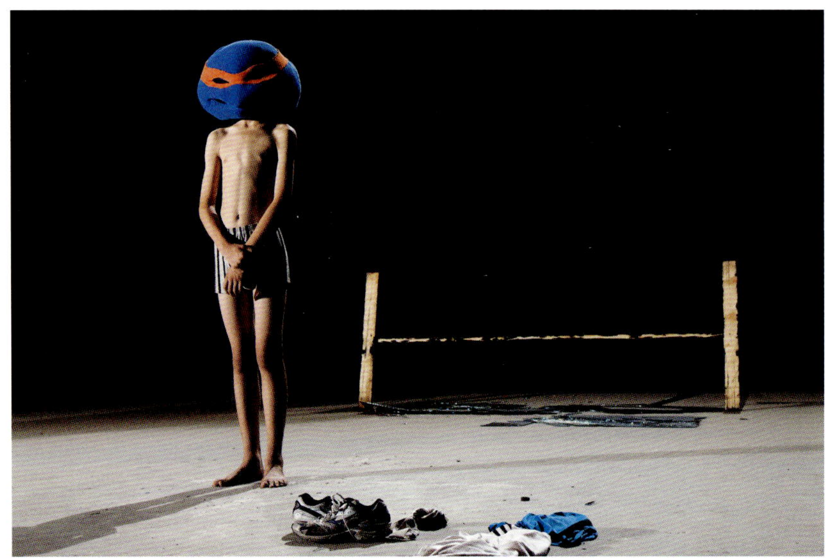

Welcome to the Desert of the Real, 2010

Performance; five-channel HD color video, with sound; and wood boxes and modified furniture, 90 min.

LEFT AND RIGHT: video stills

both a false reality and a dialectic of good and evil.[16] Žižek is, in part, applying the "desert of the real" from Jean Baudrillard's *Simulacres et simulation* (*Simulacra and Simulation*, 1981), which starts with an examination of Borges's fanciful depiction of the decline of the Empire in the guise of a "fraying" and "abstraction" of a map of its territory. "Today," writes Baudrillard, "abstraction is no longer that of the map, the double, the mirror, or the concept." Instead, he writes, "it is the generation by models of a real without origin or reality: a hyperreal."[17] For Wang, the hyperreal is key to his concept of multimedia theater as a continuous rehearsal of a performance that is both realist and abstract and brings the viewer closer to his or her own interpretation.

After producing the video for *Welcome to the Desert of the Real*, Wang rented a studio in Fangjia Hutong, near the Lama Temple, Beijing, and conducted an elaborate "rehearsal" of a durational live-theater production (see p. 35). Five contemporary dancers interacted with objects built for the performance, including wood containers that open and are easily manipulated like magicians' chests. In the background, the video, with additional animation, played continuously, and a sound piece accompanied the performance. What appears to be a series of movements is actually a meticulous dance in which each

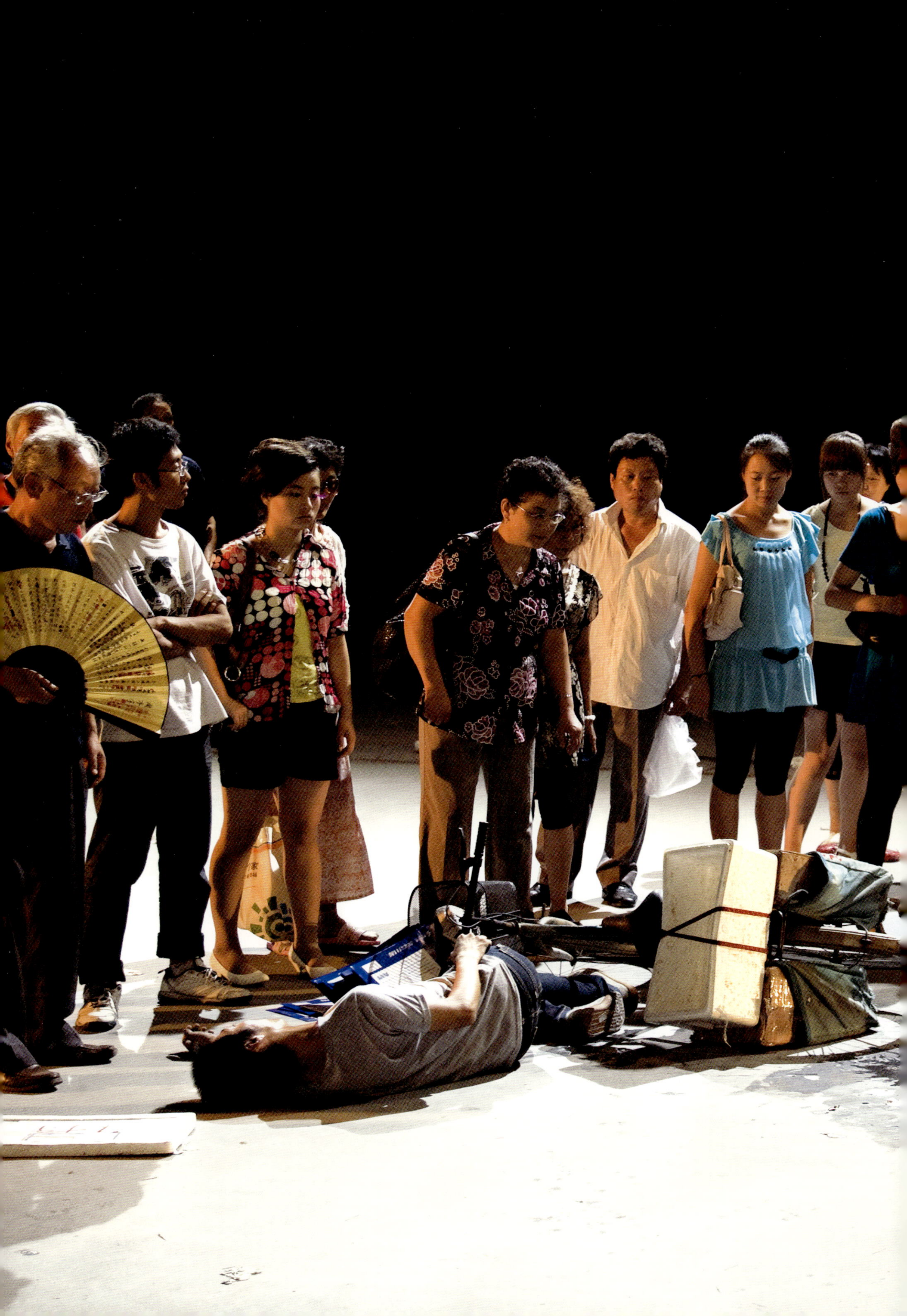

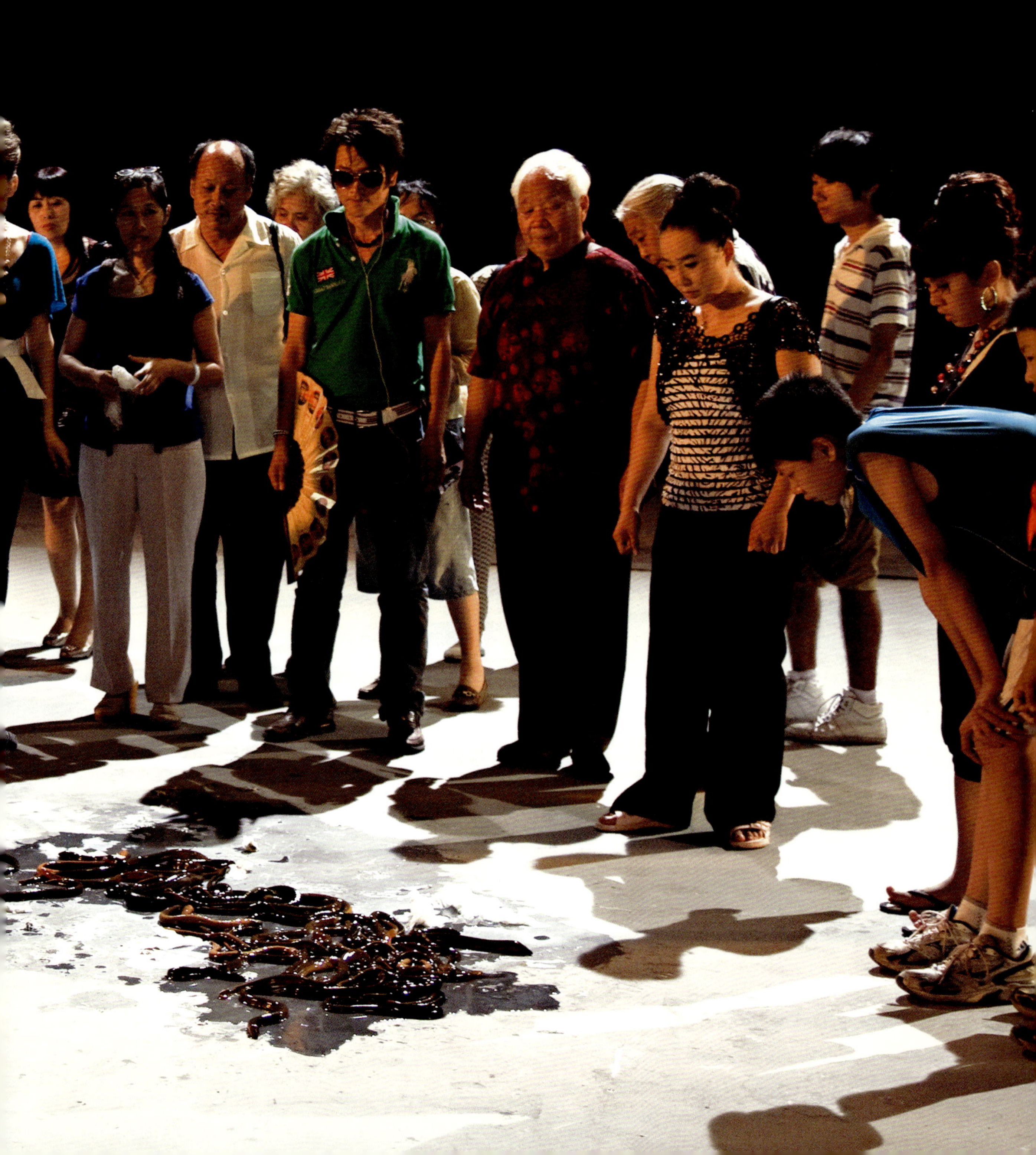

Welcome to the Desert of the Real, 2010

Performance; five-channel HD color video, with sound; and wood boxes and modified furniture, 90 min.

LEFT: video still

RIGHT: performance view: Zürcher Theater Spektakel, Zurich, September 3–5, 2010

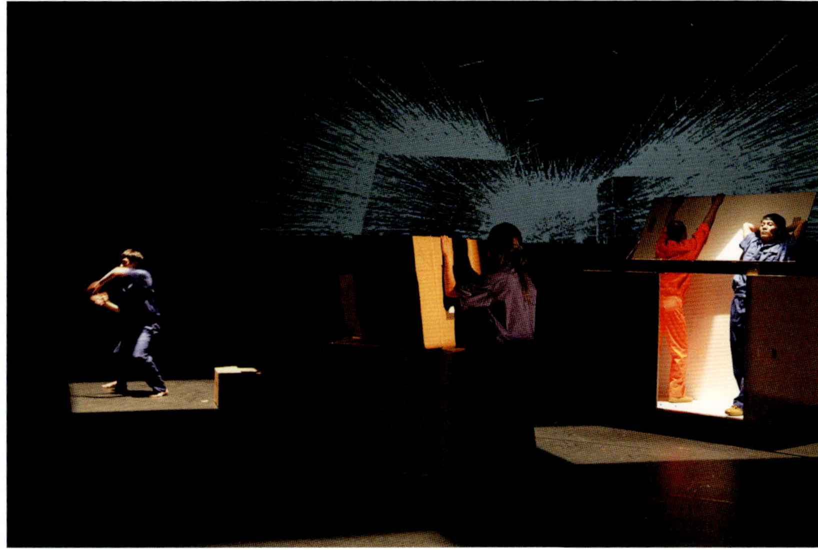

stance represents a recognizable pose in the history of body movements in China, from a martial-arts pose and a position known from traditional Beijing opera to a revolutionary stance that turns into one used in consumer advertising. For the performance part of the project, the artist choreographed a history of the social body in China.

Theater constitutes the political realm in Wang's work, in which the political is highlighted through quotidian interactions between people and between the individual and society. More recently, he has further represented the political in a series of abstract works that consider contemporary society as a gray area, one that lies between the multiple layers of reality and fiction that can be invested in creating a work of art. In 2011, that intermediate space became the basis for a five-part solo exhibition at the Ullens Center for Contemporary Art, Beijing. An elaborate project comprising theater, video, and an installation, *Yellow Signal* (2011, pp. 37–41) marks the state of being in-between, highlighting the space between dual opposites: stopping and moving, right and wrong, permission and prohibition, active and passive, engagement and reluctance. Both a warning and a possibility, a barrier and an intermediary, the yellow signal is overall a sign of choice and of action and reaction. Without it, there would be no moment to prepare to stop or go, no place to pause and reflect, no chance to initiate change. This liminal space has become very powerful for Wang, for he sees this zone of interchange as giving meaning and demanding action in one's daily experiences.[18]

Yellow Signal, 2011

Chapter One: Making do with Fakes

Eight-channel HD color video with sound; 6 min., 33 sec.; 7 min., 7 sec.; 6 min., 59 sec.; 10 min., 24 sec.; 6 min., 59 sec.; 6 min., 14 sec.; 5 min., 54 sec.; 6 min., 6 sec., respectively

RIGHT: production still

Time Temple

For the first commission of The Robert H. N. Ho Family Foundation Chinese Art Initiative, Wang Jianwei has created a labyrinth of time-based sculptures that situate form and formations in space. *Time Temple* highlights a moment of metamorphosis and the transformation of modern Chinese society. It connects the "time temple" of twenty-first-century China to the "time temple" of the Guggenheim Museum, which was founded in the twentieth century. In an early letter, Hilla Rebay, the first Guggenheim director and curator, who helped establish the museum's collection, mentions her desire to create "the temple of non-objectivity and reverence."[19] Equally inspired by the idea of art as a liberating force, Wang's temple is not only a museum, but also a collection and library for contemporary thought. Its three components—an installation of sculptures and paintings, a film, and a performance—each consider time and space as a means to connect the artist, the artwork, and the space and time of artistic production.

In the exhibition portion, viewers are confronted with a landscape of large objects, which can be perceived as sculptures, architectural forms, and physical manifestations of time-based events that reposition the time of their production. These items are essentially theatrical renderings and executions of the artist creating the works over time, and *Time Temple* positions the museum, as evidenced by the title of the performance, as a *Spiral Ramp Library*.[20] For Wang, the library "is inspired by the design of the Guggenheim Museum by Frank Lloyd Wright. It further references the 'Universe,' which some call a library, composed of an indefinite and infinite number of hexagonal spaces (galleries)."[21] This part of the work reveals the influence of Borges's short story "La Biblioteca de Babel" ("The Library of Babel," 1941), in which, among other ideas explored, the dimensions of time and space become similar in people's imaginations and create an unexpected new form.[22] In asking what it means to be contemporary, Wang thus points to the "rehearsal" and "the contemporary event," which inherently connects the time in which the work is created to the time it is presented, its contact with the viewer, and ultimately its existence as a commission and as part of the Guggenheim's programs. In other words, *Time Temple* cannot be separated from its life cycle as a work that is commissioned, exhibited, viewed, and absorbed into a collection. As the first commission in The Robert H. N. Ho Family Foundation series, it is also a starting point from which we may rethink contemporary Chinese art inside a global museum and collection.

Wang prefers not to consider China as the basis of his contemporary practices, but one can see how the idea of China is present in the work's contemplation of social change. The country has undergone rapid development in the last thirty years, and following the artist's

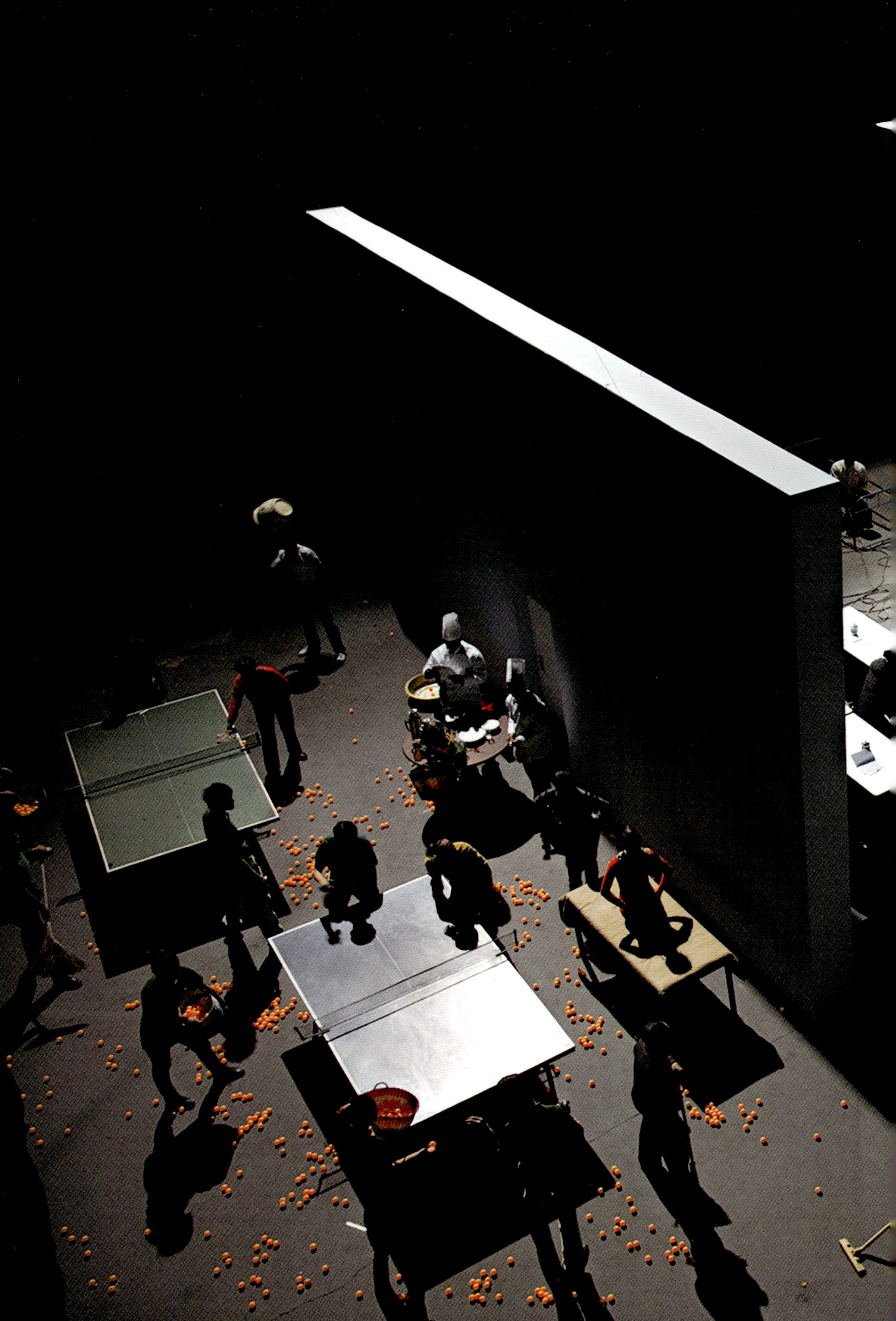

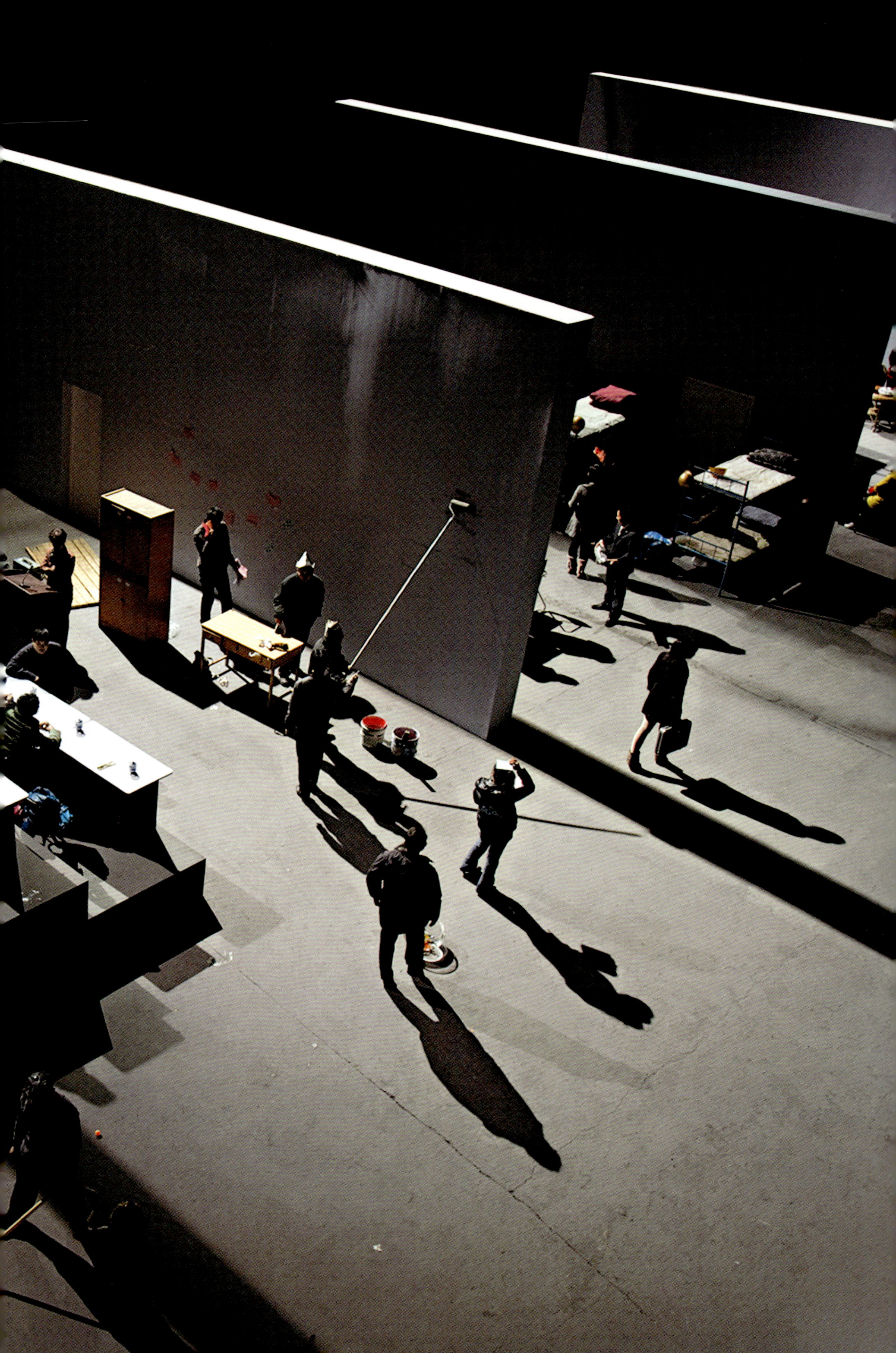

Yellow Signal, 2011

Chapter One: Making do with Fakes

Eight-channel HD color video, with sound; 6 min., 33 sec.; 7 min., 7 sec.; 6 min., 59 sec.; 10 min., 24 sec.; 6 min., 59 sec.; 6 min., 14 sec.; 5 min., 54 sec.; 6 min., 6 sec., respectively

LEFT: production still

RIGHT: installation view: Ullens Center for Contemporary Art, Beijing, April 1–24, 2011

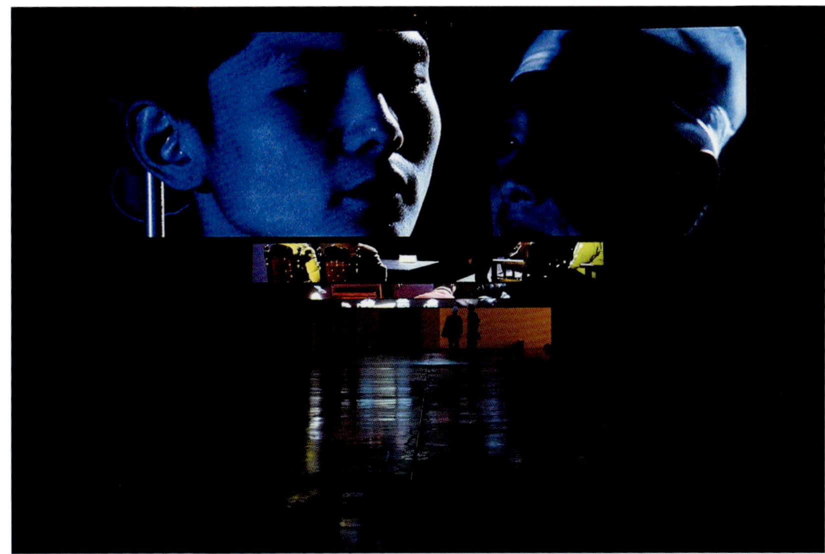

fluid, dynamic thinking, every moment and movement flows into these contemporary events and the transpiring of social and political change. As Wang has said about the installation, "since it consists of [eclectic] things, it escapes our current methods of interpretation; thus it includes resistance. Anything that contains resistance already has political attitudes and forms."[23]

This gap between perception and methods of interpretation is explored in the film portion of the commission, *The Morning Time Disappeared*, which evokes, in part, Franz Kafka's *Die Verwandlung* (*The Metamorphosis*, 1915). It also shows multiple ways of thinking through time and considers its disappearance. In the film, a young man named Xu moves to Beijing like many Chinese with fantasies about the future and a better life. As Wang summarizes, "one day when he wakes up, he finds that there is a gill on his head, and a series of transformations happens to his body."[24] Like that of Kafka's protagonist, Xu's life becomes caught between fiction and reality, a metaphor for life in China and, for that matter, elsewhere around the world today. *The Morning Time Disappeared* looks at how the boundary between everyday life and one's imagination can become blurred and abstracted, "producing a new lifestyle" within "the state of imaginary realism."[25] Through the

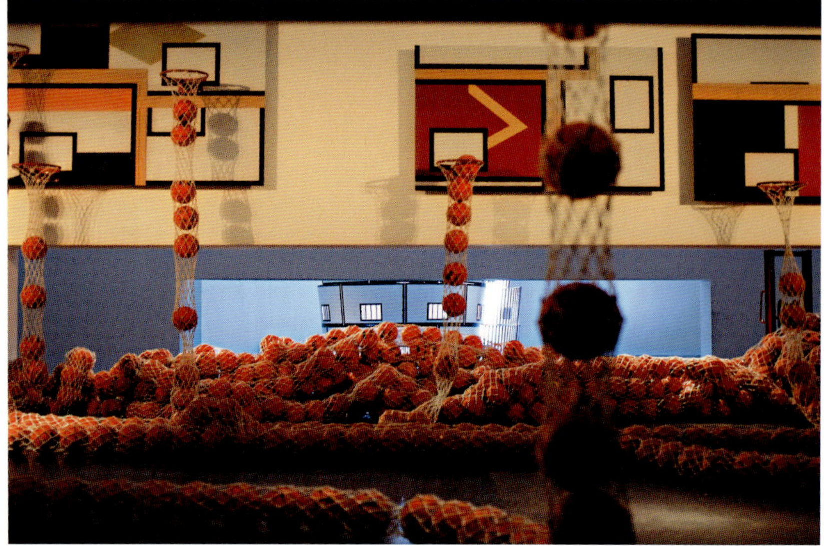

Yellow Signal, 2011

LEFT: *Chapter Two: "We know what we are doing . . . "*

Basketball boards, hoops, nets, and balls; acrylic and oil on canvas; eight bronze basketball sculptures; two washbasins with miniature basketball court; and model court of law, dimensions variable

Installation view: Ullens Center for Contemporary Art, Beijing, April 26–May 15, 2011

RIGHT, TOP: *Chapter Three: Internal Conflict*

Acrylic and oil on canvases, wood, acrylic on furniture, plastic traffic cones, fiberglass, and acrylic on board, dimensions variable

Installation view: Ullens Center for Contemporary Art, Beijing, May 17–June 5, 2011

RIGHT, BOTTOM: *Closing/Opening*

Performance; HD color video, with sound; and acrylic on wood boxes and modified furniture

Performance view: Ullens Center for Contemporary Art, Beijing, June 26, 2011

film, viewers can experience China's vision of itself as a global economic wonderland, where fantasy and real life commingle as a single illusory construction. For the commission as a whole, this presentation of China, no longer marked by fixed ideology and at a radical juncture in its history, is asserted through a new, time-inflected, durational art, in which the viewer becomes both receiver and mediator of theater as a novel abstract form.

Wang Jianwei's concept of rehearsal, which links all his practices, suggests more than any specific form of art. Rather, his iterative, repetitive process operating in the medium of time is at once precise and abstract, courageous and doubtful. Whether through polymorphic sculptures, paintings that present sequential scenes of the same configuration, or labyrinthine films and performances, Wang compels his viewers and participants to see the latent potential of any point in time. In that suspended moment, liberation from history and ideology becomes possible. *Time Temple* is the prescribed site where this encounter with infinity, in contemporary terms, unfolds.

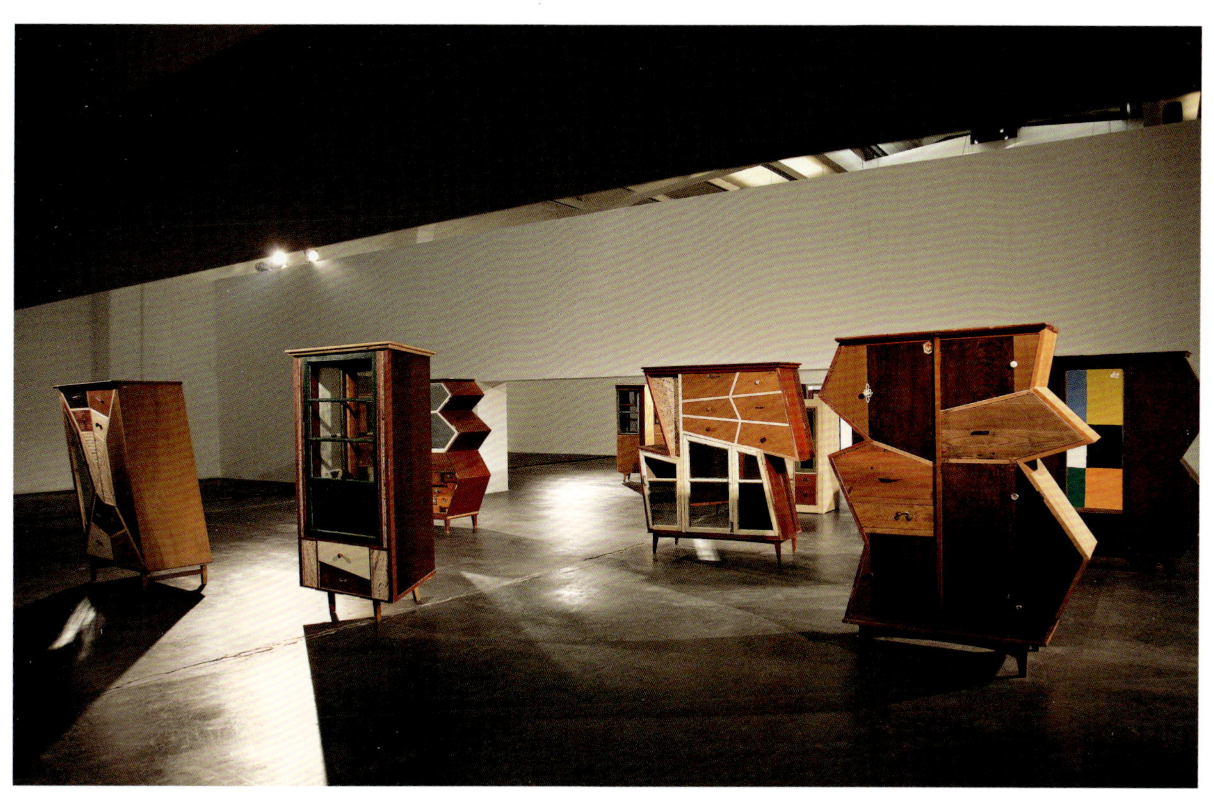

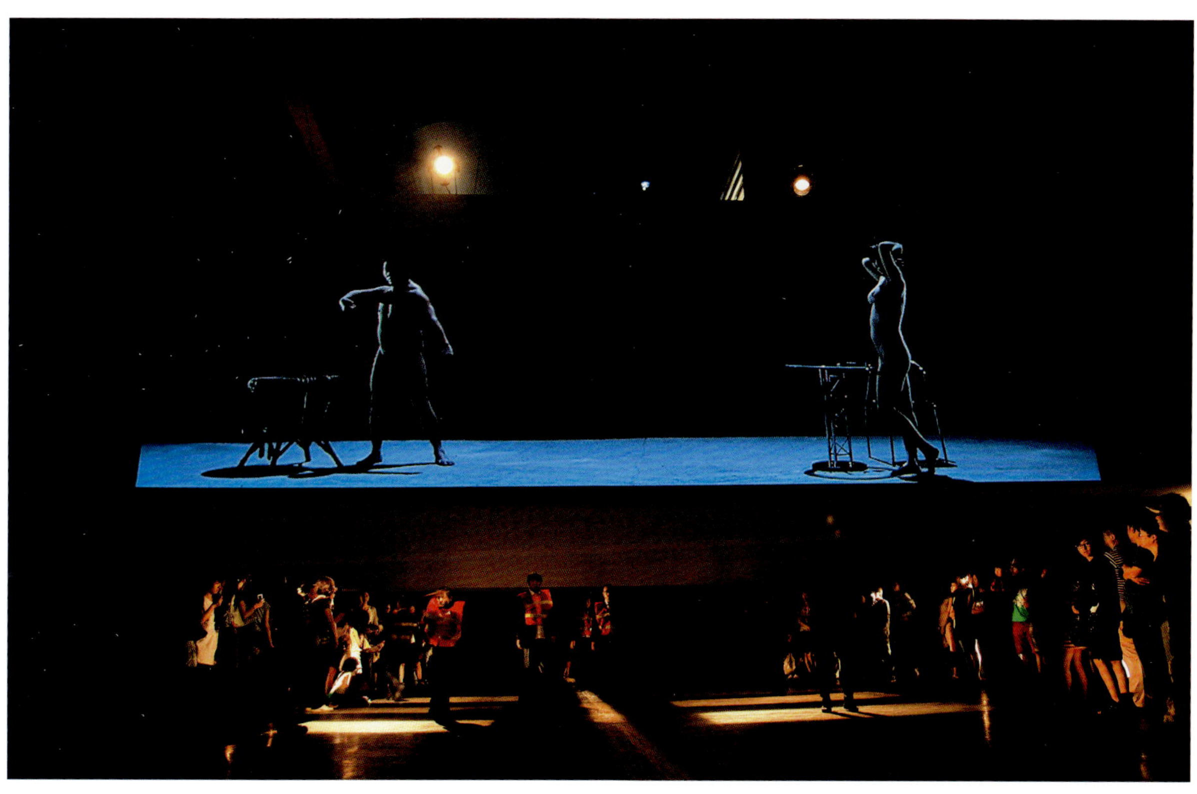

NOTES

The epigraph is from Wang Jianwei, "Rehearsal, for Things to Come," in this volume, p. 51.

1 A good introduction to art during the Cultural Revolution can be found in the documentation for *Art and China's Revolution*, curated by Melissa Chiu and Zheng Shengtian for the Asia Society Museum, New York (2008–09), at http://asiasociety.org/art-and-chinas-revolution (accessed June 2014). For more information, see Melissa Chiu and Zheng Shengtian, eds., *Art and China's Revolution* (New York: Asia Society Museum, 2008).

2 Written in 1899, *Resurrection* was first published in its entirety in 1936.

3 *Gott ist tot* ("God is dead") is a widely quoted statement from the work of Friedrich Nietzsche, including in *Die Götzen-Dämmerung, oder Wie man mit dem Hammer philosophiert* (*Twilight of the Idols, or How One Philosophizes with a Hammer*), written in 1888 and first published in 1889.

4 For more on the New Measurement Group, see Hou Hanru, "Towards an 'Un-Unofficial Art': De-Ideologicalisation of China's Contemporary Art in the 1990s," *Third Text* (London) 10, no. 34 (Spring 1996), pp. 37–52.

5 Wang Jianwei, interview with the author, Beijing, Jan. 19, 2014.

6 See Huang Zhuan, ed., *Ju chang: Wang Jianwei de yi shu*, exh. cat. OCT Contemporary Art Terminal, Shenzhen and Shanghai [Theater: The Art of Wang Jianwei] (Guangzhou: Ling nan mei shu chu ban she, 2008).

7 Wang Jianwei, interview with the author, Beijing, Jan. 20, 2014.

8 Wang Jianwei, interviews with Hans Ulrich Obrist (2001, 2003, and 2006) in *Hans Ulrich Obrist: The China Interviews*, ed. Philip Tinari and Angie Baecker (Hong Kong and Beijing: Office for Discourse Engineering, 2009), p. 277.

9 See Thomas Berghuis, "The Distance Between Us," in *Edge of Elsewhere*, ed. Lisa Havilah, exh. cat. (Campbelltown, Australia: Campbelltown Arts Centre, 2010), pp. 45–48.

10 *Hostage* was first produced as a solo exhibition at the Zendai Museum of Modern Art, Shanghai, in 2008 and was later shown in the first part of *Edge of Elsewhere*, Campbelltown Arts Centre, Australia, in 2010. See Shen Qibin, ed., *Hostage: Wang Jianwei Solo Exhibition*, exh. cat. (Shanghai: Zendai Museum of Modern Art, 2008), and Berghuis, "The Distance Between Us."

11 Wang, interview, Jan. 19, 2014.

12 "One world, one dream" was the official slogan of the games.

13 See Michèle Vicat, "Welcome to the Desert of the Real," *3 Dots Water*, Sept. 2010, http://www.3dotswater.com/pointeratwork006.html (accessed Oct. 24, 2013).

14 Undated artist statement, http://www.wangjianwei.com/hyldzssm.html (accessed May 2014).

15 *Welcome to the Desert of the Real* was produced by the Swiss cultural organization Culturescapes, Basel, and traveled to Zurich and Geneva in 2010. For more information, see "Chronology," in this volume, p. 88.

16 Slavoj Žižek, "Welcome to the Desert of the Real," *South Atlantic Quarterly* (Durham, N.C.) 101, no. 2 (Spring 2002), pp. 385–89.

17 Jean Baudrillard, *Simulacra and Simulation*, trans. Sheila Faria Glaser (Ann Arbor, Mich.: University of Michigan Press, 1994), p. 1.

18 See also Jérôme Sans, "Chronology and Entropy: Jérôme Sans Interviews Wang Jianwei," in *Wang Jianwei: Yellow Signal*, exh. cat. (Beijing: Ullens Center for Contemporary Art, 2012), pp. 15–22.

19 Hilla Rebay to Rudolf Bauer, Apr. 16, 1930, Box 84, Hilla von Rebay Foundation Archive, M0007, Solomon R. Guggenheim Museum Archives, New York. Quoted in Karole Vail, "A Museum in the Making: Two Artists and Their Patron—Hilla Rebay, Rudolf Bauer, and Solomon R. Guggenheim," in *The Museum of Non-Objective Painting: Hilla Rebay and the Origins of the Solomon R. Guggenheim Museum*, ed. Vail (New York: Guggenheim Museum, 2009), p. 28.

20 Wang Jianwei, artist statement for the *Wang Jianwei: Time Temple* exhibition proposal, Dec. 28, 2013.

21 Ibid.

22 Jorge Luis Borges, *The Library of Babel*, trans. Andrew Hurley (Boston: David R. Godine Publisher, 2000).

23 Wang, interview, Jan. 19, 2014.

24 Wang, artist statement for *Time Temple* exhibition proposal.

25 Ibid.

Time Temple: The Labyrinth of a Single Straight Line

Gao Shiming

Translated from the Chinese by Lee Ambrozy

Only through time time is conquered.
–T. S. Eliot

Temple of Time Contemplation

One summer day in 2011, in a village outside the city of Lishui in Zhejiang Province, I came upon the ruins of a temple, named the "Temple of Time Contemplation." A house of worship for both Buddhists and Daoists, it was built in 1356, during the final reign of the Yuan dynasty. It contains many traces of the ancient past as more than half of its structure was added in later periods. Therefore, I encountered not a Yuan-dynasty temple but in fact an aggregation of time. At the moment of my arrival, these rooms, constructed at various points, collapsed onto a single plane through a process of historical superposition and repeated accumulation. By viewing its continually metamorphosing body, I came into contact with the markings of many different eras. In this world, all objects are social archives and historical indices, and for Wang Jianwei, they are all sacrificial offerings at the Time Temple.

In Chinese linguistics, the word "temple" in "Time Temple" does not necessarily indicate a religious structure. The character (寺) itself combines "process/continue" (行) and "halt/pause" (止).[1] To denote a place or location, it first serves as a general term referring to a secular place to discuss business or to receive guests. In 68 CE, during the reign of Emperor Ming (25–78 CE) of the Han dynasty, sacred Buddhist texts were carried eastward on white horses, stopping first at Minghu Temple in Luoyang, Shandong Province.[2] After this event and the arrival of Buddhism in China, the character (寺) more generally connoted Buddhist places of worship and practice.

The character for "temple" (寺) is also a combination of earth (土) and *cun* (寸).[3] The glyph for "sun" (日) alongside "temple" (寺) is then "time" (時), which can measure both space and time. As discussed in the first chapter of the *Erya* (爾雅), "Explaining the Old Words" (釋詁), "time, real, is being" (時，是也),[4] and here "being" (是) is similar to the European philosophical concept of *Sein* (German for "being").[5] In the book *Explaining and Analyzing Characters* (說文解字), time is derived from the sun, following its arc, and following the *cun*. In other words, the sun is the coordinate for earthly time, which is contingent on the sun's movement, with the *cun* as its metric. A *cun* of time, that is, the shadows of light, measures time by sight. The shadows of time are perhaps visible phenomena, but what cannot be measured is one's perception and comprehension of time. Confucius (551–479 BCE), standing by a stream, said, "It passes on just like this."[6] In the *Analects* (ca. 500 BCE), he comments again, "At the distance of a hundred ages, its affairs may be known."[7] The former feels as if time begets sorrows, melancholy regains open-mindedness. In the latter, consequences drive the future, and open and upright behavior begets transparency. Nonetheless, both reflect the complex appreciation of time in Chinese culture.

"The shadows of time are the eternal passing travelers."[8] The wind and rain are merely ephemeral clouds and mist. A hundred years of human life are as fleeting as a pony's shadow glanced through a rock fissure.[9] Human existence is like "accidental [swan] claw tracks left in the slush";[10] the grand universe, with its torrent of chatter, is a mere passerby on the river of time. To transcend such a fate would require building a "Temple of Time." The ancient connotation of "Time Temple" indicates this sort of place, where time resides and is condensed. When time halts is the present; within the present, time becomes its being, known as the "temple" (寺).

The Labyrinth of a Single Straight Line

In Isaac Newton's world, time is comprised of the linkage of countless indistinguishable moments. It is indivisible, a ray pointing in a single direction. For Henri Bergson, external time does not matter. To grasp the ways of the world, "you must replace yourself within it" and "being distinctive, thus coincid[ing] with the unique, inexpressible thing."[11] In this way, the ego is always interlinked to the source of the world, and through intuition we extend the entire world. There is a living "moving eternity in which our own particular duration would be included as the vibrations are in light."[12] If Honoré Balzac's narrative belongs to Newtonian time, then Sergei Eisenstein's montage demonstrates the rupture and broken state of Newtonian time. In James Joyce's *Ulysses* (1918–20), time appears agglutinated, roundabout, and entangled in daily minutiae. Since modernity, artists' conceptions of time seem to confirm Bergson's idea of extensions; yet, the more expansive notion of time endures. Jorge Luis Borges's time is infinite, cyclic, and without beginning or end. He said, "I tend to return eternally to the Eternal Return."[13] This point is to neither enter a discussion of the endless metaphysical debates about time nor reiterate Gilles Deleuze's repeatedly tangled propositions of *Time Image*, but rather to illuminate the significance of the worldview projected in Wang's *Time Temple* (2014) before we consider how it has become manifested in the artist's work.

Time flows endlessly like water, and the zone between the states of interruption or of continuity in time is the most disruptive place. Between intermittent disturbances and continuances, there exists a potential time and space, what Wang calls the "Time Temple" or what Borges calls a "labyrinth, consisting of a single line."[14]

In the film *L'Année dernière à Marienbad* (*Last Year at Marienbad*, 1961), time suddenly freezes at a social gathering. Of course, time has not actually stopped, as the image still elapses before the viewer's eyes. Only the sculptural crowd of guests has frozen, and the camera continues to roam like a specter among the fetishlike objects. In an earlier profound cultural image, on the famous Odessa steps of *Bronenosets Po'tyomkin* (*Battleship Potemkin*, 1925), Eisenstein shreds time, only to reassemble it like a Cubist by overlapping some 150 angles repeatedly and in infinite layers. The classic montage reveals not only what film critic Erwin Panofsky has called the "spatialization of time" and "the dynamization of space,"[15] but also a dynamic unfolding of the labyrinth of a single line. A static version can be seen in the window paintings of the René Magritte, in which a window has been destroyed by an unknown force, but each shard of glass retains a fragmented image of the world–the world is saved in this pile of shattered mirrors.

Wang's *Time Temple* points toward an exceptional worldview. For the artist, the place where time pauses is the fundamental location of image. In one respect, time spent viewing liberates people from the monotony of everyday life, pushing them into an even more condensed and coherent narrative space; in another, the image is a hole excavated from time, constructing an "alternate time" within normal time, a different track. In this sense, a photograph is a denomination of time and occurrences. In the experience of modernity, the camera's intervention is intimately entangled with one's perceptions of events and feelings. The nature of the occurrence or time in photography has already been evacuated by this kind of instantaneous experience. To a large extent, the artist hopes to resist precisely this experience of time, in which it is constructed from countless instants.

Wang's work infinitely magnifies the present, breaking up a steady stream of images and routinely postponing the next moment. The axis of time is also a chain of significance derived from a specific timespan, but here the present moment is delayed again, significance is run aground, and it never reaches the other shore, becoming an absence of meaning. For Wang, an image functions similarly: it is a boat run aground on the river of time in the temple of time; "before the beginning and after the end," the river has frozen.[16]

Non-Interpretive Images

"Interpretive imagery almost completely dominates images," Wang has said. "This is proof of the image's decay."[17] The interpretive image of history, a latent captioned photograph, is also proof of historiographic decay. In that case, does a non-interpretive image exist? Wang himself has not offered an answer.

In the summer of 2011, the artist Liu Guoqiang invented a "supplemental frame camera." He affixed a miniature camera with an automatic sensor onto his glasses, and every time he blinked, the camera would take a photo. Our visual processing rarely halts, capturing the images of our lives day in and day out, but every time we blink, this continuous narrative loses a frame. The supplemental frame camera recovers those lost moments.

During Taiwan's period under Japanese rule (1895–1945), the Kōminka movement attempted to make the Taiwanese people subject to the emperor, and one of its methods was to broadcast propaganda films. The majority of locals did not understand Japanese, thus real-time interpreters were needed. Many of the translators, dubbed "sophists," were anti-Japanese, and while they translated the subtitles for the crowds, they often used the opportunity to propagate their anti-colonial sentiment. The viewing experience then turned into an absurd mélange—images of the emperor set to an anti-Japanese soundtrack, filling the minds of the audience with contrary and antagonistic ideas and images.

Along the borders of Shanxi, Hebei, Shandong, and Henan provinces in the early years of China's Civil War (1927–36), before every assault, the photographers who traveled with the army would photograph each soldier in the death squads, recording a solemn point in his life, perhaps his final moments. Due to a shortage of materials, these soldiers could vaguely intuit that the camera was likely filmless. Nonetheless, they straightened their uniforms neat and tidy, faced the camera, and posed. After completing the final and perhaps only photographic ceremony of their lives, they charged onto the battlefield against treacherous odds.

The moment when one blinks and the supplemental frame camera is activated, when the Taiwanese sophists deliver anti-Japanese voice-over to Kōminka propaganda films, when photographers lift their cameras to capture soldiers in the moment before their charge—these points in time are some of the most important in the history of images. The results, documenting what is missed, contradicted, or can never be captured (with a camera that has no film), allow us to think differently about the essence of images, and it is these images, transmitted and accumulated within our thoughts, that gradually engender a raw determination and a liberating power.

Over the past few years, from the symbolic characterization of the people in *Hostage* (2008) to the repeated performances of the nameless collective in *Yellow Signal* (2011), Wang's images have gradually divorced themselves from visualizing the social structure to collectively representing the "crowd" and "masses." Impressions that rub out the texture of reality, they no longer describe a certain actuality or realization of ideas. Instead, they have become a part of the unfolding reality. His videos are constructed through theater, and as they are filmed, they collapse the film studio and the theater into one. Through the repeated interweaving of theatrical and cinematic performance, the energy of the theatrical stage is transmitted into a performative landscape that is showcased before the camera's lens. Thus, in front of the lens, life's image instantaneously becomes a kind of living landscape. How can such living landscapes surmount the real landscape? For Wang, this is a tremendous difficulty.

As Wang has said, "Video artists should be like [Franz] Kafka's messenger, delivering a letter, but without having to know its contents."[18] The instant that a video breaks from the timeline of causal relationships is precisely the moment that it is liberated from performing as an interpretive image and can flaunt itself. Freed from the domain of interpretation, images puncture the scrim of representation and return to an undetermined status of significance. Images here translate, not elucidate, meaning. "Image" thus becomes a verb, transforming into image action. The instant that image transforms the landscape into action is also the instant when it becomes a life image.

Occurrence and Rehearsal

In September 1929, on a small island in the Sea of Marmara, near Istanbul, Bolshevik revolutionary Leon Trotsky, then fifty years old, wrote that the things he experienced in the first half of his life are the most magnificent page in human history. In retrospect, each section of that history has various different directions. What is regretful, history can only happen once. Therefore, he thought, the results were unexpected, but not accidental.[19]

Trotsky's sentiment is imbued with a type of nostalgia built on the supposition of linear time, a cross-section from which can serve as a platform of illusion. It seems that we can stand beside this platform, indeed temporarily outside history, and reflect, just as Confucius gazed on the river of time. However, our existence cannot be separated from time. As Borges said, "Time is the substance I am made of. Time is the river which sweeps me along, but I am the river; it is the tiger which destroys me, but I am the tiger; it is a fire which consumes me, but I am the fire."[20]

For Trotsky, history is a gamble. It is comprised of countless occurrences and determinate moments, and the ego is merely a pawn, subject to larger forces. Even though we are important participants in historical events and can be memorialized in the "decisive moment" of a historical image, we are only a detail in the caption. In the landscape of historiography, becoming a trivial and incomplete detail seems to be the fate of the modern human. However, history knows no end, and everything is not yet complete. The caption can be changed; occurrences are still indeterminate situations. As long as everything remains unsettled, there is always time for action.

Action images, or image actions, are images that are sustained in a continuously unfinished state. In film production, the second that the word "action" is shouted is the moment we can move and the performance begins. More precisely, that moment signifies the moment of rehearsal. For Wang, rehearsal is different from revolution. If revolution is a reversal or a beginning, then rehearsal puts things in a continual state of progress. Rehearsal tends toward future evolution, approaching an inflection point that is imminently arriving. It is not the terminus in a teleological sense or a conclusion but is an undetermined, open, and transformative process without beginning or end.

In the opening to "Brief über den Humanismus" ("Letter on Humanism," 1947), Martin Heidegger wrote that the essence of an action was in its accomplishment (*vollbringen*), and accomplishment implies that one must take something and develop it until the richness of its essence is produced.[21] In this sense, *vollbringen* is "unrealized," where what is produced is not the process of making commodities but the unfolding of an occurrence. This occurrence is neither akin to historical plots and intrigues nor what is later considered a decisive moment as judged by everyday causal correlations. In those big events, we are the details of a prescribed, captioned photograph. As the overall incident becomes more powerful, the assigned significance of its fragmented details, the daily minutia of life, becomes less important. Still, occurrences are just as contingent on the unresolved closure that is their context. They still cannot be named, are untitled, and carry historical potential and latent possibility.

Occurrences as occurrences are the time when history is cleared out and all the latent potential surges forth. This moment is not the "decisive moment" captured by documentary photographers; quite the opposite, it is a moment that "escapes history," time on an alternative track. In this supplementary time, that old, captioned photograph turns into ruined ash. This destruction is not a conclusion; as in the rehearsal, our action begins with these ruins.

In *Yellow Signal,* Wang's point of departure is the news transmitted by mass media, events that actually transpired and burst with tension. In an era of mass media, these occurrences are reduced to disposable anecdotes and vapid gossip, but Wang salvages them. Their original significance has been lost, leaving only blurry, ambiguous forms. Now, these plots, emptied of meaning, are thrust on stage and repetitively rehearsed before the camera. Their rehearsal is not to perfect their significance but merely to invalidate them of meaning. The more vague the meaning of an occurrence, the further it distances itself from becoming part of a narrative. All that remains is a throng of indeterminate masses, not the crowds of media reports, the "People" of political propaganda, or even the nameless extras on a film set. The goal of the rehearsal is to allow the crowds to liberate themselves from that captioned photograph to become the still undefined, untitled image and excavate their latent potential. In this process, each frame gathered by the crowd contains a lost historical possibility, and rehearsal strips the nameless crowd of the foregone conclusion implied in examining history. This deprivation turns the plot into an occurrence once again, uniting latent potential with the power of history.

Constantly flowing, time has no legacy. Rehearsal is an attempt to interrupt chains of causal relationships, prompting occurrences to happen anew. Only during occurrences can we become the subject, and the rehearsal aims to create a more acute reality and more powerful subject from historical relationships and the restaging of occurrences.

Rehearsal allows for a continuously evolving process. In Wang's mind, the images in *Time Temple* are in fact transpiring on a "morning time disappeared."[22] Losing time is not a state of oblivion in one's life, a blackout in a film reel, or a state of weightlessness in time. On a morning when time disappears, everything is simultaneously and eternally on set. The Temple of Time, in a state of evolution, is outside of history.

During rehearsal, Wang is no longer concerned with "conclusions or beginnings," the interests of the poet Bei Dao and his generation. Before the beginning and after the end, in the Temple of Time or at this pause in history, all origins are equally a moment of extinction.

The Temple of Time is not an altar to history. Historical significance has already been cleared; the latent energy in occurrence is accumulated and is ready to fire. In *Time Temple,* there is great serenity. In the temple of time, let the sounds of the masses rise!

NOTES

The epigraph is from T. S. Eliot, "Burnt Norton" (1936), *Four Quartets* (New York: Harcourt, Brace and World, 1968), p. 16.

1 Zhang Wenjiang, *Gu dian xue shu jiang yao* [Analysis of classic literature] (Shanghai: Shanghai Guji Publishing, 2010).

2 *Kangxi* dictionary, quoted in Gao Cheng, ed., *Shi wu ji yuan ji lei shi juan* [Recording of the origin of things] (Taibei shi, Taiwan: Xin Xing, 1976).

3 A *cun* is a traditional unit of measure, that is, the length of a thumb from the knuckle.

4 "Explaining the Old Worlds," *Erya*, no. 172. This quote is translated by Lee Ambrozy and Shu-Wen Lin. The *Erya* (229–221 BCE) is the oldest Chinese dictionary.

5 See Martin Heidegger, *Being and Time*, trans. John Macquarrie and Edward Robinson (Oxford, U.K.: Blackwell, 1967).

6 Confucius, *The Confucian Analects, The Great Learning and the Doctrine of the Mean*, trans. James Legge (New York: Cosimo, 2009), p. 222.

7 Ibid., p. 153.

8 Bai Li, "Preface to the Feast in a Peach and Plum Garden on a Spring Night," trans. Lee Ambrozy.

9 From Zhuang Zi, "Kih Pei Yu, or Knowledge Rambling in the North," in *The Sacred Books of China*, trans. James Legge (Oxford, U.K.: The Clarendon Press, 1891), p. 57.

10 Su Shi, "Written in Response to Ziyou's Poem About Days in Mianchi," *The Anchor Book of Chinese Poetry: From Ancient to Contemproary, the Full 3,000-Year Tradition*, ed. Tony Barnstone and Chou Ping (New York: Anchor Books, 2005), p. 248.

11 Henri Bergson, *Creative Evolution*, trans. Arthur Mitchell (Lanham, Md.: University Press of America, 1983), p. 308.

12 Henri Bergson, *Introduction to Metaphysics*, trans. T. E. Hulme (New York: G. P. Putnam's Sons, 1912), p. 64.

13 Jorge Luis Borges, "Circular Time," *Borges: Selected Non-Fictions*, ed. Eliot Weinberger (New York: Penguin, 1999), p. 225.

14 Jorge Luis Borges, "Death and the Compass" (1942), trans. Donald A. Yates, *Labyrinths: Selected Stories and Other Writings*, ed. Yates and James E. Irby (New York: New Directions, 1964), p. 87.

15 Erwin Panofsky, "Style and Medium in the Motion Pictures," *Three Essays on Style*, ed. Irving Lavin (Cambridge, Mass.; MIT Press, 1997), p. 96.

16 Eliot, "Burnt Norton," p. 19.

17 Wang Jianwei, interview with the author, May 25, 2014.

18 Ibid.

19 Leon Trotsky, *My Life: An Attempt at an Autobiography* (New York: Pathfinder Press, 1970).

20 Jorge Luis Borges, "A New Refutation of Time" (1944–46), trans. James E. Irby, *Labyrinths*, p. 234.

21 Martin Heidegger, "Letter on Humanism" (1947), trans. Frank A. Capuzzi, *Pathmarks*, ed. William McNeil, *Texts in German Philosophy* (Cambridge: Cambridge University Press, 1998), pp. 239–76.

22 *The Morning Time Disappeared* is the name of the film portion of *Time Temple* (2014).

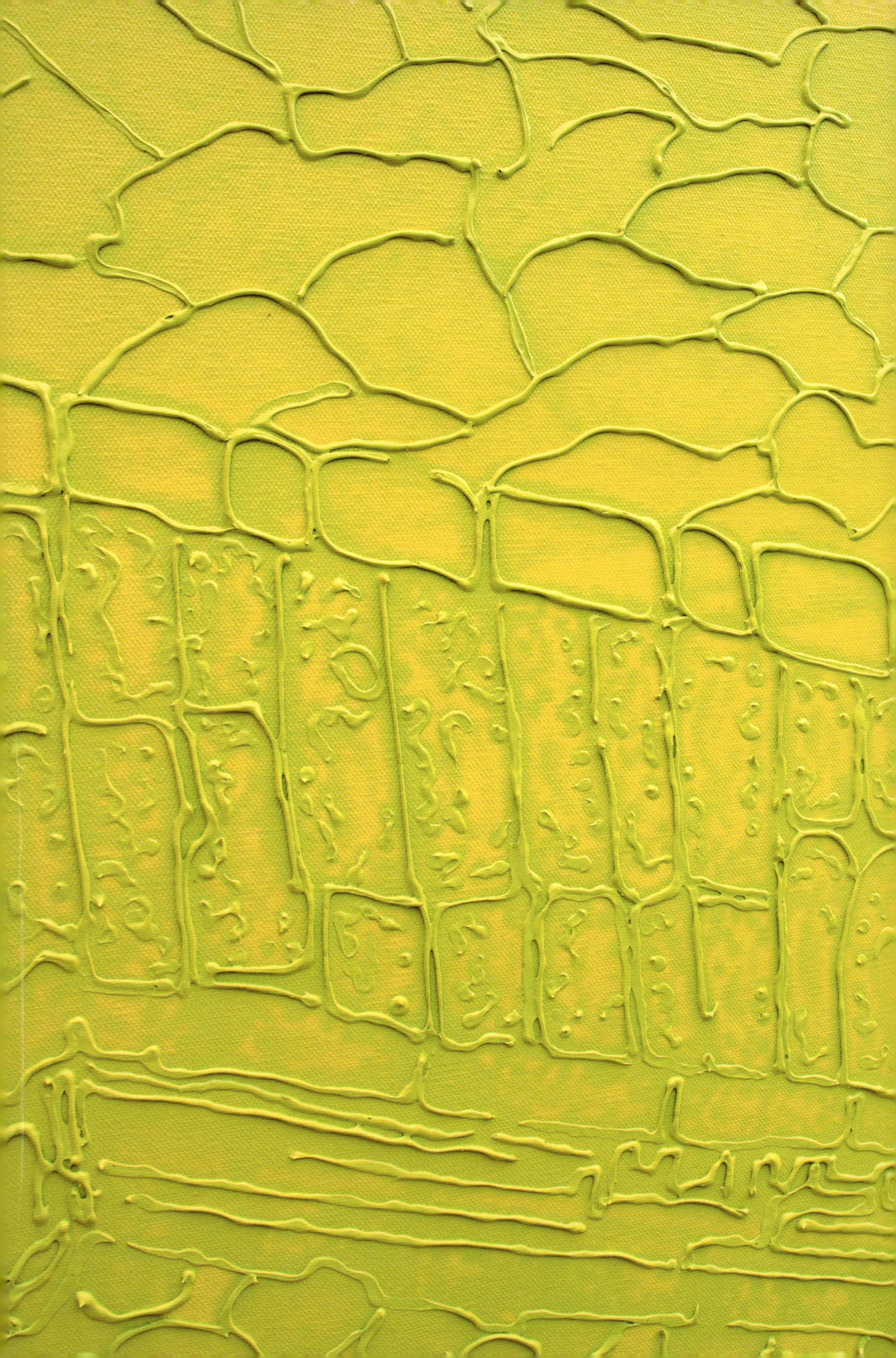

Rehearsal, for Things to Come

Wang Jianwei

Translated by Rebecca Karl and Jenny Lee

Latent Time

How to take action on something that is yet to come? Here, we are faced with a predicament of time, of how to use our experience of the present, accrued from the past, to bring to fruition a vision of the future.

A predicament also implies potential. This potential, or latent time, is constituted by anything capable of a singular mode of action yet simultaneously retaining the capacity for an entirely separate mode of action, including inaction. At the same time, the two or more capacities of this thing rely on each other and thus avoid conflict. One might also say that any object or event invariably bears a relation to a choice of openness: choosing to preserve, or not, its integrity. Notwithstanding its consistency, contradiction is a mark of authenticity. It changes how one regards an object; that is, an object can only reside in the possibility of its ability, necessary or accidental, to be perceived. In this way, the object announces its completion as a communal presence.

This type of time can be seen precisely in Stéphane Mallarmé's poem "Un Coup de dés jamais n'abolira le hasard" ("A Throw of the Dice Will Never Abolish Chance," 1897). Here, in the flash of a throw of the dice, chance is united with the inevitable. Such time furnishes a rationale through which to envision the future.

Rehearsal

This latent time and its corresponding work can be understood as a rehearsal. Rehearsal is a limitless opening, not a method. It does not wait for an accident. Rather, from the moment the rehearsal starts, it announces improvisation and randomness as enemies that resist it. Rehearsal is the activity of latency, possibility, and continuity. Such possibility also contains an impossibility. Just as I throw the dice knowing they have the potential to land in a certain position, I do not know whether they will actually land in that position. In the same way, rehearsal reveals a new kind of work that, regardless of function and composition, cannot be determined by randomness or turn into some fixed method (e.g., Conceptual, interdisciplinary, or experimental art). Instead, such rehearsal work is always situated between a chemist's laboratory and a craftsman's workshop, equally confined by elements, data, ratios, quantities, proportions, distributions, and densities, along with interrupted processes of revision and adjustment. This work leads to continuous deviation: at once losing a conventional sense of time and determining objects under the conditions of "normal" time. Such work leads precisely to a new state of being, and this collapse of inertia forecloses the possibility of naming the work process itself. With such a deficit of markers, this work employs other means of defining itself, namely quality, temporality, and parameters.

Form

Rehearsal is also the movement of form in its authentic resistance to interpretation. At the point of the instability of any given thing, rehearsal creates the conditions for an unbroken and continuous movement of self-transcendence. Within a concrete process of labor, a given thing preserves chance and necessity in its generation and activity. The thing, amid this work unlimited by quantity as well as activity unlimited by time, possesses some temporal form. The temporal form forces the object to produce an "overflow," even as it maintains its own properties. Possessed of this plurality, the thing also transcends the original value of its own self-duplication. The form of this thing lies in its own movement, that is, a rehearsal, which in turn allows it to become visible. This visible form guarantees the "materialized authenticity" of the object. Becoming form is the only mode of existence for the unknowable object. Form is thus a singular product of thought. It does not require an intellectual explanation of other content in order to become itself.

Universality

Form must furnish all humans with a nameless and total commonality. The type of universality theorized by Alain Badiou maintains the power of its own singularity from beginning to end, and it is precisely formalized power that imbues form with universality. Moreover, it is universality that allows art the ability to connect and be identified.

The form of universality that leaves no remnant behind becomes its own official elucidation of existence. Its mission is to not be admitted into the existing order of politics, as it cannot be named in this order. On the contrary, it will always be declared an exception, relegated to a place outside the normal order. At the same time, one must acknowledge that contemporary art is not a humanistic art; it should avoid being hijacked by any new romanticism (suffused with political sociality). That is, contemporary art is not a first-aid kit for humanism. Such a mission would be false and distorted. Genuine humanism offers no rescue; it only offers a universal sense of equality, which is transparent and inexplicable, all the while transcending human nature.

I think revolu
when you
anything in its
including

我認為，真正的革命是發生在對於現存

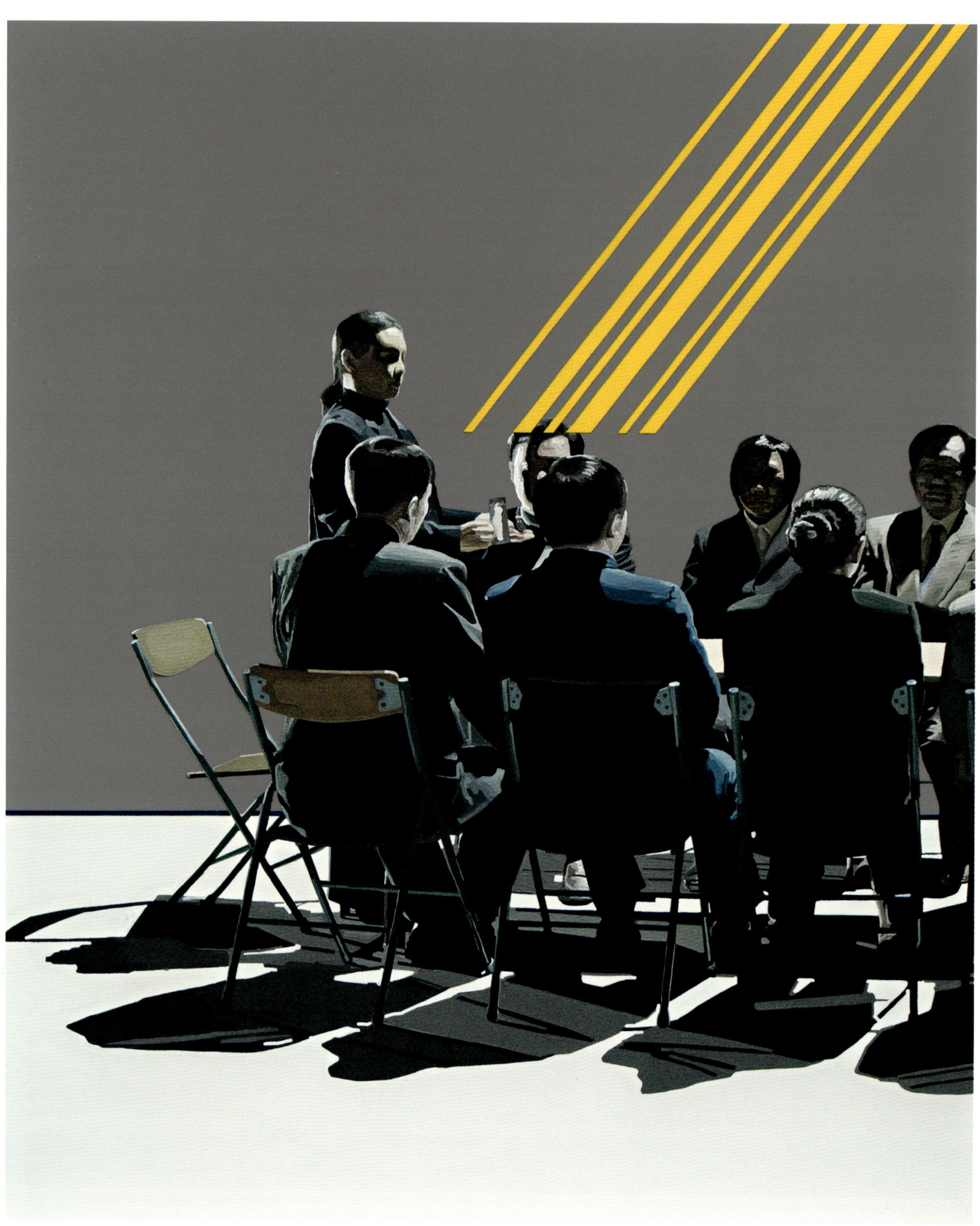

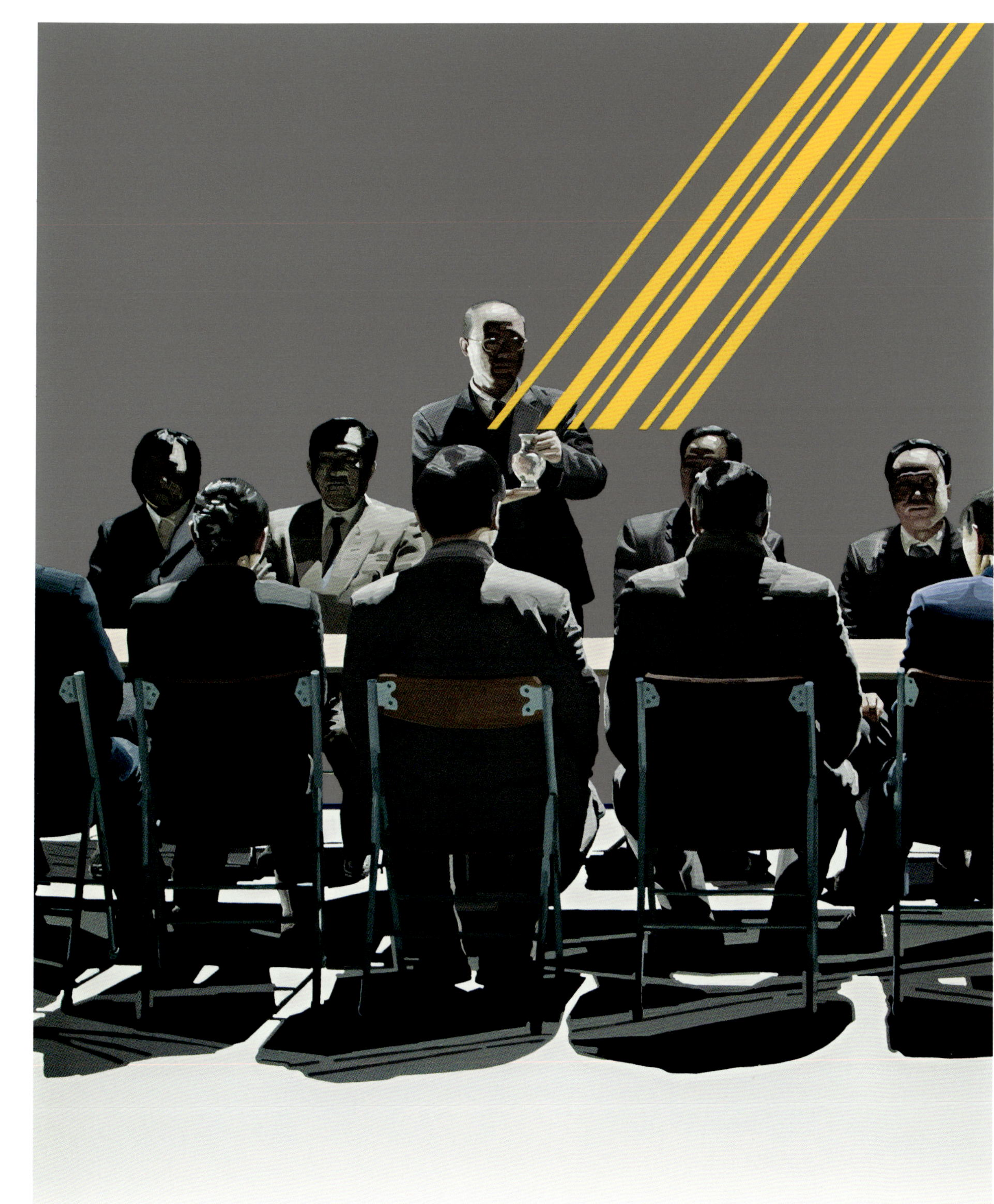

De-particularizing

Universality is vigilant toward any kind of particularity in order to clear away the remnants of details from the interpretation of things. Deep remnants are not transparent. They are obstructed by particularity and inexplicability, and genuine transparency rejects any form of suture. As a result of endless incidental conditions (region, nationality, religion, culture), particularity is incapable of embodying universality. It can only be sealed off in the exchange of such factors, in the mutual explanations that prove capable of producing a unified meaning. Unilaterally integrated into every sphere of circulation, particularity becomes a logistic, disappearing indefinitely into the supply and demand of entertainment news, political events, and public opinion. Particularity is merely domination over style and landscape.

Limits

Each day the artist's work confronts challenging environments not encountered the day before, situations that could not have been foreseen, and yet at the same time inhibit the artist's capacity for (unexpected) imaginings. The artist's work must evoke the limits on genuine thought and action. (In addition, on a purely conceptual level, the idea of thought depends on the loss of a referential "environment," which only enables thought to confine itself to the work of processing information. In a boundless state, the object of thought is lost altogether). One can no longer feign knowledge of any restrictions, which would merely force us to persist in drawing blueprints for what the future might bring. This new environment affords the artist-in-action the possibility to transcend his or her boundaries and limitations. I am unable to imagine the "unrestricted work" that such labor excludes. I am also incapable of understanding what "only free" labor even is. Would that be terror?

ution happens
u distrust
s current state,
yourself.

所有的東西不信任，包括了你自己的事情。

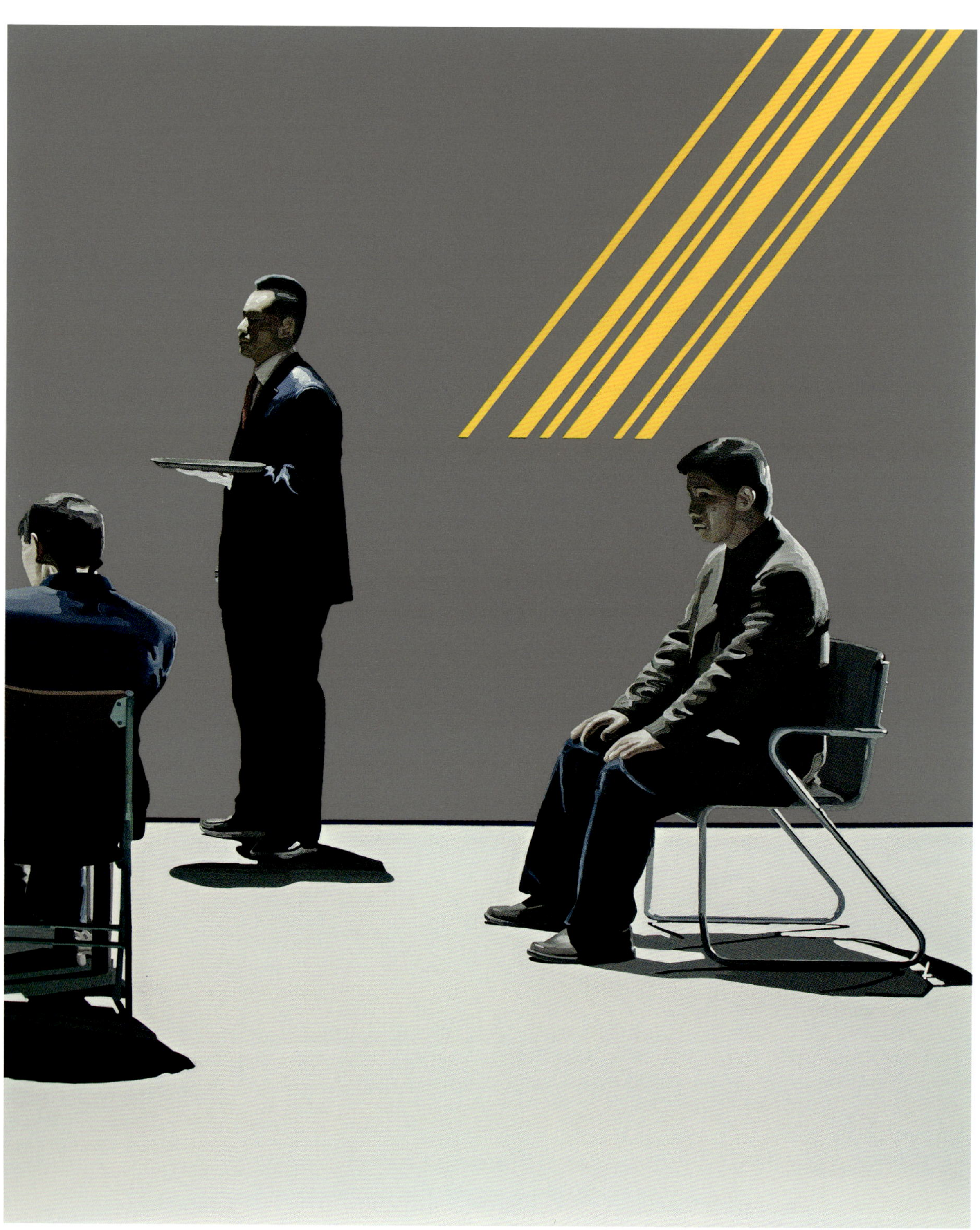

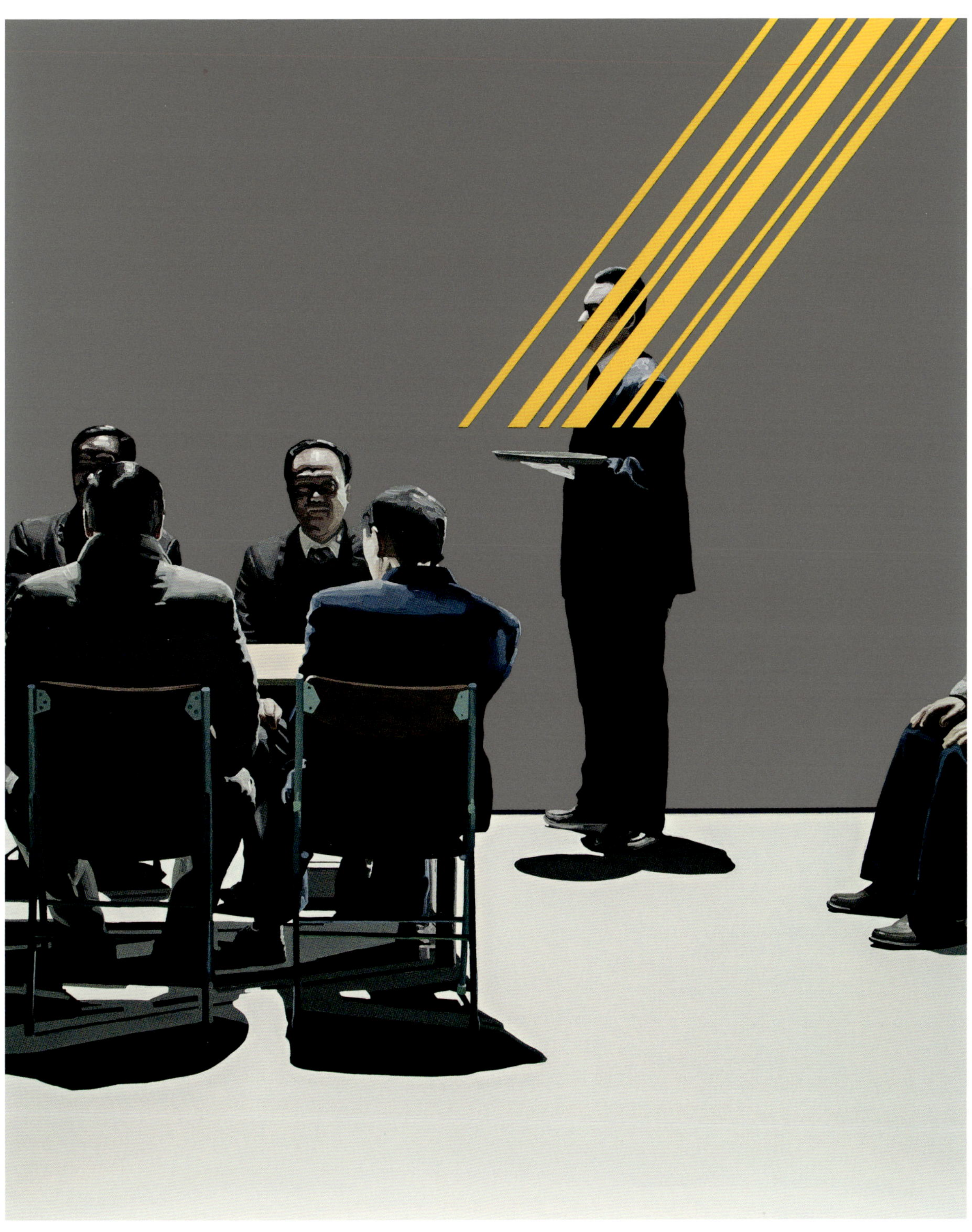

Time Temple, 2014. Acrylic and oil on canvas, four panels, 258.5 x 205.5 cm each, 258.5 x 822 cm overall

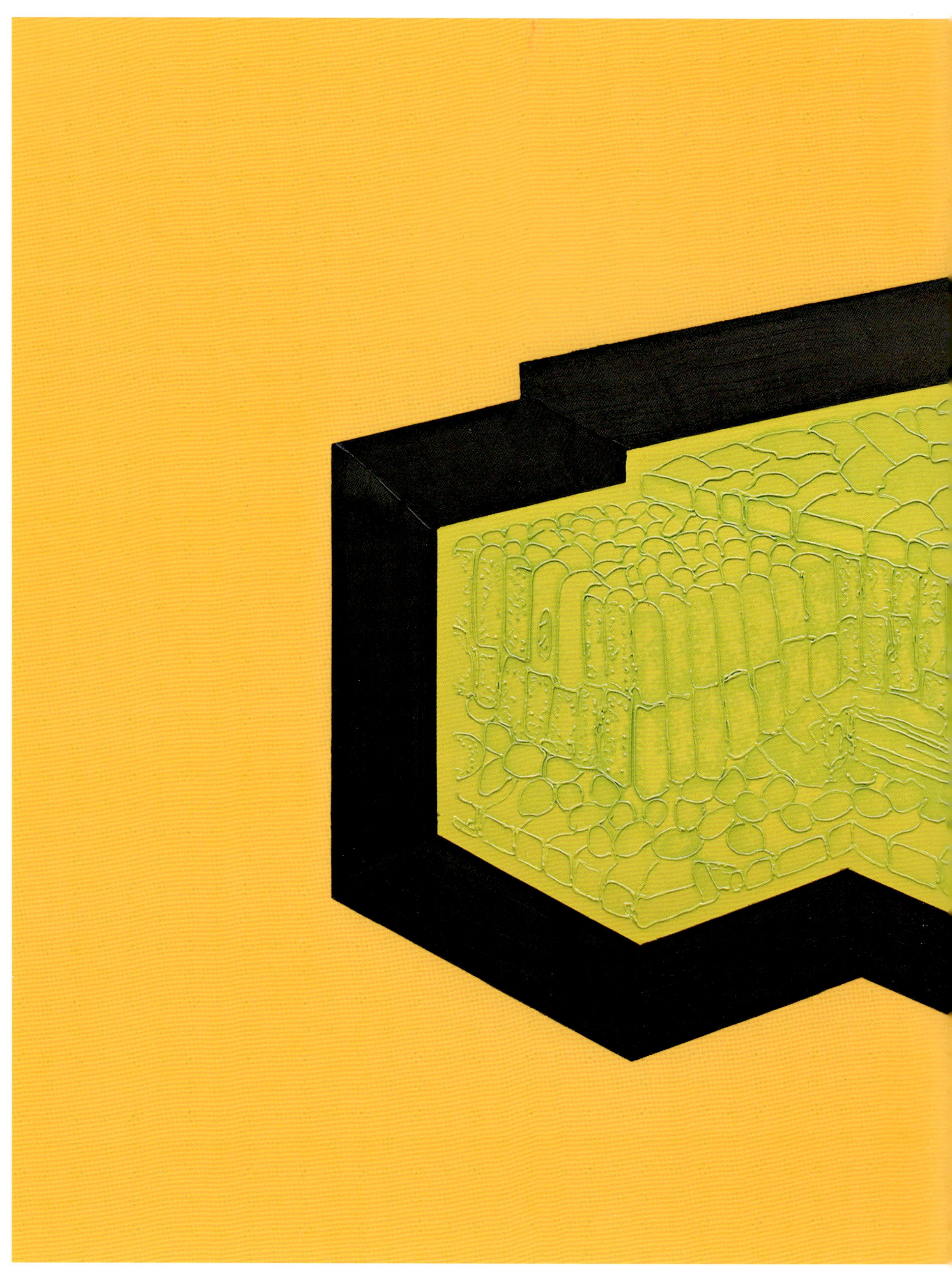

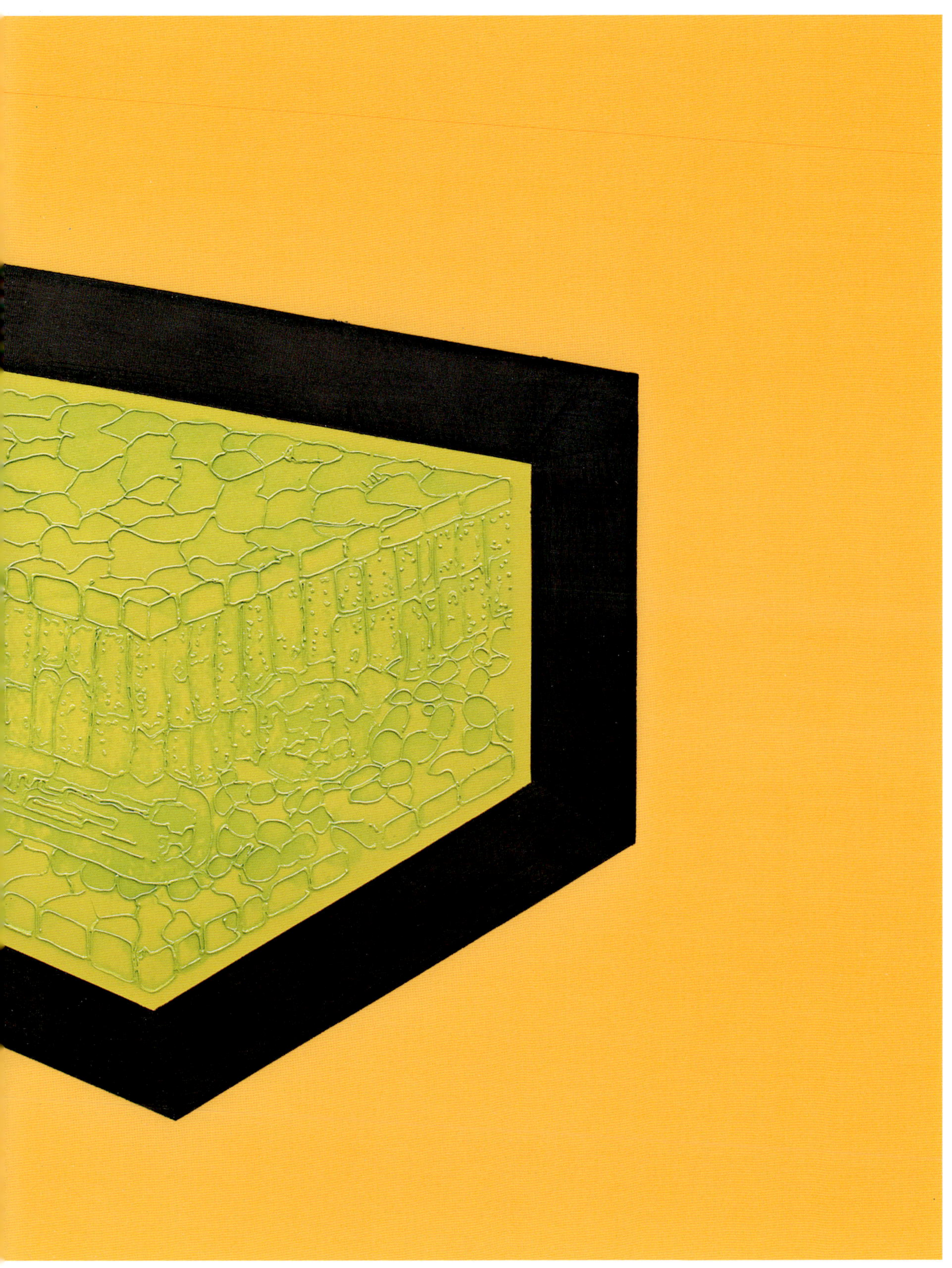

Time Temple, 2014. Acrylic and oil on canvas, 210 x 301 cm

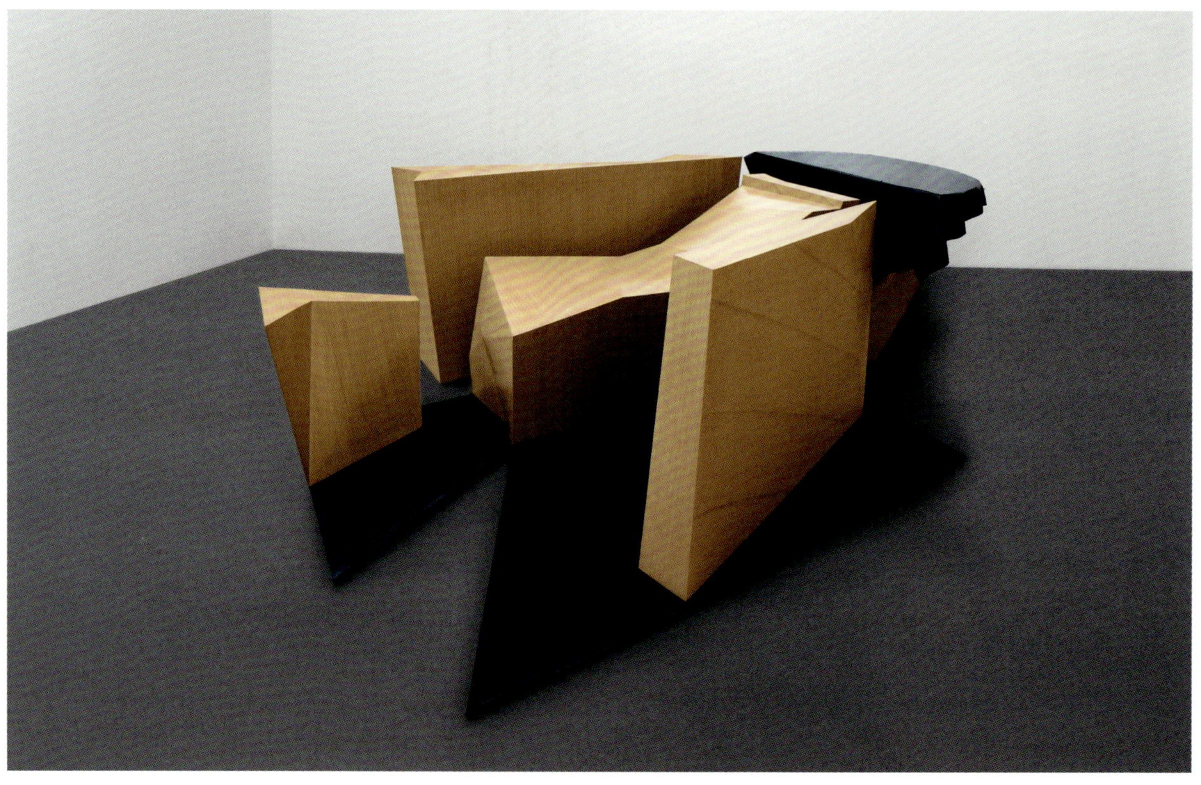

Time Temple 1, 2014. Wood and rubber, seven parts, dimensions variable overall
Right: detail

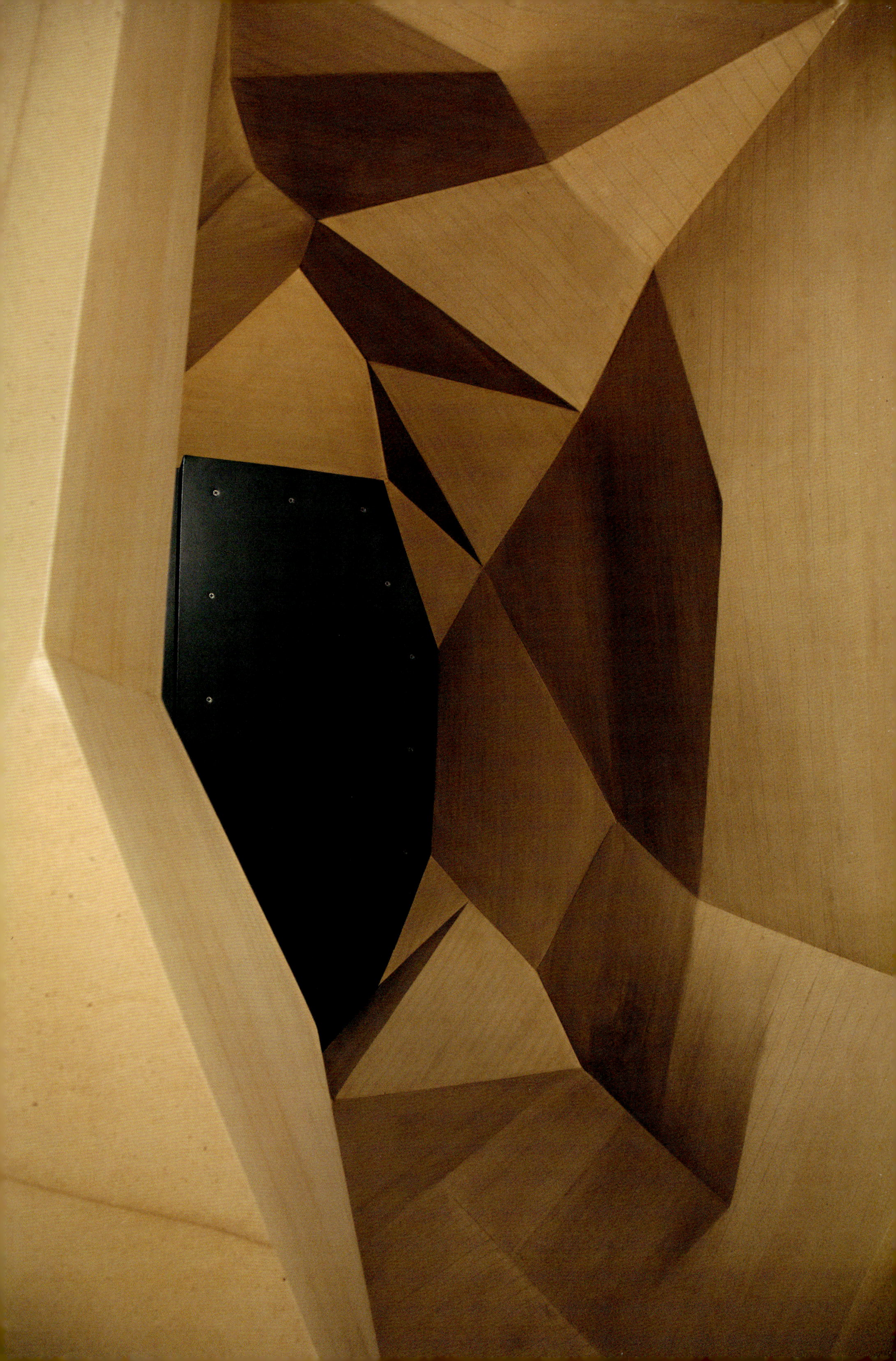

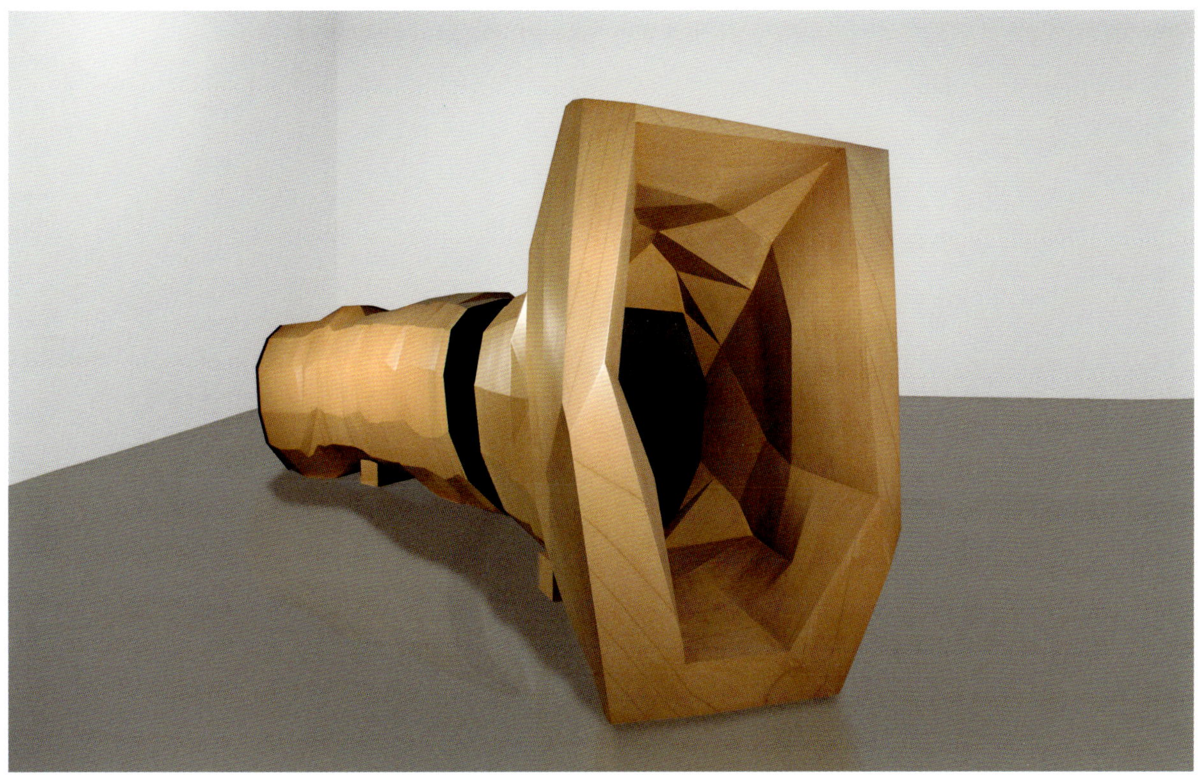

Time Temple 2, 2014. Wood, rubber, and steel, five parts, dimensions variable overall
Left: detail

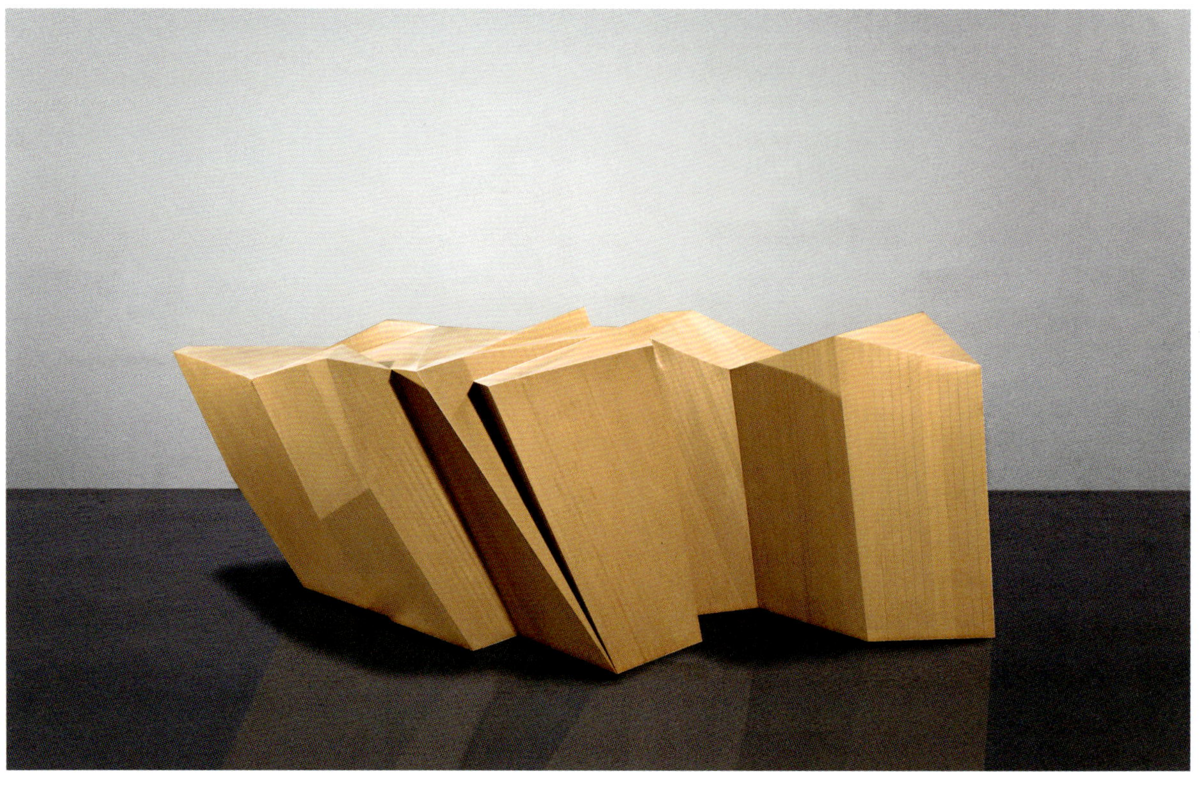

Time Temple 3, 2014. Wood, first of two parts, dimensions variable overall

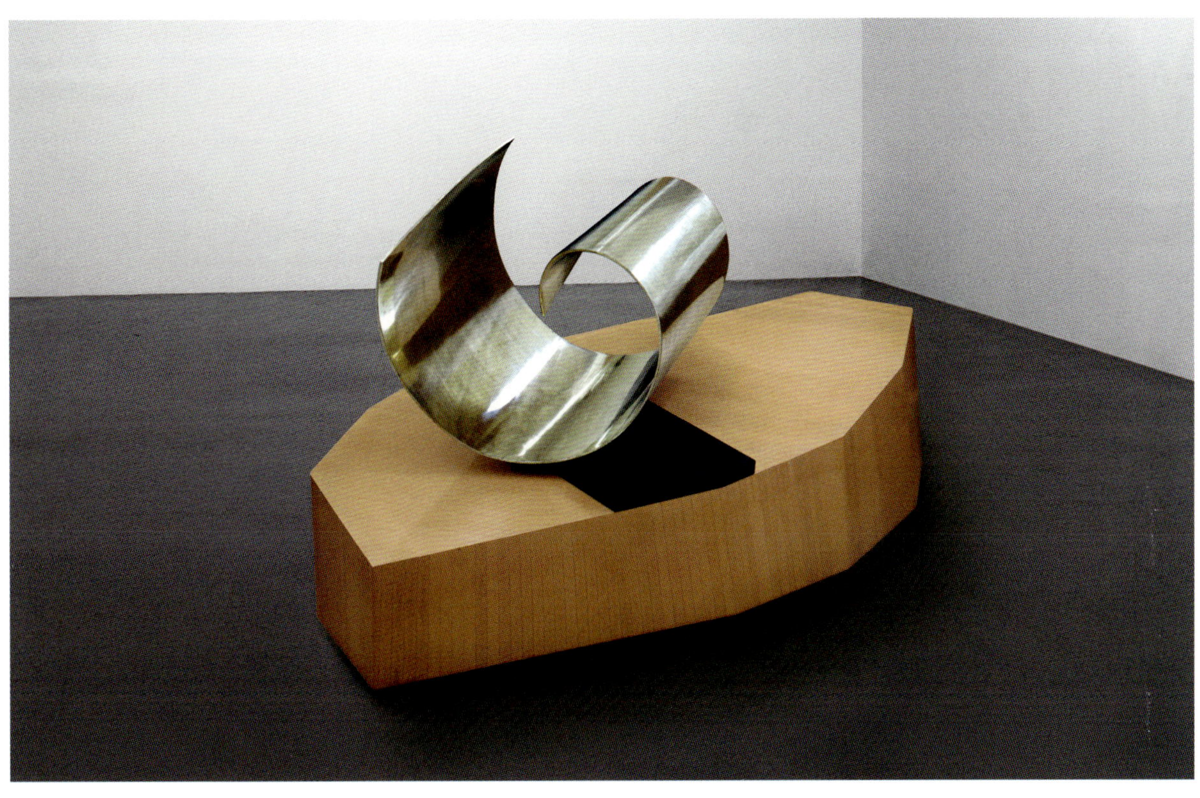

Time Temple 3, 2014. Wood, brass, and rubber, second of two parts, dimensions variable overall

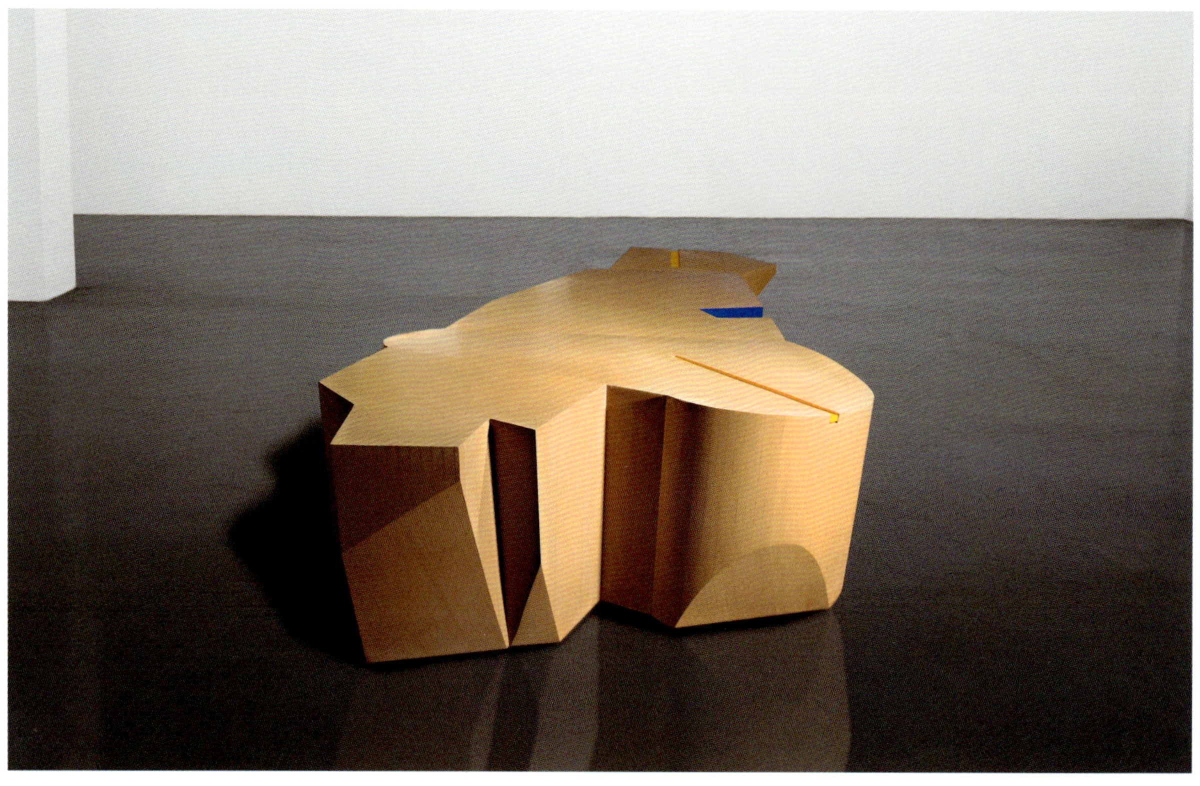

Time Temple 4, 2014. Wood and paint, one of two parts, dimensions variable overall
Right: detail

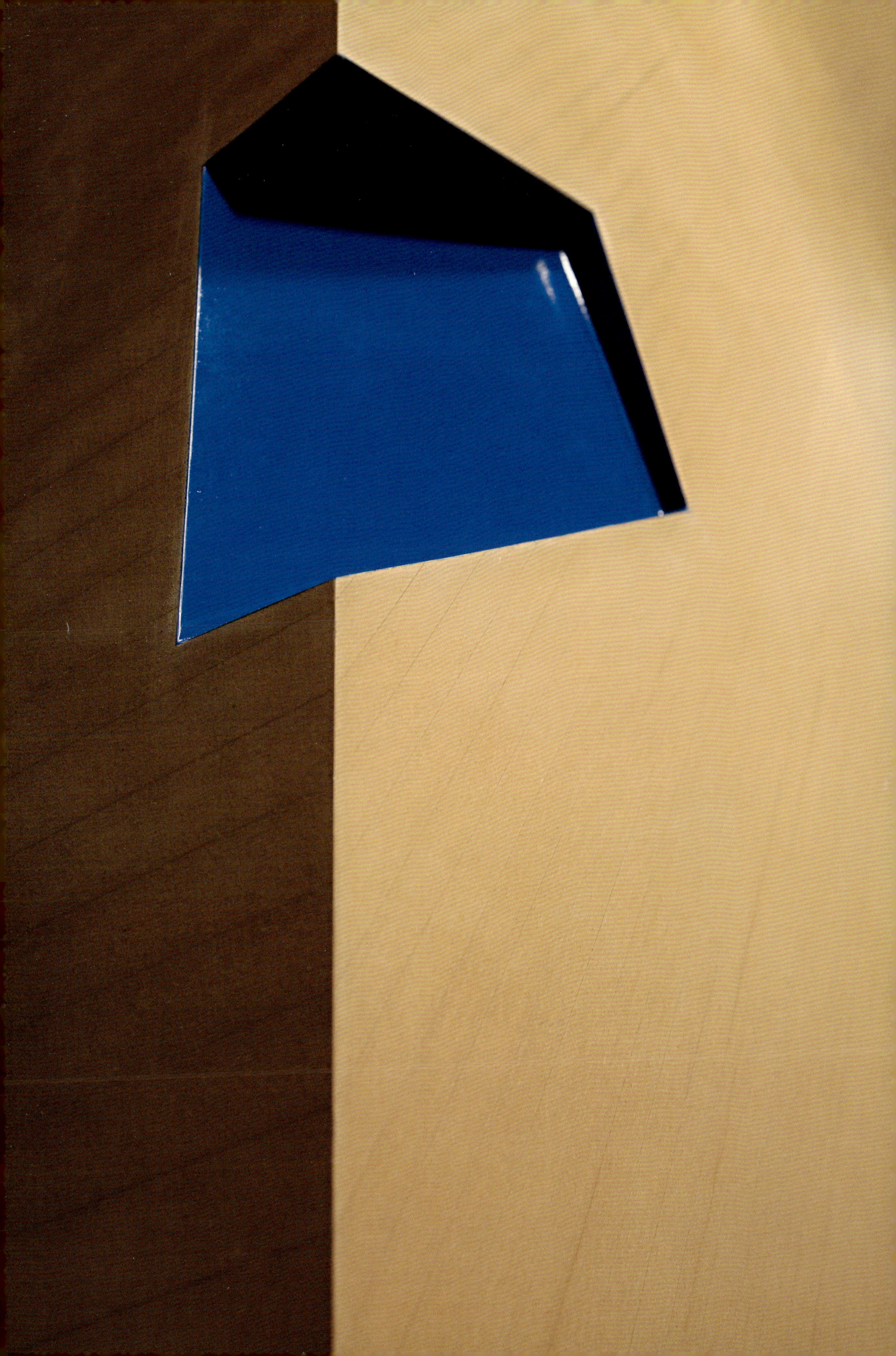

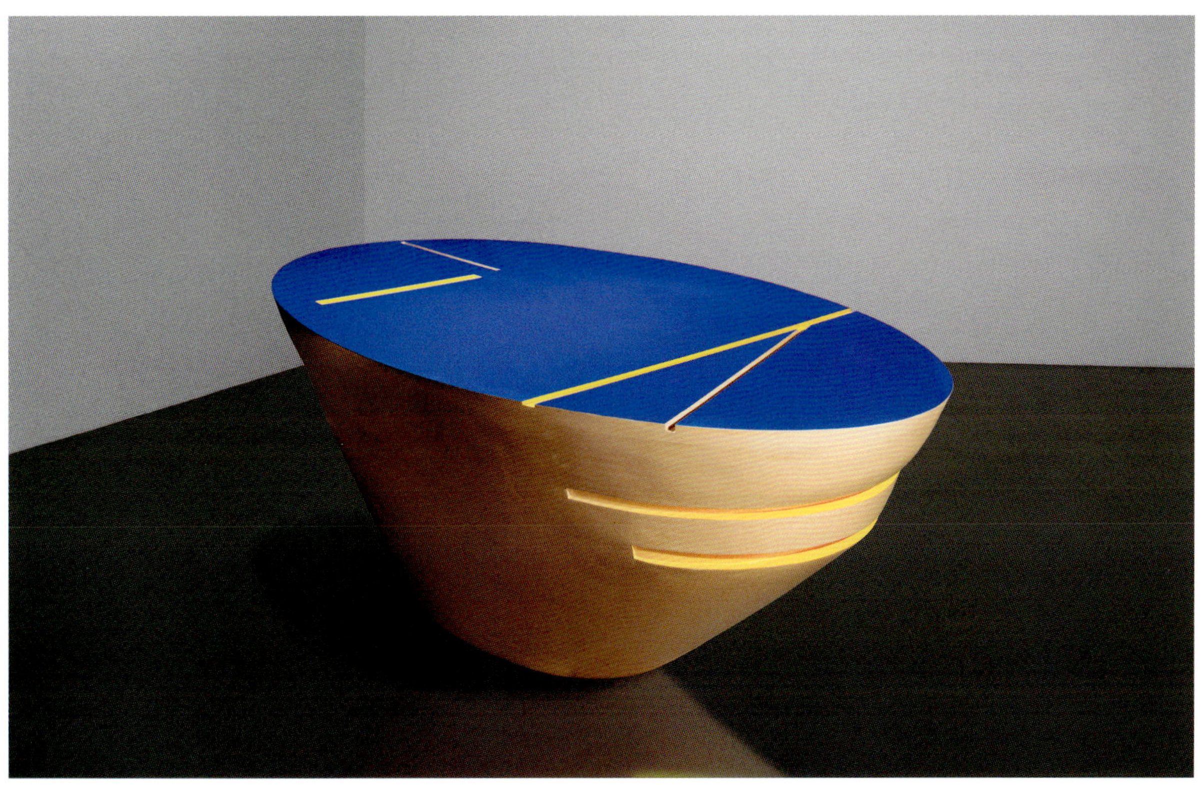

Time Temple 4, 2014. Wood and paint, one of two parts, dimensions variable overall
Left: detail

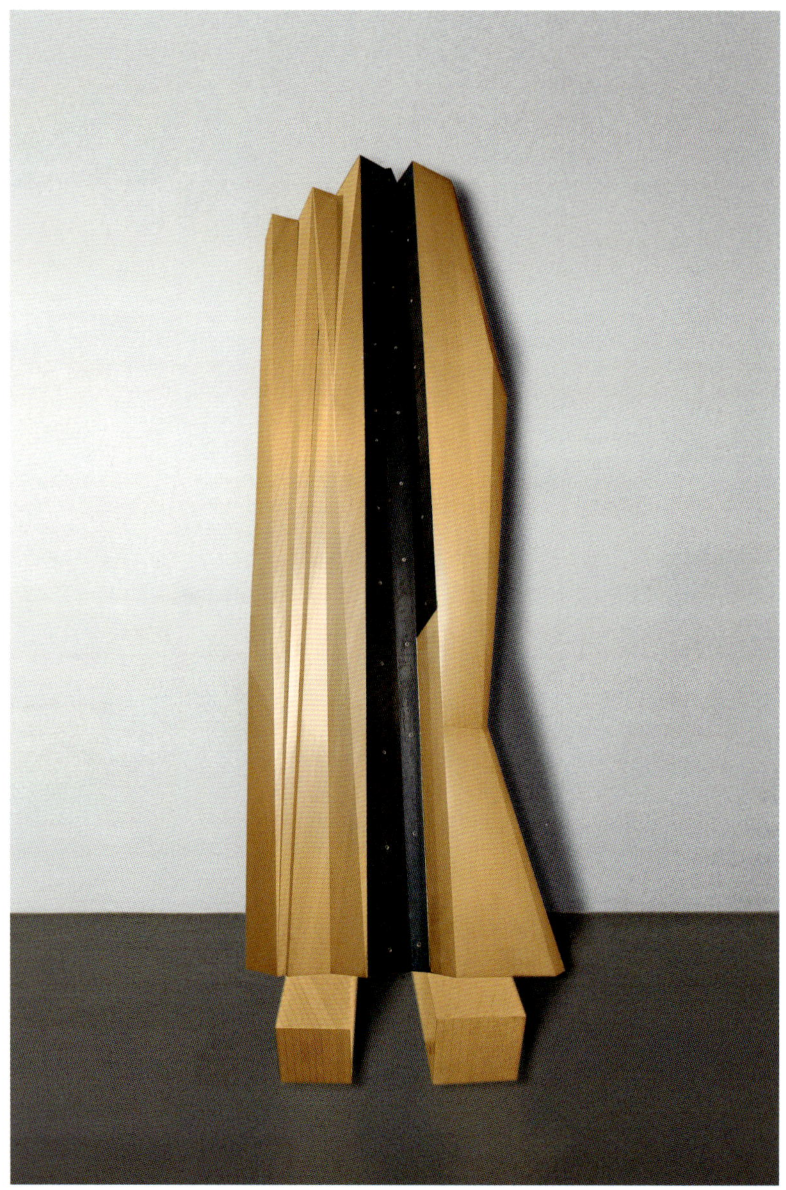

Time Temple 5, 2014. Wood and steel, three parts, dimensions variable overall
Right: detail

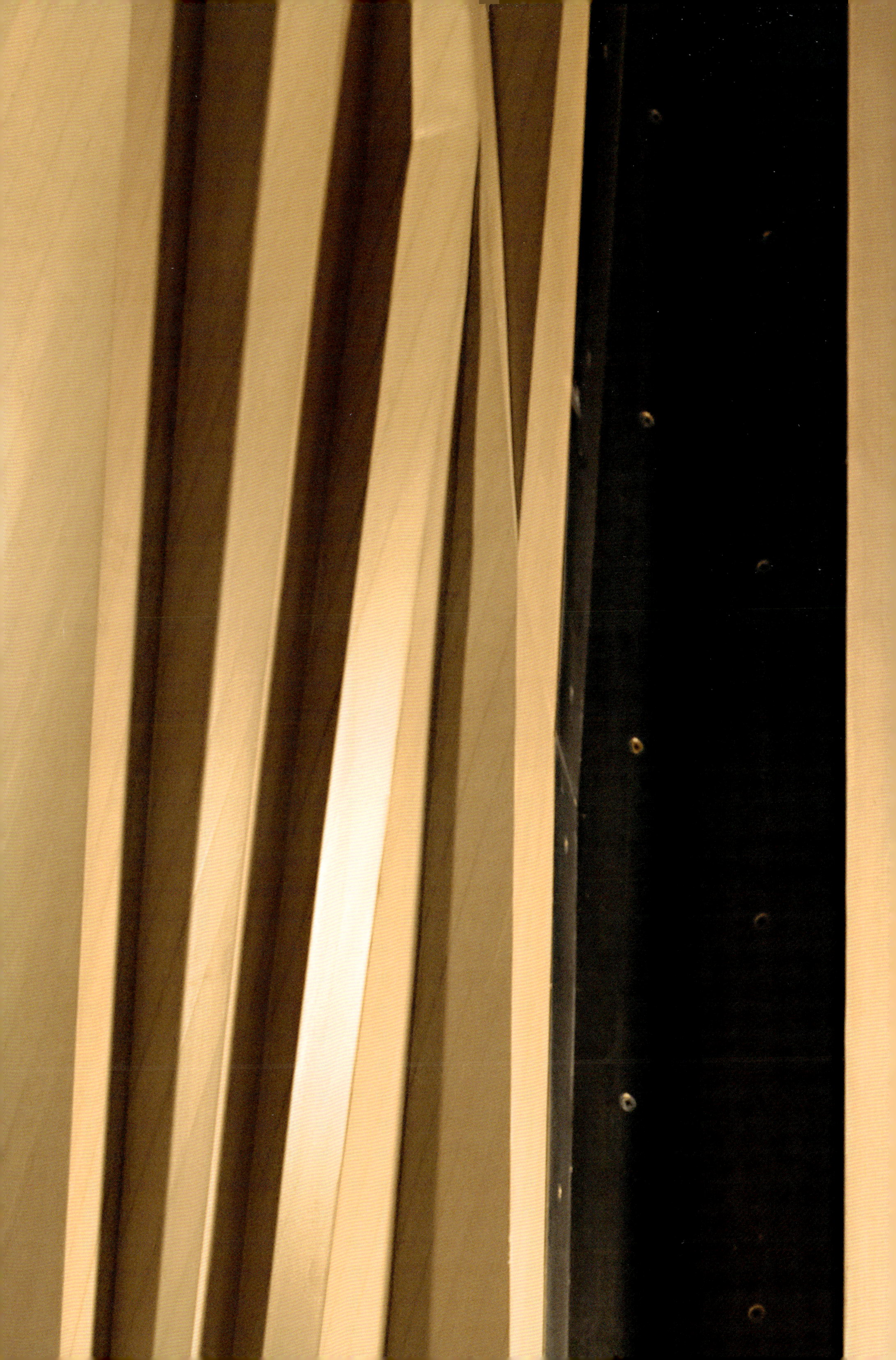

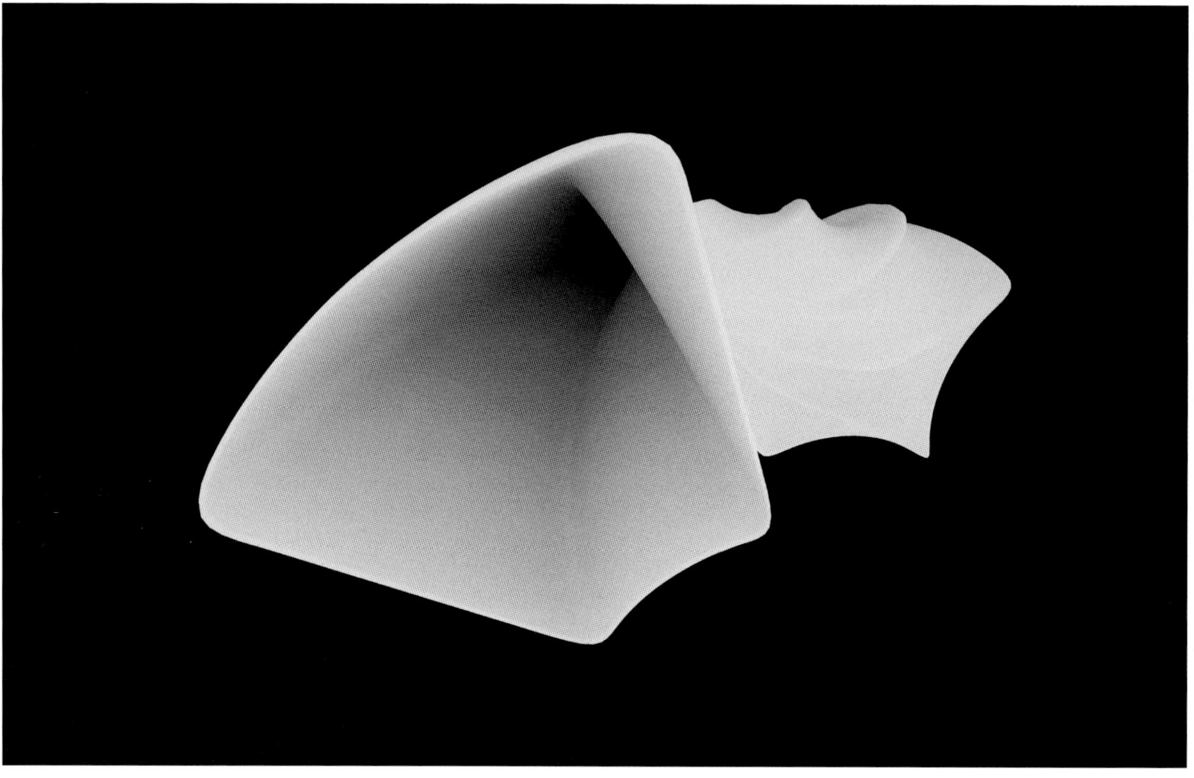

Sketch for the film *The Morning Time Disappeared*, 2014. Digital rendering, 2014

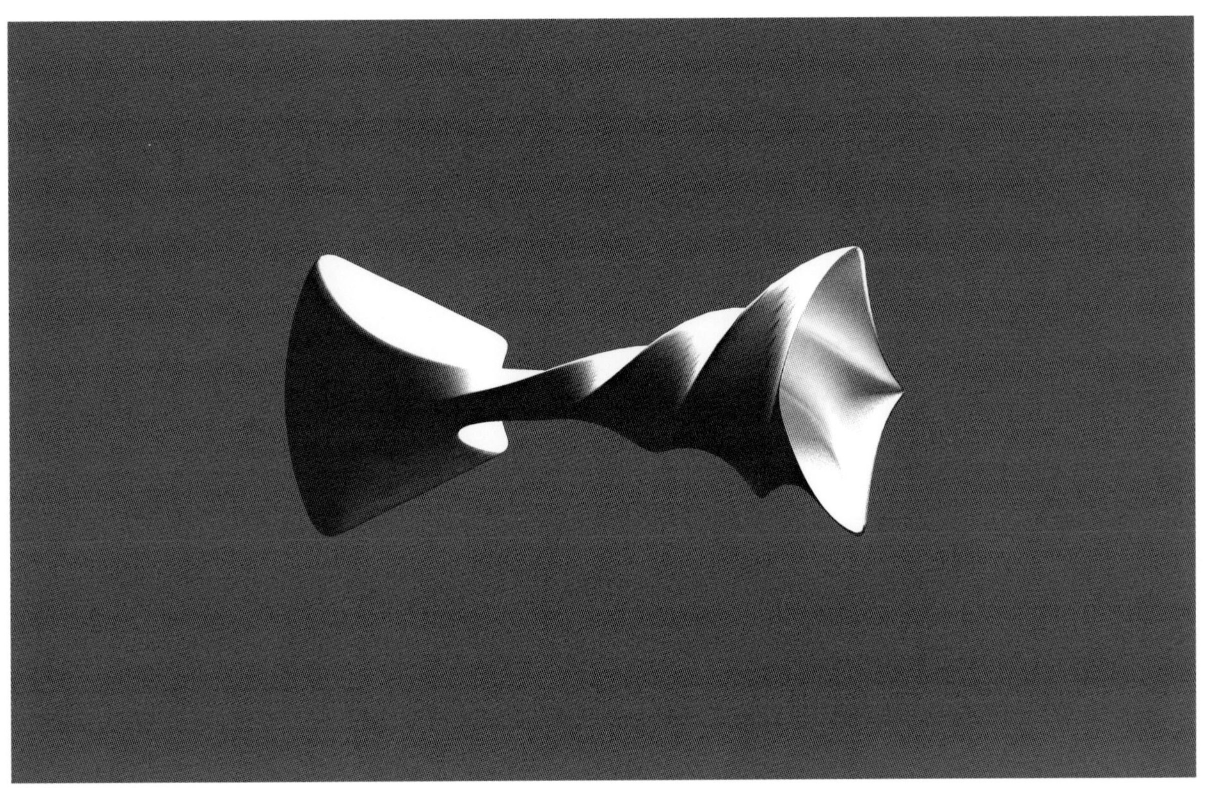

Sketch for the film *The Morning Time Disappeared*, 2014. Digital rendering, 2014

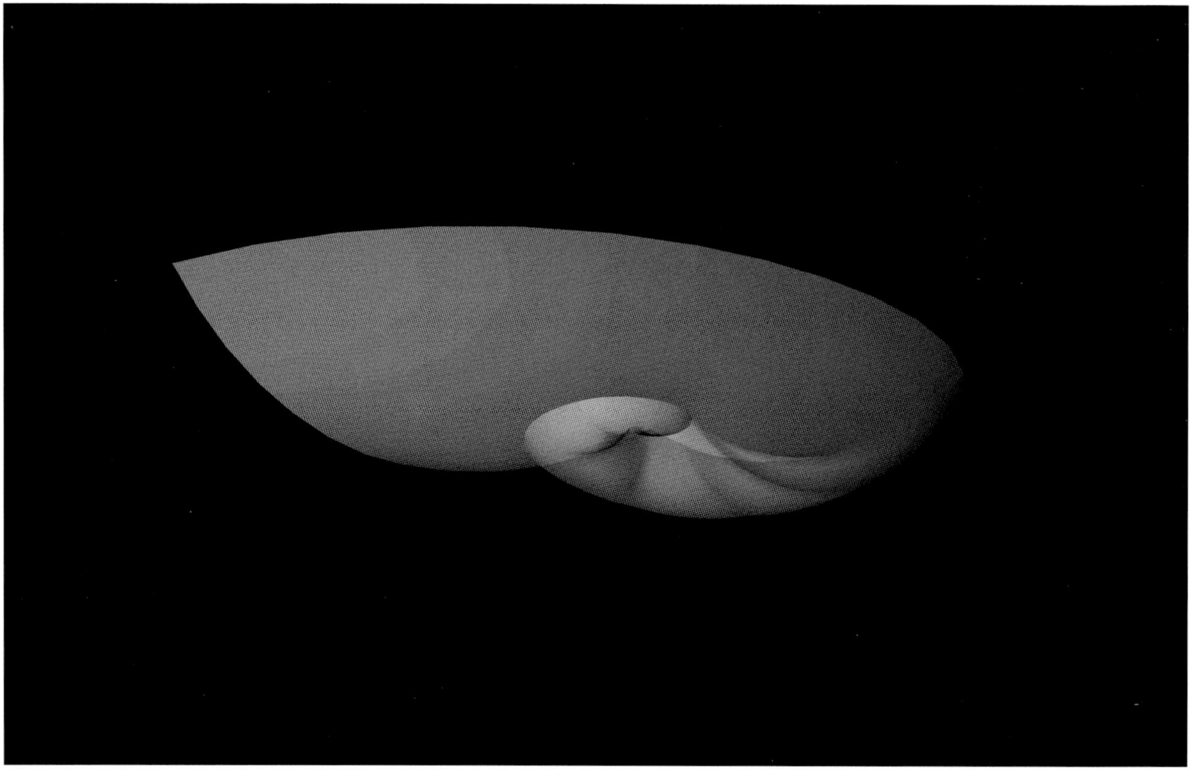

Sketch for the film *The Morning Time Disappeared*, 2014. Digital rendering, 2014

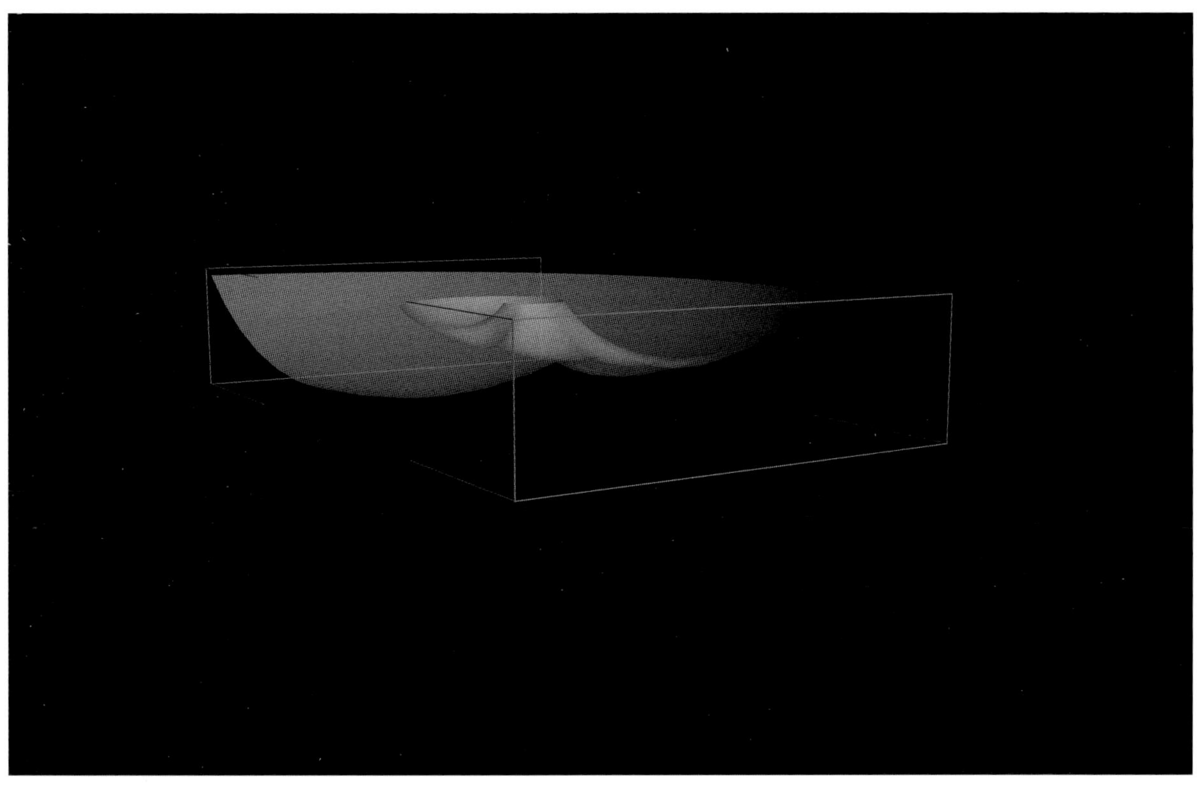

Sketch for the film *The Morning Time Disappeared*, 2014. Digital rendering, 2014

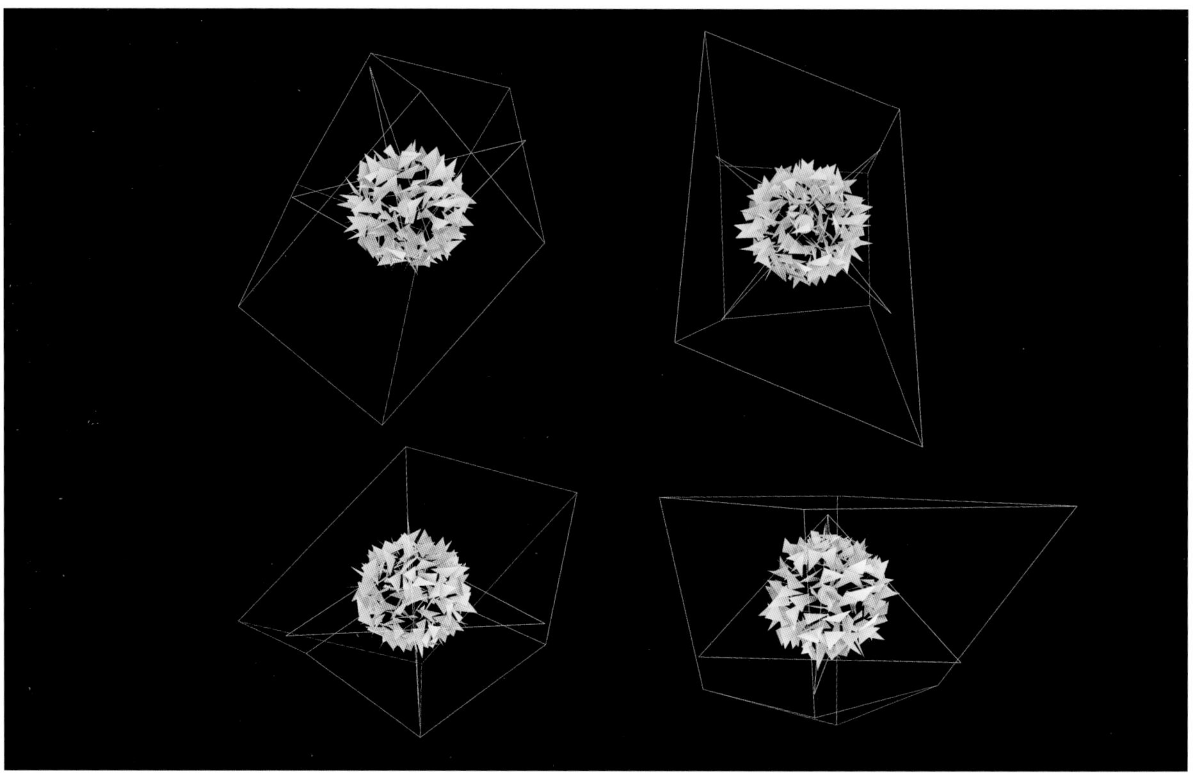

Sketch for the performance *Spiral Ramp Library*, 2014. Digital rendering, 2014

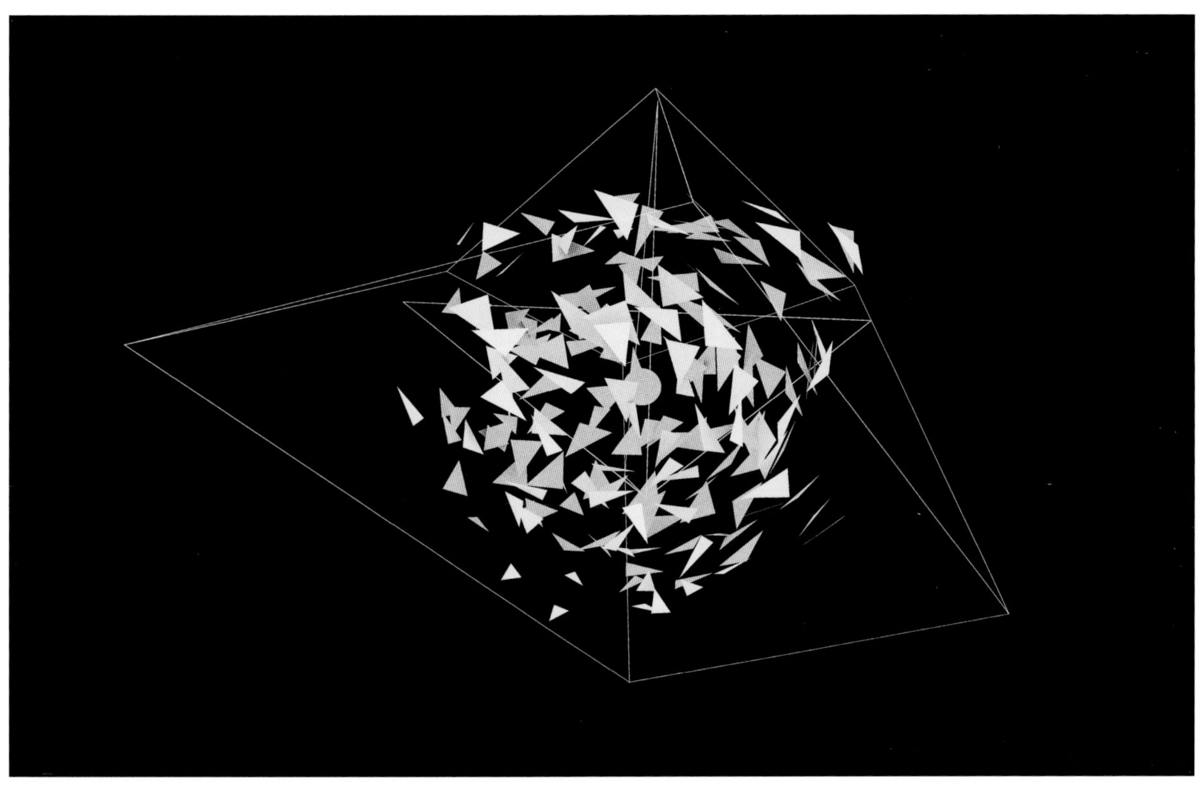

Sketch for the performance *Spiral Ramp Library*, 2014. Digital rendering, 2014

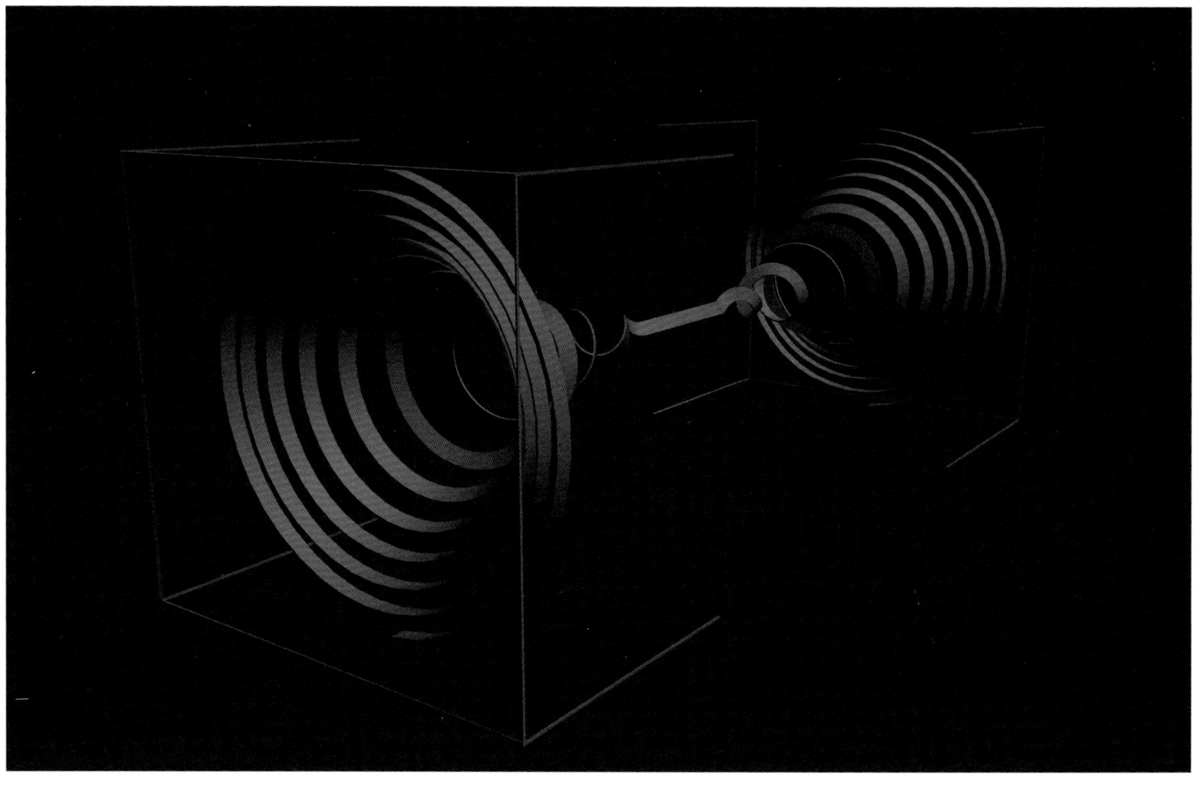

Sketch for the performance *Spiral Ramp Library*, 2014. Digital rendering, 2014

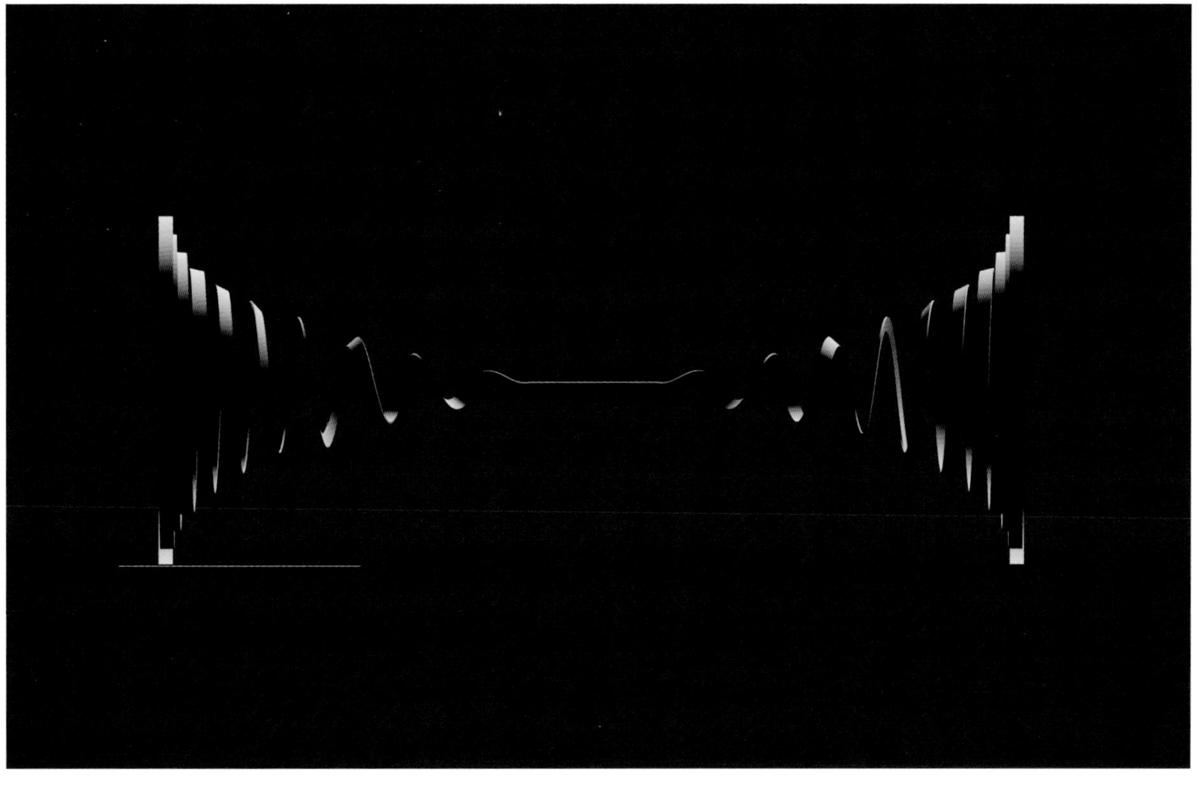

Sketch for the performance *Spiral Ramp Library*, 2014. Digital rendering, 2014

Works in the Exhibition

All works in the exhibition were commissioned by The Robert H. N. Ho Family Foundation Chinese Art Initiative at the Guggenheim and were produced in 2014, unless otherwise indicated.

Not all works in the exhibition are illustrated in this catalogue. The illustrations in the previous pages reflect possible variations as the works can be displayed together or independently in multiple iterations and formations. Dimensions of the sculptures vary with installation.

1 TIME TEMPLE

Acrylic and oil on canvas
Four panels, 258.5 x 205.5 cm each, 258.5 x 822 cm overall
Solomon R. Guggenheim Museum, New York, The Robert H. N. Ho Family Foundation Collection

The frames designed for the display of the tetraptych are not illustrated. The frames are of varying depths (35, 40, 45, and 50 cm, respectively) and create an undulation of images to the fore and back, alluding to time and movement.

Pages 54–55

2 TIME TEMPLE

Acrylic and oil on canvas
210 x 301 cm
Solomon R. Guggenheim Museum, New York, The Robert H. N. Ho Family Foundation Collection

Pages 56–57

3 TIME TEMPLE 1

Wood and rubber
Seven parts: 87 x 110 x 70 cm; 82 x 145 x 59 cm; 88.5 x 159 x 38 cm; 60 x 57 x 39 cm; 18 x 150 x 92 cm; 200 x 98 x 2 cm; 90 x 76 x 2 cm
Solomon R. Guggenheim Museum, New York, The Robert H. N. Ho Family Foundation Collection

Pages 58–59

4 TIME TEMPLE 2

Wood, rubber, and steel
Five parts: 196 x 152.5 x 123 cm; 150 x 220 x 117 cm; 147 x 97 x 102 cm; 35 x 60 x 35 cm; 35 x 60 x 35 cm
Solomon R. Guggenheim Museum, New York, The Robert H. N. Ho Family Foundation Collection

Pages 60–61

5 TIME TEMPLE 3

Wood, brass, and rubber
Two parts: 87.5 x 205 x 124 cm; 92 x 188 x 91 cm
Solomon R. Guggenheim Museum, New York, The Robert H. N. Ho Family Foundation Collection

Pages 62–63

6 TIME TEMPLE 4

Wood and paint
Two parts: 340 x 124 x 58 cm; 90 x 211.5 x 101.5 cm
Solomon R. Guggenheim Museum, New York, The Robert H. N. Ho Family Foundation Collection

Pages 64–67

7 TIME TEMPLE 5

Wood and steel
Three parts: 274 x 83.5 x 23 cm; 35 x 60 x 35 cm; 35 x 60 x 35 cm
Solomon R. Guggenheim Museum, New York, The Robert H. N. Ho Family Foundation Collection

Pages 68–69

8 THE MORNING TIME DISAPPEARED

Film, edition 1/5
Solomon R. Guggenheim Museum, New York, The Robert H. N. Ho Family Foundation Collection

Shot in Beijing in summer 2014, this experimental film explores the transformation of contemporary China and the multiple ways of experiencing time and its disappearance.

The film was in production when this publication went to press. For complete documentation, visit guggenheim.org/timetemple.

Pages 70–73

9 SPIRAL RAMP LIBRARY

Two-part performance
Solomon R. Guggenheim Museum, New York, The Robert H. N. Ho Family Foundation Collection

Spiral Ramp Library is a two-part performance staged at the Guggenheim Museum in 2014–15. It focuses on the gathering and circulation of people and ideas within the museum space.

The performance had not yet taken place when this publication went to press. For complete documentation, visit guggenheim.org/timetemple.

Pages 74–77

Selected Bibliography (English Sources)

Compiled by Stephanie Kwai

Please note that, owing to the age and obscurity of some sources, it was not always possible to provide page numbers, despite our best efforts.

BY THE ARTIST

ARTIST WRITINGS AND STATEMENTS

Sources below may also appear in other sections of the Selected Bibliography.

2002

"Views on Contemporary Chinese Art." *Yishu: Journal of Contemporary Chinese Art* (Taipei) 1, no. 1 (May 2002), p. 14.

2005

"Multiple Explanations of One Process." *In Relativism: A Flying Bird Is Motionless*, pp. 6–9. Exh. cat. New York: Chambers Fine Art, 2005. In Chinese and English.

"On 'Interval.'" In *Interval*. Exh. cat. Shanghai: Hi-Shanghai Loft, 2005. In Chinese and English.

2007

"Leave a Place for Uncertainty." In *Fang Zhenning: Interface*. Exh. cat. Beijing: Wall Art Museum, 2007. In Chinese and English.

"Towards the World and Knowledge." In *China Welcomes You . . . Desires, Struggles, New Identities*, edited by Peter Pakesch, pp. 72–73. Exh. cat. Graz, Austria: Kunsthaus Graz, 2007. In German and English.

2011

Wang Jianwei, Lu Xinghua, Gao Shiming, and Song Yi. "Historical Void, Memory, and Archive." *Yishu: Journal of Contemporary Chinese Art* (Taipei) 10, no. 2 (Mar./Apr. 2011), pp. 42–46.

"What Makes Me Understand What I Know?" In *I Am Curious Yellow, I Am Curious Blue: He An Solo Exhibition*. Exh. cat. Beijing: Tang Contemporary, 2011. In Chinese and English.

2012

"About 'Yellow Signal.'" In *Wang Jianwei: Yellow Signal*, pp. 6–7. Exh. cat. Beijing: Ullens Center for Contemporary Art, 2012. In Chinese and English.

2013

"Out with Exceptionalism." *LEAP* (Beijing) 24 (Dec. 2013), p. 22. In Chinese and English.

"Protecting the Subjectivity of Contemporary Art." *LEAP* (Beijing) 21 (June 2013), p. 25. In Chinese and English.

"Sign as Event." *LEAP* (Beijing) 19 (Feb. 2013), pp. 100–01. In Chinese and English.

"Unavoidable." *LEAP* (Beijing) 20 (Apr. 2013), p. 41. In Chinese and English.

"Wang Jianwei: The 'Us' Fight." *LEAP* (Beijing) 22 (Aug. 2013), pp. 84–85. In Chinese and English.

"Wringing Out Attitude." *LEAP* (Beijing) 23 (Oct. 2013), p. 28. In Chinese and English.

"The Wrinkles of Rebellion." *LEAP* (Beijing) 22 (Aug. 2013), p. 26. In Chinese and English.

INTERVIEWS

Sources below may also appear in other sections of the Selected Bibliography.

2000

Dal Lago, Francesca, Song Dong, Zhang Dali, Zhan Wang, and Wang Jianwei. "Space and Public: Site Specificity in Beijing." *Art Journal* (New York) 59, no. 1 (Spring 2000), pp. 74–87.

2002

Obrist, Hans Ulrich. "Chang Yungho, Wang Jianwei." In *Bridge the Gap?*, edited by Miyake Akiko and Hans Ulrich Obrist, pp. 339–411. Cologne: Verlag der Buchhandlung Walther König, 2002.

2003

Obrist, Hans Ulrich. "Wang Jianwei in Conversation with Hans Ulrich Obrist." In *Camera/Chang Yungho, Wang Jianwei, Yang Fudong*. Exh. cat. Paris: Musée d'art moderne de la Ville de Paris, 2003. In French and English.

2005

Napack, Jonathan. "Wang Jianwei." In *Relativism: A Flying Bird Is Motionless*. Exh. cat. New York: Chambers Fine Art, 2005. In Chinese and English.

2008

Binghui Huangfu. "Interview of Wang Jianwei." In *Hostage: Wang Jianwei Solo Exhibition*, edited by Shen Qibin, pp. 26–48. Exh. cat. Shanghai: Zendai Museum of Modern Art, 2008. In Chinese and English.

Li Zhenhua. "Wang Jianwei: An Intellectual Who Questions Knowledge." In *Community of Tastes: The Inaugural Exhibition of Iberia Center for Contemporary Art*, pp. 207–15. Exh. cat. Beijing: Iberia Center for Contemporary Art, 2008. In Chinese and English.

2009

Obrist, Hans Ulrich. "Wang Jianwei." In *Hans Ulrich Obrist: The China Interviews*, edited by Philip Tinari and Angie Baecker, pp. 274–85. Hong Kong and Beijing: Office for Discourse Engineering, 2009.

2010

Binghui Huangfu. "Scripted Accident." In *Edge of Elsewhere*, edited by Lisa Havilah, pp. 121–24. Exh. cat. Campbelltown, Australia: Campbelltown Arts Centre, 2010.

Obrist, Hans Ulrich. "Wang Jianwei." In *A Post-Olympic Beijing Mini-Marathon*. Zurich: JRP|Ringier, 2010.

2012

Gao, Christy Y. Q. "Wang Jianwei." In *Contemporary Titans*, pp. 225–52. Shanghai: Joint Publishing, 2012. In Chinese and English.

Obrist, Hans Ulrich, Philip Tinari, and Melissa Chiu. "From Exhibition to Book: A Questionnaire on the Future of China—Innovative Hybrid Project Surveys Artists." *Asia Society* video, 42:06. May 16, 2012. Accessed July 31, 2014, http://asiasociety.org/hong-kong/exhibition-book-questionnaire-future-china.

Sans, Jérôme. "Chronology and Entropy: Jérôme Sans Interviews Wang Jianwei." In *Wang Jianwei: Yellow Signal*, pp. 15–22. Exh. cat. Beijing: Ullens Center for Contemporary Art, 2012. In Chinese and English.

Zheng Shengtian. "Interview with Wang Jianwei on Yellow Signal." *Yishu: Journal of Contemporary Chinese Art* (Taipei) 11, no. 3 (May 2012), pp. 30–41.

ABOUT THE ARTIST

MONOGRAPHIC EXHIBITION CATALOGUES

Sources below may also appear in other sections of the Selected Bibliography.

2005

Relativism: A Flying Bird Is Motionless. New York: Chambers Fine Art, 2005. With statements by the artist and essays by Jonathan Napack and Christophe W. Mao. In Chinese and English.

Wang Jianwei: Giant Steps. Adelaide, Australia: Australian Experimental Art Foundation, 2005.

2006

Dodge. Shanghai: Shanghai Gallery of Art, 2006. In Chinese and English.

2007

Mao, Christophe W., and John Tancock, eds. *Dilemma: Three Way Fork in the Road—Recent Works by Wang Jianwei*. Beijing: Chambers Fine Art, 2007. With essays by Anselm Franke and Christophe W. Mao. In Chinese and English.

2008

Shen Qibin, ed. *Hostage: Wang Jianwei Solo Exhibition*. Shanghai: Zendai Museum of Modern Art, 2008. With essays by Binghui Huangfu, Marianne Brouwer, and Shen Qibin. In Chinese and English.

2012

Wang Jianwei: Yellow Signal. Beijing: Ullens Center for Contemporary Art, 2012. With statements by the artist and essays by Lu Jie, Jérôme Sans, Paula Tsai, and Zhu Wen. In Chinese and English.

GROUP EXHIBITION CATALOGUES

Sources below may also appear in other sections of the Selected Bibliography.

1987

Beyond the Open Door: Contemporary Paintings from the People's Republic of China, p. 73. Pasadena, Calif.: Pacific Asia Museum, 1987.

1993

China's New Art, Post-1989, pp. 40–41. Hong Kong: Hanart TZ Gallery, 1993. In Chinese and English.

Dorana, Valerie, and Melanie Pong. *New Art from China, Post-1989*. London: Marlborough Fine Art, 1993.

Mao Goes Pop: China Post-1989. Sydney: Museum of Contemporary Art, 1993.

1995

Gwangju Biennale '95: Beyond the Borders Gwangju, South Korea: Gwangju Biennale Foundation, 1995. In Korean and English.

Minamishima, Hiroshi, Arata Tani, and Huang Zhuan. *New Asian Art Show 1995: China, Korea, Japan*. Osaka: Committee of International Contemporary Art, 1995. With an essay by Huang Zhuan. In Japanese and English.

1996

The Second Asia-Pacific Triennial of Contemporary Art: Brisbane, Australia, 1996, p. 73. Brisbane, Australia: Queensland Art Gallery, 1996.

1997

Another Long March: Chinese Conceptual and Installation Art in the Nineties. Breda, Netherlands: Fundament Foundation, 1997.

David, Catherine, and Jean-François Chevrier. *Politics, Poetics: Documenta X, the Book*. Ostfildern-Ruit, Germany: Hatje Cantz, 1997.

Hanru, Hou, and Hans Ulrich Obrist. *Cities on the Move*. Ostfildern-Ruit, Germany: Hatje Cantz, 1997.

In & Out: Contemporary Chinese Art from China and Australia, pp. 52–55, 78. Singapore: LaSalle-SIA College of the Arts, 1997. In Chinese and English.

Journey to the East '97: Installation Arts from Beijing, Shanghai, Taipei and Hong Kong. Hong Kong: Hong Kong Arts Centre and Hong Kong Institute of Contemporary Culture, 1997. In Chinese and English.

1998

Cai Qing and Feng Boyi. *Trace of Existence: A Private Showing of Chinese Contemporary Art '98*, pp. 10–11, 14, 134–37. Beijing: Art Now Studio, 1998.

Cities on the Move: Contemporary Asian Art on the Turn of the 21st Century. Vienna: Wiener Secession, 1998.

1999

Engberg, Juliana. *Signs of Life: Melbourne International Biennial 1999*. Melbourne: City of Melbourne, 1999.

Fast>>Forward: New Chinese Video Art, p. 34. Hong Kong: Hanart TZ Gallery, 1999. In Chinese, Portuguese, and English.

10th Yamagata International Documentary Film Festival. Yamagata, Japan: Museum of Art, Yamagata, 1999. In Japanese and English.

2000

Post-Material: Interpretations of Everyday Life by Contemporary Chinese Artists. Beijing: Red Gate Gallery, 2000. In Chinese and English.

13th Festival International de Programmes Audiovisuels. Biarritz, France: FIPA, 2000. In French and English.

2001

Obrist, Hans Ulrich, and Barbara Vanderlinden, eds. *Laboratorium*, pp. 452–53. Antwerp, Belgium: DuMont, 2001.

2002

Compound Eyes: Contemporary Video Art from China, pp. 64–71, 91–92. Singapore: LaSalle-SIA College of the Arts, 2002.

The First Guangzhou Triennial: Reinterpretation—A Decade of Experimental Chinese Art (1990–2000), pp. 256–57, 448–49. Chicago: Art Media Resources, 2002.

Synthetic Reality, pp. 66–73. Beijing: East Modern Art Center, 2002. In Chinese and English.

2003

Alors, la Chine?, pp. 254, 327, 421. Paris: Editions du Centre Pompidou, 2003. In French and English.

Camera/Chang Yungho, Wang Jianwei, Yang Fudong, pp. 13–17, 37–39, 44–49. Paris: Musée d'art moderne de la Ville de Paris, 2003. With an essay by Michel Nuridsany. In French and English.

Control Z. Beijing: Taikang Space, 2003. In Chinese and English.

How Latitudes Become Forms: Art in a Global Age, pp. 244–47, 351. Minneapolis: Walker Art Center, 2003.

New Zone: Chinese Art. Warsaw: Zachęta National Gallery of Art, 2003. In Polish and English.

Second Hand Reality: Pre-Reality. Beijing: Today Art Museum, 2003. In Chinese and English.

2004

Between Past and Future: New Photography and Video from China, pp. 108–09, 163. Chicago: David and Alfred Smart Museum of Art, University of Chicago; New York: International Center of Photography; Göttingen, Germany: Steidl, 2004.

Devenport, Rhana, and Leng Lin, eds. *Slow Rushes: Takes on the Documentary Sensibility in Moving Images from Around Asia and the Pacific*. Vilnius, Lithuania: Contemporary Art Centre, 2004. In Lithuanian and English.

18 Solo Exhibitions. Kinmen, Taiwan: Bunker Museum of Contemporary Art, 2004. In Chinese and English.

Past in Reverse: Contemporary Art of East Asia, pp. 34, 114–17, 165. San Diego: San Diego Museum of Art, 2004.

2005

Beyond Boundaries: Shanghai Gallery of Art '04–'05, pp. 124–29. Shanghai: Shanghai Gallery of Art, 2005. With an interview by Zhu Qi. In Chinese and English.

Variation Xanadu. Taipei: Museum of Contemporary Art, 2005. In Chinese and English.

2006

Gao Shiming and Noah Ng Fong Chao, eds. *Micrology: The Politics of Realism, Chinese Contemporary Art Exhibition*, pp. 120–24. Macao: Macao Museum of Art, 2006. In Chinese and English.

Jiang Hu, pp. 5, 58–59. New York: Tilton Gallery, 2006. In Chinese and English.

2007

Beyond Icons: Chinese Contemporary Art in Miami, unpaginated. Hong Kong: Timezone 8, 2007.

China: Facing Reality, pp. 88–93. Vienna: Museum moderner Kunst Stiftung Ludwig Wien, 2007. In German and English.

China Onward: The Estella Collection—Chinese Contemporary Art, 1966–2006, pp. 278–79. Humlebæk, Denmark: Louisiana Museum of Modern Art, 2007.

The First Today's Documents 2007: Energy, Spirit, Body, Material. Beijing: Today Art Museum, 2007. In Chinese and English.

Net: Reimagining Space, Time and Culture. Beijing: Chambers Fine Art, 2007.

Pakesch, Peter, ed. *China Welcomes You . . . Desires, Struggles, New Identities*. Exh. cat. Graz, Austria: Kunsthaus Graz, 2007. With a statement by the artist. In German and English.

Sustainable Imagination: Media Art in China, Exhibition Series 1999–2007. Beijing: Arario Gallery, 2007.

2008

China Power Station Part III. Luxembourg: Mudam Luxembourg, 2008. In French, German, and English.

Community of Tastes: The Inaugural Exhibition of Iberia Center for Contemporary Art, pp. 207–19. Beijing: Iberia Center for Contemporary Art, 2008. With an essay by Li Zhenhua. In Chinese and English.

Inward Gazes: Performance Art in Asia—Exhibition by Invitation 2008, pp. 58–59, 91. Macao: Macao Museum of Art, 2008. In Chinese, Portuguese, and English.

Map Games: Dynamics of Change. Beijing: Today Art Museum, 2008. In Chinese and English.

Our Future: The Guy & Myriam Ullens Foundation Collection. Beijing: Ullens Center for Contemporary Art, 2008. In Chinese and English.

Wang Jianwei, Ni Haifeng, and Tiong Ang. *Between the Light and the Dark: On the Borders of Chineseness*, pp. 16–21, 38–41, 66–69. Amstelveen, Netherlands: Canvas International, 2008. With statements by the artist and essays by Marianne Brouwer and Simon Ferdinando.

2009

Bourgeoisified Proletariat, pp. 13, 53, 64–65, 78, 96, 112, 128, 142, 158. Shanghai: Shanghai Songjiang Creative Studio, 2009. In Chinese and English.

Deep Images: Why We Need Images to Live?, p. 49. Yokohama: International Festival for Arts and Media Yokohama, 2009. In Japanese and English.

Huang Zhuan, ed. *State Legacy: Research in the Visualisation of Political History*. Manchester, UK: Righton Press, 2009. In Chinese and English.

Shan Shui: Nature on the Horizon of Art. Beijing: Beijing Center for the Arts, 2009. In Chinese and English.

2010

Havilah, Lisa, ed. *Edge of Elsewhere*. Campbelltown, Australia: Campbelltown Arts Centre, 2010. With an interview by Binghui Huangfu and an essay by Thomas Berghuis.

Long March Project: Ho Chi Minh Trail. Beijing: Long March Space, 2010. In Chinese and English.

Museum on Paper: Twelve Chinese Artists, pp. 171–77, 287–88. Beijing: Iberia Center for Contemporary Art, 2010. In Chinese and English.

Reshaping History: Chinart from 2000 to 2009. Beijing: China National Convention Center, 2010. In Chinese and English.

2011

Out of the Box: The Threshold of Video Art in China (1984–1998). Guangzhou: Times Museum, 2011.

2012

Face, pp. 80–84. Shanghai: Minsheng Art Museum, 2012. In Chinese and English.

Rosenthal, Stephanie, ed. *Art of Change: New Directions from China*, pp. 84–99. London: Hayward Publishing, 2012. With an essay by Karen Smith.

The 7th Shenzhen Sculpture Biennale: Accidental Message—Art Is Not a System, Not a World. Shenzhen: OCT Contemporary Art Terminal, 2012. In Chinese and English.

BOOKS

This section includes books, chapters, and sections of books unrelated to exhibitions.

2006

Berghuis, Thomas J. "Performance in New Media, 1997–2004." In *Performance Art in China*, pp. 128–50. Hong Kong: Timezone 8, 2006.

2007

Chiu, Melissa. *Breakout: Chinese Art outside China*, pp. 24–25. Milan: Edizioni Charta, 2007.

2008

Albertini, Claudia. "Wang Jianwei." In *Avatars and Antiheroes: A Guide to Contemporary Chinese Artists*, pp. 104–07. New York: Kodansha Ltd., 2008.

Vine, Richard. "From Film to Video." In *New China New Art*, pp. 164–70. Munich: Prestel, 2008.

2009

Smith, Karen. "Wang Jianwei: Does Grey Matter?" In *Nine Lives: The Birth of Avant-Garde Art in New China*, updated edition, pp. 418–67. New York: AW Asia, 2009.

2010

Wu Hung and Peggy Wang, eds. *Contemporary Chinese Art: Primary Documents*, pp. 182, 242, 340–41, 424. Durham, N.C.: Chesham/Duke University Press, 2010.

2011

Burris, Jon. *At Work: Twenty-Five Contemporary Chinese Artists*, pp. 144–51. San Francisco: Long River, 2011.

Chen Xhingyu. "Wang Jianwei." In *Chinese Artists: New Media 1990–2010*, pp. 28–33. Atglen, Penn.: Schiffer, 2011.

Vine, Richard. *New China New Art*, pp. 166–73. New York: Prestel Publishing, 2011.

2012

Gao, Christy Y. Q. "Wang Jianwei." In *Contemporary Titans*, pp. 225–52. Shanghai: Sang Lian Books, 2012. In Chinese and English.

Nuridsany, Michel. *China Art Now*, pp. 74–81. Paris: Flammarion, 2012. In French and English.

Smith, Karen. "Wang Jianwei | Making Do with Fakes." In *As Seen 2001*, pp. 67–72. Hong Kong: Commercial Press, 2012.

ARTICLES AND ESSAYS

This section includes texts appearing in periodicals, collections of essays, and monographic and group-exhibition catalogues. Some sources may also appear in other parts of the Selected Bibliography.

1996

Hou Hanru. "Towards an 'Un-Unofficial Art': De-Ideologicalisation of China's Contemporary Art in the 1990s." *Third Text* (London) 10, no. 34 (Spring 1996), pp. 37–52.

2000

Pijnappel, Johan. "Wang Jianwei—Screen: Screen." In *18th World Wide Video Festival Amsterdam*, edited by Leo Reijnen and Johan Pijnappel, pp. 442–53. Exh. cat. Amsterdam: World Wide Video Festival, 2000.

2001

Phillips, Christopher. "Factual Fictions." *Art in America* (New York) 89, no. 3 (2001), pp. 46–51.

2002

Pijnappel, Johan. "Wang Jianwei: Material for Thinking." *ArtAsiaPacific* (Hong Kong) 34 (2002), p. 64.

Wu Hung. "Self and Environment." In *The First Guangzhou Triennial: Reinterpretation—A Decade of Experimental Chinese Art (1990–2000)*, pp. 251–55. Exh. cat. Chicago: Art Media Resources, 2002.

2003

Binghui Huangfu. "Wang Jianwei: Working on the Boundaries." *Artlink* (Tel Aviv) 23, no. 4 (Dec. 2003), pp. 58–62.

Hou Hanru. "Looking for a Place, for Yourself, and for All the Others." In *Camera/Chang Yungho, Wang Jianwei, Yang Fudong*, pp. 13–17. Exh. cat. Paris: Musée d'art moderne de la Ville de Paris, 2003. In French and English.

Nuridsany, Michel. "Wang Jianwei: Public Space, Private Space." In *Camera/Chang Yungho, Wang Jianwei, Yang Fudong*, pp. 40–47. Exh. cat. Paris: Musée d'art moderne de la Ville de Paris, 2003. In French and English.

Rehberg, Vivian. "Three Men and a Camera: Chang Yungho, Wang Jianwei, and Yang Fudong." *Yishu: Journal of Contemporary Chinese Art* (Taipei) 2, no. 3 (Sept. 2003), pp. 62–63.

2004

McNeil, David. "Wang Jianwei: Giant Steps." *Broadsheet/Contemporary Visual Art + Culture* (Adelaide, Australia) 33, no. 2 (June/July/Aug. 2004), p. 50.

Pollack, Barbara. "Mainland Dreams on Tape." *Art in America* (New York) 92, no. 6 (June/July 2004), pp. 130–34.

2007

Chan, David Ho Yeung. "Starting from Zero: Wang Jianwei." *Yishu: Journal of Contemporary Chinese Art* (Taipei) 6, no. 1 (Mar. 2007), pp. 34–38.

Franke, Anselm. "The Ghosts Crossing the Smokescreen: On the Position of Wang Jianwei's Work in an Emerging Debate." In *Dilemma: Three Way Fork in the Road—Recent Works by Wang Jianwei*, edited by Christophe W. Mao and John Tancock, pp. 10–13. Exh. cat. New York: Chambers Fine Art, 2007.

2008

Binghui Huangfu. "Scripted Accident." In *Hostage: Wang Jianwei Solo Exhibition*, edited by Shen Qibin, pp. 10–17. Exh. cat. Shanghai: Zendai Museum of Modern Art, 2008. In Chinese and English.

Borysevicz, Mathieu. "Wang Jianwei: Zendai Museum of Modern Art." *Artforum* (New York) 47, no. 2 (2008), p. 404.

Brouwer, Marianne. "Producing the Real." In *Hostage: Wang Jianwei Solo Exhibition*, edited by Shen Qibin, pp. 18–25. Exh. cat. Shanghai: Zendai Museum of Modern Art, 2008. In Chinese and English.

Shen Qibin. "Uncertainty, Possibility & Grey Area." In *Hostage: Wang Jianwei Solo Exhibition*, edited by Shen Qibin, pp. 4–7. Exh. cat. Shanghai: Zendai Museum of Modern Art, 2008. In Chinese and English.

2010

Berghuis, Thomas. "The Distance Between Us." In *Edge of Elsewhere*, edited by Lisa Havilah, pp. 45–48. Exh. cat. Campbelltown, Australia: Campbelltown Arts Centre, 2010.

"Building a Yellow Light Commonwealth." Long March Project—Ho Chi Minh Trail, June 10, 2010. Accessed Oct. 24, 2013, http://www.hochiminhtrailproject.com/html/e-discourse0.html.

Vicat, Michèle. "Wang Jianwei's Symptom at Nyon." *3 Dots Water*, Apr. 2010. Accessed Oct. 24, 2013, http://www.3dotswater.com/pointeratwork002.html.

———. "Welcome to the Desert of the Real." *3 Dots Water*, Sept. 2010. Accessed Oct. 24, 2013, http://www.3dotswater.com/pointeratwork006.html.

Wang Jiahao. "Wang Jianwei: Time—Theatre—Exhibition." *LEAP* (Beijing) 1 (Feb. 2010), pp. 190–93. In Chinese and English.

2011

Li Xiaonan. "Museum on Paper: Twelve Chinese Artists." *LEAP* (Beijing) 8 (May 2011), pp. 198–201. In Chinese and English.

Whittaker, Iona. "Wang Jianwei: Man In-Between." *LEAP* (Beijing) 9 (June 2011), pp. 99–105. In Chinese and English.

Young, Michael. "Beijing Iberia Center for Contemporary Art: Museum on Paper." *ArtAsiaPacific* (Hong Kong) 73 (2011), p. 139.

2012

Guo Juan. "Theory Fever: From Phenomena Onward." *LEAP* (Beijing) 14 (May 2012). In Chinese and English.

Lu Jie. "Encountering Yellow Signal." In *Wang Jianwei: Yellow Signal*, pp. 23–24. Exh. cat. Beijing: Ullens Center for Contemporary Art, 2012. In Chinese and English.

Smith, Karen. "Wang Jianwei: The Measure of Disorder." In *Art of Change: New Directions from China*, edited by Stephanie Rosenthal, pp. 84–89. Exh. cat. London: Hayward Publishing, 2012.

Tang Lingjie. "Face." *LEAP* (Beijing) 15 (July 2012). In Chinese and English.

Tsai, Paula. "Engineering the In-Between." In *Wang Jianwei: Yellow Signal*, pp. 230–33. Exh. cat. Beijing: Ullens Center for Contemporary Art, 2012. In Chinese and English.

Wang, Sue. "'Intimation and Illusion': Taking 'Yellow Signal' for Instance to Comment on the Artistic Language of Borrowing and Ambiguity of Wang Jianwei." CAFA Art Info, Mar. 9, 2012. In Chinese and English. http://en.cafa.com.cn/intimation-and-illusion-taking-yellow-signal-for-instance-to-comment-on-the-artistic-language-of-borrowing-and-ambiguity-of-wang-jianwei.html.

Zheng Shengtian. "Contemporary Chinese Art in Vancouver: Introduction to Yellow Signal—New Media in China." In *Yishu: Journal of Contemporary Chinese Art* (Taipei) 11, no. 3 (May 2012), pp. 6–12.

Zhu Wen. "The Endless Gleam of 'Yellow Signal.'" In *Wang Jianwei: Yellow Signal*, pp. 4–5. Exh. cat. Beijing: Ullens Center for Contemporary Art, 2012. In Chinese and English.

Compiled with the assistance of Siqiao Lu, Xiaorui Zhu, and Ying Zhu.

Selected Exhibition History

Compiled by Stephanie Kwai

Exact dates for some exhibitions were undiscoverable. In these instances, either the opening date or the month is noted. Where neither could be determined, the date field has been left blank.

SELECTED SOLO EXHIBITIONS

1991

Cultural Palace of Nationalities, Beijing, *Wang Jianwei.*

1992

Hong Kong Arts Centre, *Wang Jianwei.*

1993

Hong Kong Arts Centre, *Incident—Process, State.*

2003

Institute of Contemporary Arts, London, *Ceremony*, Oct. 23–26.

2004

4A Centre for Contemporary Asian Art, Sydney, *Wang Jianwei: Giant Steps*, Mar. 11–May 15. Traveled to Australian Experimental Art Foundation, Adelaide, Australia, Feb. 25, 2004–Apr. 2, 2005. Exh. cat.

2005

Chambers Fine Art, New York, *Relativism: A Flying Bird Is Motionless*, Oct. 27, 2005–Dec. 22, 2006. Traveled to Arario Gallery, Beijing, Apr. 1–May 14, 2006. Exh. cat.

2006

Shanghai Gallery of Art, *Dodge*, May 20–July 9.

2007

Hebbel am Ufer, Berlin, *Cross Infection*, June 1–10.

Chambers Fine Art, New York, *Dilemma: Three Way Fork in the Road—Recent Works by Wang Jianwei*, Oct. 4–Nov. 3. Exh. cat.

2008

Zendai Museum of Modern Art, Shanghai, *Hostage*, Apr. 19–May 18. Exh. cat.

OCT Contemporary Art Terminal, Shenzhen, *Symptom: A Large Stage Work by Wang Jianwei*, June 28–July 28. Exh. cat.

2009

Today Art Museum, Beijing, *Time·Theatre·Exhibition*, Nov. 22.

2011

Ullens Center for Contemporary Art, Beijing, *Wang Jianwei: Yellow Signal*, Apr. 1–June 26. Exh. cat.

2013

Long March Space, Beijing, *. . . the event matured, accomplished in sight of all non-existent human outcomes*, Sept. 14–Oct. 13.

SELECTED GROUP EXHIBITIONS

1984

National Art Gallery (now National Art Museum of China), Beijing, *Sixth National Fine Arts Exhibition*, Oct. 1–7. Exh. cat.

1987

Pacific Asia Museum, Pasadena, Calif., *Beyond the Open Door: Contemporary Paintings from the People's Republic of China*. Exh. cat.

1993

Hong Kong Arts Centre and Hong Kong City Hall (organized by Hanart TZ Gallery, Hong Kong), *China's New Art, Post-1989*, Jan. 1–Feb. 1. Traveled to Marlborough Fine Art, London, Dec. 7, 1993–Feb. 12, 1994. Exh. cat.

Museum of Contemporary Art, Sydney, *Mao Goes Pop: China Post-1989*, June 2–Aug. 15. Exh. cat.

1995

Gwangju Biennale Exhibition Hall, Gwangju Biennial, South Korea: *Beyond the Borders*, Sept. 20–Nov. 20. Exh. cat.

Kirin Plaza Osaka, *New Asian Art Show 1995: China, Korea, Japan*. Exh. cat.

1996

Queensland Art Gallery, Brisbane, Australia, Asia Pacific Triennial of Contemporary Art, Sept. 27, 1996–Jan. 19, 1997. Exh. cat.

1997

LaSalle-SIA College of the Arts, Singapore, *In & Out: Contemporary Chinese Art from China and Australia*, May 14–June 21. Traveled to RMIT Gallery, Royal Melbourne Institute of Technology University, Australia, July 18–Aug. 30; SCA Gallery, The Sydney University, Sept. 4–28; Plimsoll Gallery, Tasmania University, Hobart, Australia, Mar. 1998; Australian National University, Canberra, Aug. 1998. Exh. cat.

Chassé Kazerne, Breda, Netherlands (organized by Fundament Foundation), *Another Long March: Chinese Conceptual and Installation Art in the Nineties*, May 31–Aug. 3. Exh. cat.

Kassel, Germany, Documenta X, June 21–Sept. 28. Exh. cat.

Yamagata Museum of Art, Japan, Yamagata International Documentary Film Festival, Oct. 6–13. Exh. cat.

Wiener Secession, Vienna, *Cities on the Move*, Nov. 26, 1997–Jan. 18, 1998. Traveled to Centre d'art plastiques contemporains, Bordeaux, June 5–Aug. 30, 1998; P.S. 1 Contemporary Art Center (now MoMA PS1), New York, Oct. 18, 1998–Jan. 10, 1999; Louisiana Museum of Modern Art, Humlebæk, Denmark, Jan. 29–Apr. 21, 1999; Hayward Gallery, London, May 13–June 27, 1999; Museum of Contemporary Art Kiasma, Helsinki, Nov. 5–Dec. 19, 1999. Exh. cat.

1998

Beijing Art Now Studio, *Trace of Existence: A Private Showing of Chinese Contemporary Art '98*, opened Jan. 2. Exh. cat.

Hong Kong Institute of Contemporary Culture and the Hong Kong University of Science and Technology Center for the Arts, *Journey to the East '97*, Jan. 22–24. Exh. cat.

1999

Contemporary Art Centre of Macao, *Fast>>Forward: New Chinese Video Art*, Mar. 19–May 30. Exh. cat.

Chinese Pavilion, Melbourne Biennial: *Signs of Life*, May 14–June 27. Exh. cat.

Provincial Museum of Photography, Antwerp, Belgium, *Laboratorium*, June 27–Oct. 3. Exh. cat.

Yamagata Museum of Art, Japan, Yamagata International Documentary Film Festival, Oct. 19–25. Exh. cat.

Institute of Contemporary Arts, London, *Beijing in London*.

2000

Biarritz, France, Festival international de programmes audiovisuels, Jan. 18–23. Exh. cat.

Brighton Dome, UK, Brighton Festival, May 3–25.

M.A.P. Brussels, Kunstenfestivaldesarts, May 5–27.

Melkweg, Amsterdam, World Wide Video Festival, Sept. 16.

Red Gate Gallery, Beijing, *Post-Material: Interpretations of Everyday Life by Contemporary Chinese Artists*, Oct. 21–Nov. 30. Exh. cat.

Shanghai Art Museum, Shanghai Biennial: *Shanghai Spirit*, Nov. 6, 2000–Jan. 6, 2001.

2001

Haus der Kulturen der Welt, Berlin, *Translated Acts: Performance and Body Art from East Asia*, Mar. 8–May 27. Traveled to Queens Museum of Art, New York, Oct. 28, 2001–Feb. 17, 2002.

LaSalle-SIA College of the Arts, Singapore, *Compound Eyes: Contemporary Video Art from China*, June 8–July 18. Traveled to He Xiangning Art Museum, Shenzhen, Oct.; Ivan Dougherty Gallery, University of New South Wales, Australia, July 4–Aug. 10, 2002. Exh. cat.

Tokyo Opera City Art Gallery, *My Home Is Yours/Your Home Is Mine*, July 1–Sept. 16.

China Academy of Art, Hangzhou, The New Media Art Festival: *Non-Linear Narrative*, Sept.

Hamburger Bahnhof, Berlin, *Living in Time: 29 Contemporary Artists from China*, Sept. 19, 2001–Jan. 6, 2002.

KW Institute for Contemporary Art, Berlin, *The State of Things*.

2002

Pavilhão Ciccillo Matarazzo, Parque do Ibirapuera, São Paulo Biennial, Mar. 23–June 2.

M.A.P. Brussels, Kunstenfestivaldesarts, May 3–25.

Luding Bridge, Sichuan, *The Long March: A Walking Visual Display*, June 5–Oct. 25.

Earl Lu Gallery, Singapore, *Site + Sight: Translating Cultures*, June 7–July 26.

Guangdong Museum of Art, Guangzhou Triennial, Nov. 18, 2002–Jan. 19, 2003. Exh. cat.

East Modern Art Center, Beijing, *Synthetic Reality*, Dec. 14–30. Exh. cat.

2003

Walker Art Center, Minneapolis, *How Latitudes Become Forms: Art in a Global Age*, Feb. 3–May 4. Traveled to Fondazione Sandretto Re Rebaudengo, Turin, June 1–Sept. 14, 2003; Contemporary Arts Museum Houston, July 17–Sept. 19, 2004. Exh. cat.

Musée d'art moderne de la Ville de Paris, *Camera: Chang Yungho, Wang Jianwei, Yang Fudong*, Feb. 7–Mar 23. Traveled to National Museum of Contemporary Art, Bucharest, Romania, opened Oct. 29, 2004. Exh. cat.

Arsenale, Venice Biennale, June 15–Nov. 2. Exh. cat.

Centre Georges Pompidou, Paris, *Alors, la Chine?*, June 25–Oct. 13. Exh. cat.

Taikang Space, Beijing, *Control Z*, Sept. 16–20. Exh. cat.

Today Art Museum, Beijing, *Second Hand Reality: Pre-Reality*, Sept. 17–Oct. 16. Exh. cat.

Edwin's Gallery, Jakarta, *Interplay: Chinese Contemporary Art*, Oct. 2–21. Exh. cat.

Centre Georges Pompidou, Paris, Festival d'Automne à Paris, Oct. 8–11.

Zachęta National Gallery of Art, Warsaw, *New Zone: Chinese Art*, Dec. 1, 2003–Feb. 1, 2004. Exh. cat.

2004

Museum of Modern Art, New York, *China Now*, Feb. 12–16.

M.A.P. Brussels, Kunstenfestivaldesarts, May 5–27.

International Center of Photography and Asia Society, New York, *Between Past and Future: New Photography and Video from China*, June 11–Sept. 5. Traveled to Smart Museum of Art, University of Chicago, and Museum of Contemporary Art, Chicago, Oct. 2, 2004–Jan. 16, 2005; Seattle Art Museum, Feb. 10–May 1, 2005; Victoria and Albert Museum, London, Sept. 15, 2005–Jan. 15, 2006; Santa Barbara Museum of Art, July 1–Sept. 17, 2006; The Nasher Museum of Art at Duke University, Durham, N.C., Oct. 26, 2006–Feb. 18, 2007. Exh. cat.

Shanghai Gallery of Art, *Space Anew*, June 26–July 11.

Contemporary Art Centre, Vilnius, Lithuania, *Slow Rushes: Takes on the Documentary Sensibility in Moving Images from Around Asia and the Pacific*, Sept. 10–Oct. 31. Exh. cat.

Bunker Museum of Contemporary Art, Kinmen, Taiwan, *18 Solo Exhibitions*, Sept. 11, 2004–Feb. 18, 2005. Exh. cat.

Centre Georges Pompidou, Paris, Festival d'Automne à Paris, Sept. 13–Dec. 19.

Shanghai Art Museum, Shanghai Biennial: *Techniques of the Visible*, Sept. 28–Nov. 27.

San Diego Museum of Art, *Past in Reverse: Contemporary Art of East Asia*, Nov. 6, 2004–Mar. 6, 2005. Traveled to Kemper Museum of Contemporary Art, Kansas City, Mo., June 3–Sept. 4, 2005; Hood Museum of Art, Dartmouth College, Hanover, N.H., Jan. 15–Mar. 12, 2006. Exh. cat.

Seoul Museum of Art, Seoul International Media Art Biennial, Dec. 15, 2004–Feb. 6, 2005.

2005

Greater Union City Cinema, Adelaide, Australia, Adelaide Film Festival: *Image Is Everything*, Feb. 18–Mar. 3.

Museum of Contemporary Art, Taipei, *Variation Xanadu*, Aug. 6–Sept. 25. Exh. cat.

OCT Contemporary Art Terminal, Shenzhen, *Plato and His Seven Spirits*, Sept. 23–Nov. 7. Traveled to OCT Contemporary Art Terminal, Shenzhen, June 3–30, 2006. Exh. cat.

Albright-Knox Art Gallery, Buffalo, N.Y., *The Wall: Reshaping Contemporary Chinese Art*, Oct. 21, 2005–Jan. 29, 2006. Exh. cat.

Guangdong Museum of Art, Guangzhou Triennial: *Beyond—An Extraordinary Space of Experimentation for Modernization*, Nov. 18, 2005–Jan. 15, 2006.

OCT Contemporary Art Terminal, Shenzhen Biennial of Urbanism/Architecture, Dec. 10, 2005–Mar. 10, 2006.

2006

Macao Museum of Art, *Microcosm*, Mar. 18–June 18. Exh. cat.

Tilton Gallery, New York, *Jiang Hu*, May 24–June 30. Exh. cat.

Museum Boijmans Van Beuningen, Rotterdam, *China Contemporary: Architecture, Art and Visual Culture*, June 10–Aug. 13.

2007

Lewis Glucksman Gallery, Cork, Ireland, *The Year of the Golden Pig: Contemporary Chinese Art from the Sigg Collection*, Mar. 13–June 17.

Arario Gallery, Beijing, *Sustainable Imagination: Media Art in China, Exhibition Series 1999–2007*, Apr. 29–June 10. Exh. cat.

Hebbel am Ufer, Berlin, *Circuitry China*, June 1–6.

Kunsthaus Graz, Austria, *China Welcomes You . . . Desires, Struggles, New Identities*, June 6–Sept. 7. Exh. cat.

Museum Het Domein, Sittard, Netherlands, *Chinergie: China Summer Show*, Aug. 11–Sept. 2. Exh. cat.

24HR Art/Northern Territory Centre for Contemporary Art, Darwin, Australia, *Changes: Video Art from China*, Sept. 14–Oct. 20.

The Israel Museum, Jerusalem, *Made in China: The Estella Collection*, Sept. 18–Mar. 1. Traveled to Louisiana Museum of Modern Art, Humlebæk, Denmark, Mar. 16–Aug. 5. Exh. cat.

Chambers Fine Art, Beijing, *Net: Reimagining Space, Time and Culture*, Sept. 20–Nov. 3. Exh. cat.

Today Art Museum, Beijing, *Energy, Spirit, Body, Material*, Oct. 17–Nov. 13. Exh. cat.

Museum moderner Kunst Stiftung Ludwig Wien, Vienna, *China: Facing Reality*, Oct. 25, 2007–Feb. 10, 2008. Exh. cat.

Newton Building, Art Basel Miami Beach: *Beyond Icons: Chinese Contemporary Art in Miami*, Dec. 6–9. Exh. cat.

2008

Canvas International Art, Amstelveen, Netherlands, *Between the Light and the Dark: On the Borders of Chineseness*, Feb. 16–Mar. 22. Exh. cat.

Mudam Luxembourg, *China Power Station Part III*, Apr. 26–Sept. 15. Exh. cat.

Iberia Center for Contemporary Art, Beijing, *Community of Tastes: The Inaugural Exhibition of Iberia Center for Contemporary Art*, Apr. 29–June 9. Exh. cat.

Arario Gallery, Beijing, *Between the Light and the Dark*, June 10–July 26.

Today Art Museum, Beijing, *Map Games: Dynamics of Change*, June 18–28. Traveled to Birmingham Museums and Art Gallery, UK, Oct. 18, 2008–Jan. 4, 2009; Centro arti opificio siri and Palazzo Primavera, Terni, Italy, Mar. 28–May 10, 2009. Exh. cat.

Ullens Center for Contemporary Art, Beijing, *Our Future: The Guy & Myriam Ullens Foundation Collection*, July 19–Aug. 10. Exh. cat.

Beijing Center for the Arts, *Shan Shui: Nature on the Horizon of Art*, Sept. 19–Oct. 31. Exh. cat.

Macao Museum of Art, *Inward Gazes: Performance Art in Asia—Exhibition by Invitation 2008*, Nov. 8, 2008–Feb. 15, 2009. Exh. cat.

2009

Holden Gallery, Manchester, UK, *State Legacy: Research in the Visualisation of Political History*, Apr. 2–May 24. Traveled to OCT Contemporary Art Terminal, Shenzhen, Oct. 17–Nov. 30. Exh. cat.

Shenzhen Art Museum, *Historical Image: 2009 Chinese Contemporary Art Invitational Exhibition*, Apr. 24–May 24. Traveled to Hubei Art Museum, China, June 12–July 12.

Shanghai Songjiang Creative Studio, *Bourgeoisified Proletariat*, Sept. 10–14. Exh. cat.

Queensland Art Gallery, Brisbane, Australia, *The View from Elsewhere*, Oct. 7–Nov. 15. Exh. cat.

Central Academy of Fine Arts Museum, Beijing, *Collision–Experimental Cases of Contemporary Chinese Art*, Oct. 10–16.

Museo Nacional de Belles Artes de La Habana, Havana, *Beijing–Havana: The New China Contemporary Art*, Oct. 30, 2009–Jan. 15, 2010.

Shinko Pier Exhibition Hall, Yokohama, *CREAM: International Festival for Arts and Media Yokohama 2009*, Oct. 31–Nov. 29. Exh. cat.

Arario Gallery, Beijing, *Himalaya Project: Wang Jianwei & Nalini Malani*, Nov. 21, 2009–Jan. 24, 2010.

Matadero Madrid, *Beijing Time. La hora de China*, Dec. 18, 2009–Mar. 21, 2010.

2010

Iberia Center for Contemporary Art, Beijing, *Museum on Paper: Twelve Chinese Artists*, Jan. 6–Mar. 6. Exh. cat.

Campbelltown Arts Centre, Australia, *Edge of Elsewhere*, Jan. 16–Mar. 14. Exh. cat.

Times Museum, Guangdong, *Out of the Box—Threshold of Video Art in China*, Mar. 26–May 4.

China National Convention Center, Beijing, *Reshaping History: Chinart from 2000 to 2009*, May 4–21. Exh. cat.

Arario Gallery, Cheonan, China, *Weight of Floating Time*, June 29–Aug. 15.

Red Diamond Theater, 46 Fangjia Hutong, Beijing, *Welcome to the Desert of the Real*, Aug. 17–19.

Zürcher Theater Spektakel, Zurich, Sept. 3–5.

Long March Space, Beijing, *Long March Project: Ho Chi Minh Trail*, Sept. 4–Nov. 14. Exh. cat.

La Bâtie—Festival de Genève, Geneva, Sept. 7–8.

Kaserne Basel, Culturescapes, Sept. 15.

Shanghai Art Museum, Shanghai Biennial: *Rehearsal*, Oct. 24, 2010–Jan. 23, 2011.

Boers-Li Gallery, Beijing, *Out of the Box*, Dec. 16, 2010–Jan. 31, 2011. Exh. cat.

2011

Long March Space, Beijing, *Spring Group Exhibition in Long March Space*, Feb. 18–Apr. 7.

Artsonje Center, Seoul, *H BOX: A Nomadic Video Art Screening Room*, Feb. 25–May 1. Traveled to Today Art Museum, Beijing, June 11–July 11.

Long March Space, Beijing, *ACTΔTION*, June 25–Aug. 21.

Museum of Contemporary Art, Chengdu, *Collecting History: China New Art*, July 1–Aug. 31.

Minsheng Art Museum, Shanghai, *Thirty Years of Chinese Contemporary Art: Moving Image in China 1988–2011*, Sept. 7–Nov. 27.

Iberia Center for Contemporary Art, Beijing, *The Shape of Time: The Multinarrative History in Contemporary Chinese Art*, Sept. 17–20.

Artplay Design Center, Moscow Biennial of Contemporary Art: *Rewriting Worlds*, Sept. 22–Oct. 30.

Osage Gallery, Hong Kong, *One World Exposition*, Dec. 10, 2011–Jan. 8, 2012.

2012

Minsheng Art Museum, Shanghai, *Face*, Mar. 11–May 20. Exh. cat.

Centre A (Vancouver International Centre for Contemporary Asian Art), *Yellow Signal: New Media in China*, Mar. 17–Apr. 28.

Centro per l'arte contemporanea Luigi Pecci, Prato, Italy, *Moving Image in China 1988–2011*, Apr. 22–Aug. 9.

OCT Contemporary Art Terminal, Shenzhen Sculpture Biennial: *Accidental Message: Art Is Not a System, Not a World*, May 12–Aug. 31. Exh. cat.

National Museum of Modern and Contemporary Art, Seoul, *Move: Art and Dance since the 1960s*, June 6–Aug. 12.

Hayward Gallery, Southbank Centre, London, *Art of Change: New Directions from China*, Sept. 7–Dec. 9. Exh. cat.

National Portrait Gallery, Canberra, Australia, *Go Figure! Contemporary Chinese Portraiture*, Sept. 13, 2012–Feb. 17, 2013. Exh. cat.

Shanghai Art Museum, *Omen 2012: Chinese New Art*, Sept. 15–Sept. 25.

Guangdong Museum of Art, Guangzhou Triennial: *The Unseen*, Sept. 28–Dec. 16.

Centro cultural general San Martín, Buenos Aires, Bienal de la Imagen en Movimiento, Oct. 29–Nov. 4.

2013

Sharjah Art Foundation, Sharjah Biennial: *Re:emerge—Towards a New Cultural Cartography*, Mar. 13–May 13.

University of Television and Film, Munich, Kino der Kunst, Apr. 24–28.

Arsenale, Venice (organized by Museum of Contemporary Art, Chengdu), *Passage to History: 20 Years of La Biennale di Venezia and Chinese Contemporary Art*, June 1–Nov. 24.

Today Art Museum, Beijing, *2013 Martell Artists of the Year Winning Artists Group Exhibition*, June 16–30.

Museum of Old and New Art, Hobart, Australia, *The Red Queen*, June 18, 2013–Sept. 15, 2014.

Power Station of Art, Shanghai, *Portrait of the Times: 30 Years of Chinese Contemporary Art*, Aug. 18–Nov. 10.

AWARDS

1984

Gold Award for *Dear Mother* (1983), *Sixth National Fine Arts Exhibition*, National Art Gallery (now the National Art Museum of China), Beijing.

2008 (February)

Annual Grant Recipient, Foundation for Contemporary Arts, New York.

2011 (December)

Credit Suisse Today Art Award, Today Art Museum, Beijing.

2013 (June)

Martell Artist of the Year Award, Today Art Museum, Beijing.

EXHIBITION CURATED BY WANG JIANWEI

2009

Ullens Center for Contemporary Art, Beijing, *He An: What Makes Me Understand What I Know?*, Feb. 7–Mar. 22. Exh. cat.

Compiled with the assistance of Siqiao Lu.

Chronology

Compiled by Stephanie Kwai

1958

Wang Jianwei is born on October 28 in the village of Shuining, Sichuan Province, in the southwestern region of the People's Republic of China (PRC).

1958–66

Wang Jianwei lives in a traditional military family; both of his parents are soldiers. He spends his childhood in military camps, commonly referred to as *budui dayuan*.

1966–76

Chinese Communist Party (CCP) leaders including Chairman Mao Zedong launch the Great Proletarian Cultural Revolution in 1966, advocating "the abolishment of the four olds" (old ideas, old culture, old customs, and old habits). The movement's ideological aims are to cleanse the CCP of what in China are considered bourgeois values and counterrevolutionary activities. Politically, the Cultural Revolution aims to purge the CCP of Mao's rivals, casting them as "revisionist" authorities. The revolution results in massive violence against millions of people and cultural property perpetrated by groups of militant high-school and university-student rebels known as Red Guards. The nation's schools and universities are shut down amid the call for a massive youth mobilization against traditional and bourgeois values and lack of revolutionary spirit. Wang Jianwei's family is strongly affected; his father is treated violently and relocated to a village farm.

1972

Millions are sent to the countryside to be reeducated by peasants and workers in a campaign, instigated by Mao, known as the Up to the Mountains and Down to the Countryside Movement (Shang shan xia xiang, jieshou pinxia zhongnong zai jianyu).

1974

Wang Jianwei's father is released from the farm, reunited with his family, and allowed to return to his job.

1975

Wang Jianwei graduates from high school and is relocated to the countryside to be reeducated by peasants. During his free time, he bikes into town to privately study painting with a stage designer who works for a local Sichuan opera company. Through forbidden books, he acquaints himself with Russian literature and painting. During this time, he also begins learning to paint in a realist style.

1976

On September 9, Mao Zedong dies. A month later, the Cultural Revolution, now described as "ten years of catastrophe," ends with the arrest of four politburo members known as the Gang of Four (Zhang Chunqiao, Jiang Qing, Yao Wenyuan, and Wang Hongwen) for attempting to split the CCP and seize power. After Mao's death, Hua Guofeng is appointed chairman of the CCP.

1977–83

After two years of reeducation, Wang Jianwei is conscripted to join the People's Liberation Army (PLA). He serves as a military engineer and operations specialist in the PLA and is stationed in a barrack in Qinghe County, Hebei Province, south of Beijing. As part of his job, Wang is charged with drawing maps. He does not produce any art during his time in the army.

1978

Deng Xiaoping is restored as deputy chairman of the CCP, officially expels the Gang of Four from the party, and introduces policies of reform.

As paramount leader of China from 1978 to 1992, Deng advances his open-door policy to encourage foreign direct investment and to boost the Chinese economy, affording the opportunity for more liberal international cultural exchange.

1978–79

The Xidan Democracy Wall Movement (Xidan minzhu qiang) commences in Beijing. Chinese citizens vent their grievances and openly express their criticisms of the government via pro-democracy posters posted along a brick wall in the Xidan area, near Tiananmen Square in the center of the city. Hundreds of these handmade posters, known as big character posters (*dazibao*), are mounted. The movement comes to an abrupt end when criticism focuses on Deng Xiaoping, who subsequently has the Xidan Democracy Wall leaders arrested for counterrevolutionary activities.

1983

Wang Jianwei is discharged from the army and introduced to Zhu Guangyan (b. 1956, Beijing), an army nurse. Less than a year after they meet, Wang marries Zhu. They live apart for nearly seven years due to strict government policies on residency locations, known as the *hukou* household registration system. While Wang's papers tie him to his parents' residency in Chengdu (the capital of Sichuan Province), Zhu is registered in Beijing.

1983–85

In January 1983, Wang Jianwei is assigned by the military to a post as store manager at the Chengdu Painting Institute (Chengdu huayuan) at the Chengdu Art Academy (Chengdu shi meishuguan). During this time, he gains access to a variety of Western art catalogues and begins copying works of Western artists. He hopes to expose himself to the work of other artists and paint. Until now, he has had little formal art training. As an employee of the institute, he finds time to study art and examine life in the city of Chengdu. During this time, Wang creates a series of pen drawings and sketches of patrons at a local teahouse. Five years later, in 1988, these drawings will form the basis for a group of paintings known as the *Tea House* series (1988–90).

1983

Wang Jianwei paints *Dear Mother* (1983), a work that renews the academic realist style of the Sichuan Painting School (Sichuan haipai), a style developed by students of Sichuan Fine Arts Institute (Sichuan meishu xueyuan) that focuses on the details of everyday life and yields works that are often melancholic and poetic in nature. The work depicts a PLA soldier drafting a letter to his mother in the trenches of a battlefield; it refers to his personal experience of a maneuver during the 1979 Sino-Vietnamese War. *Dear Mother* is unique in that it documents the artist's emotional experience in the context of the rapid changes in China. At this time, Wang is heavily influenced by the Wanderers (Peredvizhniki), a group of Russian Realist painters formed at the Imperial Academy of Arts in Saint Petersburg in 1863, known for their humanistic narrative genre paintings that intertwine individual experiences, memory, and major historical and social events. By painting *Dear Mother*, Wang draws attention to the work of Wanderers Vasily Ivanovich Surikov (1848–1916) and Ilya Yefimovich Repin (1844–1930), noted for capturing the lives and history of individuals in late-nineteenth-century Russia in a similarly dramatic way.

1984

Wang Jianwei's painting *Dear Mother* wins the Gold Award in its category at the *Sixth National Fine Arts Exhibition* (*Di liu jie quangquo meishu zuopin zhanlan*) at the National Art Gallery (now National Art Museum of China), an exhibition that includes works from young academic graduates and established artists in China. For Wang, the experience raises questions about the designation of the term "artist."

Wang meets his future teacher Zheng Shengtian in Shenyang, a northern city in China. Zheng, just having returned to China from the United States, has many materials that reference Western contemporary art. This is the first time that Wang sees documentation of installation and environmental art, which has a profound impact on him.

1985–89

The '85 New Wave Art Movement ('85 Xinchao meishu yundong) is a nationwide avant-garde movement that is stimulated by increasing contact and exchange with the contemporary international art world. Pursuing experimental art and humanist philosophy, the movement advocates individual self-expression and "nonofficial art" over the prevailing strictures of party-sanctioned "official art" and cultural policy. The movement flourishes as self-organized avant-garde art groups and individuals organize exhibitions, hold conferences, and write about new conceptual directions with an international perspective for art in China.

1985

Wang Jianwei is introduced to the work of Robert Rauschenberg through the Rauschenberg Overseas Culture Interchange (ROCI) project hosted at the National Art Gallery. More than 300,000 people attend the exhibition, which includes the graphic mural *Chinese Summerhall* (1982–83) and examples of installation art, graphic art, Combines, and experimental theater, which have never been seen in China before. The event has significant impact on emerging avant-garde artists scene and specifically on the development of installation art in China.

1985–87

Wang Jianwei pursues graduate studies in oil painting at the Zhejiang Academy of Fine Arts (Zhejiang meishu xueyuan), now China Academy of Art (Zhongguo meishu xueyuan), in Hangzhou, Zhejiang Province. While attending the academy, Wang spends much time in the library reading books on Western literature and philosophy that had been banned from the Chinese academic curriculum while he was growing up. Existentialists such as Jean-Paul Sartre, Albert Camus, and Jorge Luis Borges greatly impact him.

1987

Wang Jianwei graduates from the Zhejiang Academy of Fine Arts.

1988–90

Wang Jianwei produces his *Tea House* series, paintings that depict elderly residents drinking tea and passing time in local teahouses. He develops what becomes a signature style, employing a documentary practice of studying, observing, sketching, and interacting with his subjects. In essence, he is performing a cultural study of a microsociety. Although Wang would not be introduced to the work of Francis Bacon until 1999, his visual treatment of the passage of time and movement of the subjects is similar.

1989

The '85 New Wave Art Movement inspires an important exhibition of new Chinese art, the 1989 *China/Avant-Garde* (*Zhongguo xiandai yishuzhan*) show at the National Art Gallery. *China/Avant-Garde* is the first nationwide survey of nonofficial Chinese art ever presented in a national institution, and the first show in China to be curated by art critics rather than museum or academic officials. The exhibition establishes experimental practices including installation art and forms of conceptual art as a major new development of modern art (*xiandai yishu*) in Chinese culture. During its two-week run, the exhibition is closed twice by the authorities. The *China/Avant-Garde* exhibition is held up by officials as a typical example of bourgeois liberalism.

Pro-democracy demonstrations gather momentum in the wake of the death of CCP reformist Hu Yaobang in April. For three months, demonstrations take place in cities across China, with protesters putting forward demands for democracy and freedom. The events in Beijing are the most extreme, and martial law is declared in parts of the city. On June 3, PLA troops and the People's Armed Police (Renmin wuzhuang jingcha) enter Tiananmen Square to clear it of demonstrators. Their militant crackdown on mainly student protesters in the square through June 4 is the bloodiest in modern Chinese history and marks a watershed moment for the Chinese government, which effectively purges the CCP of reformists and redirects focus on China's economic prosperity rather than on political reform.

1990

As a result of the 1989 reversion to stricter and more conservative regulation, avant-garde activity declines. Meanwhile, Chinese avant-garde art is drawing increased international attention.

Wang Jianwei becomes familiar with the Beijing-based art group called the New Measurement Group (Xin kedu). Members include Chen Shaoping, Gu Dexin, and Wang Luyan. This conceptual art group's experimental practice shares many of Wang's perspectives across various disciplines, influencing each other's art practice and methods of art making.

1991

Wang Jianwei's *Tea House* series is shown in a solo exhibition at the Cultural Palace of Nationalities (Minzu wenhua gong) in Beijing. This series exploring Wang's interest in capturing time further reflects his interest in art as social analysis, as he begins to deconstruct Chinese cultural traditions, social relationships, behavior, and community. Wang considers extending his practices to installation and conceptual art and increasingly approaches art, science, and philosophy as methodologies via which to reconsider new policies and research strategies for China's future.

1992

Wang Jianwei becomes interested in the "gray system," also known as "gray relational analysis." This systems theory, introduced by the Chinese mathematician Deng Julong in 1982, provides a methodology that focuses on the study of problems using partial or uncertain information. Because uncertain systems exist commonly in nature, the application for gray systems analysis to monitor behavior gained currency in the field of natural science, both among Chinese and international researchers. By the 1990s, the gray system had become widely adopted in China, in fields ranging from regional economic planning agriculture, irrigation, and weather forecasting.

Wang creates his first elaborate conceptual installation work, *Document* (1992), at his house. With *Document*, Wang aims at activating what he terms the "gray zone," or "in-between" space, signaling predictions in a combined artistic and scientific experimental process.

1993

Wang Jianwei continues to consider the gray system in *Incident—Process, State* (1993), an installation including video, text, and sculpture at the Hong Kong Arts Centre. He begins reading scientific works written by such giants as Niels Henrik David Bohr and Albert Einstein, which transform his thinking about art and his working methods. Via his new experimental model, Wang seeks to blur the distinctions between art, science, and philosophy, and between the individual and society, to evoke a complex social experiment and experience.

1993–94

Inspired by a book written by a biologist about the science of crop growth, Wang Jianwei returns to the village where he was sent during the Up to the Mountains and Down to the Countryside Movement and collaborates with a local farmer to stage a performance on a plot of agricultural land. *Circulation—Sowing and Harvesting* (1993–94) is a durational performance in which Wang and the farmer prepare, plant, and harvest a new species of wheat, going through an entire cycle of farming. The work illustrates Wang's interest in a laboratory for biological study and social activity and his continued exploration of process as an integral aspect of his work.

1995

Wang Jianwei participates in the First Gwangju Biennial in South Korea, Asia's first contemporary art biennial, whose inaugural theme is "Beyond the Borders." Wang exhibits *Reproduction* (1995), an installation featuring video and sculpture.

1997

Interested in space and language, Wang Jianwei makes the video *Production* (1997), which is characteristically representative of his earlier works that juxtapose everyday living spaces and spaces of cultural production. The work documents social interaction in selected public spaces in seven cities around Sichuan Province. Employing techniques similar to those used in sociological surveys, Wang investigates how personal spaces are derived from intimate conversations within a public space, and studies how complicated relationships overlap within everyday spaces.

In May, Wang participates in the exhibition *Another Long March*, which is the first survey in the West with a focus on Chinese conceptual and installation art in the nineties, at Chassé Kazerne in Breda, Netherlands. During the exhibition, he meets Catherine David, curator for Documenta X, the tenth iteration of an exhibition of contemporary art that takes place every five years in Kassel, Germany.

In June, Wang and Feng Mengbo become the first Chinese contemporary artists to participate in Documenta. Wang's *Production* is shown.

November marks the start of the exhibition *Cities on the Move*, curated by Hou Hanru and Hans Ulrich Obrist, at Wiener Secession in Vienna, with a thematic focus on "Contemporary Asian Art on the Turn of the 21st Century." Chinese participants in the exhibition that tours venues around the world include Cai Guo-Qiang, Huang Yong Ping, Wang, and Zhang Peili, among others.

1998–99

Wang Jianwei produces *Living Elsewhere* (1999–2000), a documentary film that examines the effect on rural communities of China as the city encroaches. It follows the lives of a group of farmers who sell their land to a developer with plans to build luxury residential homes. After the developer goes broke, the farmers move back into the unfinished luxury homes on the outskirts of Chengdu.

2000

Wang Jianwei participates in the Third Shanghai Biennial at the Shanghai Art Museum (*Shanghai meishu guan*) with the title *Shanghai Spirit* (*Haishang, Shanghai*). Hou Hanru heads the curatorial team, which includes Toshio Shimizu, Zhang Qing, Li Xu, and Fang Zengxian. *Shanghai Spirit* is the first Chinese biennial to include international and new-media artists in addition to traditional art forms.

Wang abandons his documentary format to create works that integrate visual art and a new form of experimental theater. Seeing no separation between art and society, responsibility, and progressive thinking, he produces *Paravent* (2000), a nonlinear narrative theater performance and video about rethinking history exhibited at Kunstenfestivaldesarts in Brussels and at the Brighton Festival in Brighton, UK. It is his first multimedia performance work and his first work featuring actors. The actions of the performers draw from modern and traditional Chinese and Western theater, and from contemporary Western dance and multimedia art practices, as do the set, video installations, sound pieces, and texts.

2002

Wang Jianwei participates in the Twenty-Fifth São Paulo Biennial.

2003

Wang Jianwei participates in the Fiftieth Venice Biennale.

Wang is artist-in-residence at the Walker Art Center in Minneapolis. With local workers, he presents the performance and multimedia installation *Movable Taste*. In addition, he exhibits *Living Elsewhere* at the Walker as part of *How Latitudes Become Forms: Art in a Global Age*, an international group show that examines how the shifting perceptions of place affect contemporary art making and its absorption by the culture at large.

2004

Wang Jianwei's work *My Visual Archive* (2003) is exhibited in *Alors, la Chine?* at the Centre Georges Pompidou in Paris, which is cosponsored by the Chinese and French ministries.

In the same year, Wang attends the Festival d'Automne à Paris. Wang presents *Ceremony* (2003), a large-scale multimedia work that includes theater, performance, and new media, at the Centre Georges Pompidou. *Ceremony* explores historical interpretation and its relationship to understanding reality today, specifically in China. In this work, the stage becomes an intersection of past and present where everybody (actor and audience) is given a role of "performer" and speaker.

2005

Wang Jianwei creates his first video installation, *Flying Bird Is Motionless*, which explores time.

2006

Wang Jianwei creates *Dodge* (2006), a two-part work shown at the Shanghai Gallery of Art (Hushen hualang). The work stems from *El libro de los seres imaginarios* (*The Book of Imaginary Beings*, 1957) by Jorge Luis Borges, who understands reality and daily life as a series of uncertain relationships. The concept touches on a reconfiguration of time and space through a large sculptural piece composed of architectural fragments and abstracted human figures, accompanied by a video that depicts overlapping activities and spaces (karaoke bars, train stations, hospitals). *Dodge* illustrates Wang's continued exploration of theatrical spaces; he uses the complex intersection of environments and activities to reflect contemporary life in China, showing it marked by pleasure, economy, and disease.

2007

Wang Jianwei's solo exhibition *Cross Infection* is held at Hebbel am Ufer in Berlin.

2008

China welcomes the international community to Beijing as it hosts the Twenty-Ninth Summer Olympic Games.

Wang Jianwei shows a major installation, *Hostage* (2008), at the Zendai Museum of Modern Art (Zhengda yishu) in Shanghai. The work, conceived specifically for the space, is comprised of a series of large sculptures of machinery and technology that appear to be exploding, melting, and/or being consumed by themselves, and depicts the breakdown of industry and thought as China becomes a major player on the world stage. Accompanying the work is a video that reconstructs daily life on a Cultural Revolution–era commune. *Hostage* explores the different layers of social phenomena and considers how dreams and ambitions are "held hostage" by established systems of power such as knowledge, history, and ideology, at a time of rapid economic prosperity, industrialization, and modernization in China.

Wang presents his multimedia theatrical work, *Symptom*, at OCT Contemporary Art Terminal in Shenzhen.

2010

Titled *Better City, Better Life*, Expo 2010 Shanghai China is the largest and most expensive of the world fairs to date, with 192 countries participating—the greatest number yet. Wang Jianwei did not participate.

Wang's project *Welcome to the Desert of the Real* (2010), organized by Culturescapes, Basel, employs performance, animation, theater production for film, and a five-channel video component. The work is based on a story of an adolescent boy who moves from rural China to the city with his parents and becomes addicted to computer games. He grows to inhabit a virtual reality online. The boundaries of his reality and fiction become blurred, and he stabs someone to death on a busy market street. Initially conceived as a play performed for the camera, the film and accompanying animation in *Welcome to the Desert of the Real* become the backdrop for a live performance. Eight performances are held during a monthlong tour. It is presented first in Beijing, then at Zürcher Theater Spektakel, an annual international theater and performing arts festival held in Zurich; at La Bâtie—Festival de Genève, a multidisciplinary performing arts festival held annually in Geneva; and as part of Culturescapes, an annual arts festival devoted to intercultural exchange, which this year showcases China. This work is significant in Wang's oeuvre, as it is predicated on the performances as events and underscores his philosophy that the production of art is a constant rehearsal in which a continuous process becomes central.

2011

The installation of *Yellow Signal* (2011) at the Ullens Center for Contemporary Art in Beijing marks Wang Jianwei's largest solo project, and his largest solo exhibition, to date. The immersive installation comprises film, theater, performance, sculpture, painting, and photography. Unlike earlier works, in which theater, process, and rehearsal are contained within the performance, video, or film, *Yellow Signal* expands beyond these frames and reemphasizes process and the idea of rehearsal as integral to Wang's work, including to installation and painting. The piece unfolds in four chapters over four months with a final closing ceremony performance asking the public to return to the venue multiple times to experience it. *Yellow Signal* challenges conventional structures of contemporary art—its purpose, its form, and how audiences are asked to engage and interact with it.

2013

The five-channel-video component from *Welcome to the Desert of the Real* is featured in the Eleventh Sharjah Biennial.

Wang Jianwei has a solo exhibition at the Long March Space (Chang zheng kongjian) in Beijing titled *. . . the event matured, accomplished in sight of all non-existent human outcomes* (*. . . Huozhe shijian daozhi le maiyige wuxiao de jieguo*, 2013). The title is taken from a line in the 1897 poem by Stéphane Mallarmé "Un Coup de dés jamais n'abolira le hasard" ("A Throw of the Dice Will Never Abolish Chance"), an experiment in deconstruction and implied meaning. The exhibition is comprised of painting, sculpture, and installation without the additional use of live performance or video. Wang pays great attention to the relationship and interaction of the individual works in the exhibition—the installation is seen as an entirety, but each work can also be considered a stand-alone piece. An abstract painting of a yellow square on a copper-colored background is also a representation of an enlarged image of a molecule inside a petri dish of brown liquid that reveals the abstraction of scientific form. A three-paneled realistic painting contains moments of superimposed abstraction. Viewed together, these works consider the inversion of realism into abstraction and abstraction into realism. Wang produced the installation's sculptures through a laborious and iterative process of cutting, joining, layering, and sculpting many layers of wood, metal, and rubber into solid formations, considering the time of production a rehearsal. Together and in their individual forms, these exhibition components explore the idea of uncertainty and potentiality, and express time and movement. Here, too, the artworks are seen as part of a rehearsal through physical form and representations of faceted reality in the overall time-based and continual process and continuity of making contemporary art.

汪建偉：時間寺

何鴻毅家族基金引言

何猷忠

何鴻毅家族基金主席

約十年前，家父何鴻毅創辦了家族基金，專注弘揚中華文化藝術及佛教哲學這兩個重要範疇。我們廣泛地接觸中華文化，支持彰顯其淵博歷史遺產，和鼓勵當代藝文發展的計劃。

何鴻毅家族基金和所羅門・R・古根海姆美術館近年在數個計劃上進行合作，彼此的夥伴關係建基於一個共同的策略性願景，即推動當代藝術領域的發展；而現代中華文化和社會若缺乏這方面的工作，將是不完整的。我們很高興贊助「何鴻毅家族基金中國當代藝術計劃」，因為它不僅有助於實踐這個願景，更為現時中華文化全球化下備受關注之一的當代藝術，注入一股推動力。我們相信在古根海姆專業的監督之下，這個計劃將促進當代藝術的創造力與完整性，並使其相關知識語言、學術研究以及思想大幅躍進。

汪建偉自1980年代已是一位深度地參與中華當代藝術社群的藝術家。他運用不同媒界的傑出表現廣為人知；對中華當代藝術與社會的觀察和評論，充滿睿智且發人深省，備受認可。作為如此多元且具影響力的藝術家，他替「何鴻毅家族基金中國當代藝術計劃」的第一個委約項目創作作品，毋庸置疑。我們對《時間寺》展覽感到非常欣喜，並誠摯期望所有參與展覽及其相關推廣與教育活動的觀眾，對於中國當前與過去的視覺文化，將獲更深一層的了解。

在館長Richard　Armstrong率領下的古根海姆美術館整體工作人員，他們於項目裏展示了卓越的遠見和專業精神，謹此，我們致以最衷心的謝意。

何鴻毅家族基金
THE ROBERT H. N. HO FAMILY FOUNDATION

SRGM前言

Richard Armstrong

所羅門．R．古根海姆美術館與基金會館長

所羅門．R．古根海姆美術館長久以來支持著從瓦西里．康丁斯基（Vasily Kandinsky）到提諾．塞過爾（Tino Sehgal）、從路易絲．布爾喬亞（Louise Bourgeois）到安尼許．卡普爾（Anish Kapoor）等，在世藝術家們有前瞻性且往往是富含挑戰意味的作品；最近，為了展示現代及當代藝術的全球景觀，我們加強了策展與教育部門。這些豐富且多元的視角，不單單開拓大眾的思維，也將延伸古根海姆美術館在我們的時代中，對於藝術持續不斷的參與。選擇汪建偉作為古根海姆「何鴻毅家族基金中國當代藝術計劃」的首位委約藝術家，這個計劃將促進美術館探索有潛力激發當代的創意表現、批判思考與文化理解，卻較少被檢視的當代藝術軌跡。

《汪建偉：時間寺》是這位駐北京具有影響力的藝術家與思考家，在北美的第一個美術館展覽。在汪橫越三十年的職業生涯中，他是一位先鋒藝術家，他的作品兼備中國古典思想、後現代哲學和當代視覺文化。古根海姆很榮幸地呈獻這個規模恢宏的展覽，用雕塑、繪畫、視頻影像與現場戲劇的結合，展示了汪建偉全幅的創造力。

這個展覽在「何鴻毅家族基金中國當代藝術計劃」的支持下得以發展和實現，來自基金會主要的贈款包括創立一個新的策展職位，專攻中國藝術，並且在五年內，委託來自中國、台灣、香港或澳門，三位或是一群藝術家們製作重要的作品；新的委約作品將以何鴻毅家族基金藏品的方式進到古根海姆的永久館藏。每一個委託項目，將在2014到2017年間於紐約古根海姆展出，展覽更將伴隨豐富的出版物發行、系列講座與教育活動。

我們由衷的珍惜長期與何鴻毅家族基金間的合作關係，而且感激與之在一個蘊育創造力並提升中國當代藝術國際交流的項目上合作。對創辦人何鴻毅與主席何猷忠，我們在此表達最誠摯的感謝，他們從項目的一開始即大力擁護，認同委任中國藝術家在古根海姆全球化的收藏與計劃，這樣的背景範疇下，呈現其作品的重要性。行政總裁黎義恩與政務總監鄭景翔促使我們和基金會間的良好工作，這個計劃是不可能在失去了他們的鼎力相助與建議下被推行。

《汪建偉：時間寺》由在2013年加入古根海姆，作為何鴻毅家族基金中國藝術策展人的湯偉峰（Thomas J. Berghuis）所策劃；作為該計劃第一個委約項目，他和汪及其工作室密切的工作表現上，反映他全面性廣泛的知識和經驗，確保了這個項目歷久不衰的影響力。湯在亞洲藝術界深度的經營，也同時為美術館加強了學術機制網絡，推動在未來計劃上的合作關係。

在三星亞洲藝術資深策展人孟璐（Alexandra Munroe）的率領下，亞洲藝術行動已經走到了第八個年頭，該藝術行動持續推廣並宣揚亞洲現代與當代藝術的成就，擴大在全球的藝術相關活動。通過將作品納入館藏、國際化的展覽和諸如此類針對學者及大眾的教育推廣行動，我們意旨在實踐我們全球化的承諾。

古根海姆國際化的藝術活動受到所羅門．R．古根海姆基金董事會始終如一的支援。我們特別感謝主席Jennifer Blei Stockman的鼓勵，及榮譽董事John S. Wadsworth和他的妻子Susy用以關注亞洲當代藝術，傑出的慈善事業。

我謹代表董事會的成員們，向汪建偉對他在「何鴻毅家族基金中國當代藝術計劃」中的付出，與為委託計劃所製作的卓越作品，獻上最深摯的感謝；他的作品將帶著古根海姆的歷史，促進對今日中國藝術的理解與鑑賞。

銘謝

湯偉峰

何鴻毅家族基金中國藝術策展人
所羅門 · R · 古根海姆美術館

《汪建偉：時間寺》是對駐北京藝術家汪建偉高度革新的作品，做出一份及時的認可，也同時，作為即將以何鴻毅家族基金藏品進入古根海姆永久館藏，三個委約中國藝術家系列展的首展。

在此，我希望對所羅門 · R · 古根海姆美術館與基金會館長Richard Armstrong致上最深摯的謝意，在他的領導之下，古根海姆在全球的範疇中持續發起鞭辟入裡的策展計劃，Richard以他總是如先賢般的建議，給予這個項目滿載的關注、熱情和支持。我由衷的感激副館長Nancy Spector與所羅門 · R · 古根海姆基金會首席策展人Jennifer和David Stockman的督導和卓越的策展支援。所羅門 · R · 古根海姆美術館，三星資深策展人孟璐（Alexandra Munroe）一直是一位真正的良師益友、一位舞動士氣的同事，在這個項目企圖拓展中國當代藝術中的知識語彙之時，她以嚴謹與實事求是的精神，使其充分發揮潛力。

汪建偉作為中國當代藝術的先鋒，他所創造的作品值得更進一步的關注與探討；汪思索在當代藝術中重要的新方向，使用以時間為根基的處理過程，綜合繪畫、雕塑、裝置、戲劇、表演與影片製作到他的藝術實踐之中；他的作品反映今日中國的當代藝術是在瞬息萬變的背景下被製作。我謝謝藝術家偉大的視野、深度的研究，和對古根海姆美術館的歷史及願景通透的體會，為當代藝術創造一個「時間寺」。汪也是我所合作過最慈悲為懷的藝術家，我更要特別感謝他的妻子朱光燕小姐，在這個新項目發展過程中，無可比擬的支援，在我多次造訪北京的旅程中，她是一位如此美好的女主人。

在汪建偉工作室裡，藝術家暨工作室經理徐伯欣、工作室協調專員吳非與其全體工作人員，他們在過程中的努力和付出值得真摯的感謝。我要謝謝北京長征畫廊創辦人盧杰、畫廊總監董道茲、國際項目總監梁中蘭和其團隊對汪作品的支持，給整體委約項目的規劃起了很大的作用。紐約前波畫廊創辦人兼總監茅為清和總監John Tancock提供他們長期對藝術家作品的支援，並在他們位於紐約和北京的畫廊空間，促進對中國當代藝術的廣泛興趣。

這個展覽無法在失去由何鴻毅與何猷忠所指導的何鴻毅家族基金下被推行，他們悠久的慈善事業，在世界各地宣揚對中國藝術與文化的理解；何鴻毅將中國文化裡博大精深的知識投資到這個計劃上；我和何猷忠分享了許多關於當代藝術的重要談話；何鴻毅家族基金行政總裁黎義恩提供他強而有力的見解，與他對中國文化和藝術的深入了解；計劃總監黃美儀、公共關係及傳訊經理湯惠德協助了這個計劃的進行；對營運總裁繆永珍她如沐春風的個人特質、重要的見解和對當代中國藝術的熟悉度，我要表達特別的感謝。

在2006年成立的古根海姆亞洲藝術委員會，作為一個策展智囊團，今天在亞洲文化研究、全球藝術歷史和藝術作品實踐這些部分，對新興的關鍵性問題提供咨詢；委員會為此計劃貢獻了周密的指導，我們希望提及2014年的委員會成員們：Apinan Poshyananda（泰國文化部常務次長暨代理文化部長）、Geremie Barmé（中華全球研究中心館長、坎培拉澳洲國立大學中國歷史學教授）、Iftikhar Dadi（紐約州伊薩卡康乃爾大學，美術學系系主任及副教授）、Jane DeBevoise（香港與紐約亞洲藝術文獻庫董事會主席）、Okwui Enwezor（慕尼黑Haus der Kunst館長）、特裏克．弗洛斯（Jorge B. Vargas美術館與菲律賓文化研究中心策展人、奎松市菲律賓國立大學Diliman校區，藝術研究學系教授）、Geeta Kapur（新德里藝評暨策展人）、Mami Kataoka（東京森美術館首席策展人）、Hongnam Kim（獨立策展人、首爾韓國國家美術館前館長）、郭建超（新加坡國家美術館資深顧問）、黎光頂（駐胡志明市藝術家）、邱志杰（藝術家、杭州中國美術學院綜合藝術系教授）、Enin Supriyanto（駐雅加達獨立策展人）、田霏宇（北京尤倫斯當代藝術中心館長）、巫鴻（藝術史暨東亞語言及文化學系中國藝術史Harrie A. Vanderstappen特別貢獻教授、芝加哥大學東亞藝術中心主任），及鄭勝天（溫哥華《藝術》雜誌責任編輯）。

我永遠無法用足夠的言語描述「何鴻毅家族基金中國當代藝術行動」古根海姆工作團隊，助理策展人桂嘉慧與資深項目經理Elissa Edgerton Black卓越的工作表現；嘉慧密切地和項目團隊及藝術家工作室合作，為這個委約展覽、畫冊和相關計劃的實行提供協助；她以在古根海姆策展部門的工作經驗、嚴峻縝密的學術精神、一絲不苟的管理，成功且完美地確認《時間寺》的具體實現。Elissa專業的為這個跨國際的項目，在古根海姆各部門間管理每一項層面，她和香港基金會及北京藝術家工作室進行聯繫，以實踐這個項目的野心。「何鴻毅家族基金中國當代藝術行動」從根本上奉獻於教育推廣，我們非常感激和副理事Kim Kanatani、教育部門主任Gail Engelberg，與其他名列在項目團隊的同事們間的合作；企業與機構發展部門副理事John L. Wielk、機構發展主任Kerri Schlottman-Bright在聯合何鴻毅家族基金與古根海姆間的合作，扮演關鍵性的角色。

如此的跨國行動，影響幅員將被用來衡量它的成功；在這方面，我們很幸運的有全球通訊部門副理事暨主席Eleanor Goldhar領導的專業團隊，其中包括：媒體與公共關係前任總監Betsy Ennis、外國事務副經理Renee Dumouchel與資深公關Keri Murawski。

特別的感激之情要獻給出版與數位媒體常務理事Elizabeth Levy、編輯部門副主任，同時是《汪建偉：時間寺》的項目經理Elizabeth Franzen、製作經理Minjee Cho、出版與數位媒體部門助理責任編輯Katherine Atkins，我謝謝他們持續不懈的奉獻及對策展願景的支持，和在製作此畫冊複雜的編輯過程中，所展現的幽默風趣與良好精神；我希望對MGMT才華洋溢的畫冊設計師Sarah Gephart和Federico Pérez Villoro答謝，他們如此優美地呈現了藝術家的方法論。

這樣高知識水平的項目需要藝術家、作家、策展人和批判考思考家等等，許多同儕的參與和投入；我尤其要感謝中央美術學院跨媒體藝術學院院長高士明，他幫此書提供了細密推敲的文稿；藝術家邱志傑和宋冬、紀錄片製作人吳文光早先指導我關於在當代中國裡藝術的價值；駐北京獨立策展人暨藝評栗憲庭啓發我在中國藝術領域中的工作，他應得特別的感謝；雪梨大學藝術史與電影研究系所名譽教授John Clark和我分享他對亞洲藝術史的深切了解；香港M+美術館烏利．希克（Uli Sigg）中國藝術策展人暨資深策展人皮力，同樣的也提供他對中國當代藝術寶貴的知識。

在香港亞洲藝術文獻庫，徐文玠及整體團隊支援了我們的研究工作；在紐約，多位亞洲藝術的先驅們對我的到來表示歡迎，包括：華府赫胥鴻博物館雕塑花園館長，前亞洲協會博物館館長招穎思、哥倫比亞大學藝術史與考古學系客座教授John Rajchman、國際攝影中心策展人Christopher Phillips，以及Jane DeBevoise。

我要謝謝我的家人們，我的母親Annette Fehrmann、姊姊Laura Fehrmann和已逝先父Jaap Berghuis，他們支持我從荷蘭出發到世界各地的探險。最後，我更要感謝我的太太王豔儀、女兒Anouk Berghuis與剛剛出生的小兒子Jakob Eli Berghuis，他們總是在我身邊，沒有他們無條件的愛和支持，就沒有今天在這裡的我。

萬花筒

湯偉峰

「排演是對於潛在的、可能性的、持續性的行為。」——汪建偉，2014年

對汪建偉而言，藝術製作是一場不間歇的排演；他採用一個反覆演練的實踐手段，以過程為基礎，將劇場與時間效益性的表演跟他的繪畫、裝置與錄像作品結合，複雜化傳統媒材之間的疆界。汪的作品是觀念導向並且同時紮根於日常生活，埋藏在縝密交織的歷史、現實和記憶層次之中。他主動的以中國社會的運作方式，和個人如何體現自身的自由來挑戰觀者；藉此，他將觀眾拉入中國社會和政治生活的多重視角——一個並置現實、奇觀與虛構的萬花筒。汪認為他的藝術是一種實踐手段，讓人們在文化、社會及日常生活的互動中，產生不同的、創新的連結，除此之外，他對中國當代社會現實的檢視，更說明了他和中國與和世界的關係。

在無產階級文化大革命期間（1966–76年）[1]，汪和他的家人跟許多中國人一樣被下放到鄉間，當時，正式教育不被許可，而多數的學習資源是罕見的。汪回憶起在1975年他十七歲的時候，閱讀了俄國作家暨哲學家列夫．托爾斯泰（Leo Tolstoy）《復活》（Voskreseniye，1899年）的部分譯本；早自二十世紀起，中國現代的知識份子就受到托爾斯泰的文學及哲學作品影響。《復活》描述一個男人因所處社會中的不公義和自我放縱的後果，導致他被迫面對自己道德感觀的折磨[2]；當時汪手中的副本僅有故事的中間段落，將遺失的開頭和結尾留給他發揮想像。自文學汲取靈感，和對填補故事消失章節的迫切需求，都是藝術家重要的驅動力。

1980年代期間，因為藝術家、作家和知識份子們為了社會，企圖尋求新的人文價值，存在主義文學在中國開始受到歡迎。法國作家與哲學家阿爾貝．卡繆（Albert Camus）的《薛西弗斯的神話》（Le Mythe de Sisphye，1942年）是其中獨具影響力的作品之一，此篇短文在失去了神、意志、真理和普世價值的世界裡，荒謬地搜尋意義，尤其適用在中國正在脫離根深蒂固的毛澤東信仰的學術氛圍；這個年代，更甚至見證了對德國哲學家弗里德里希．尼采（Friedrich Nietzsche）逐漸高漲的興趣，密切地用他主張的「上帝已死」[3]，來對照毛澤東及毛主義的死亡。不僅於此，還有魔幻現實主義及荒誕小說，這些文學影響建立汪對人類生存條件的具體思維。當汪在1986到1988年間，於杭州浙江美院（現中國美院）攻讀研究所時，他接觸了阿根廷作家豪爾赫．路易斯．博爾赫斯（Jorge Luis Borges）的著作，博爾赫斯想像力洋溢的小說挑戰了主流的存在主義及自然主義，他假定現實是一系列未知的連結，將故事的重心放在迷宮、夢境、圖書館、鏡子和「無窮」這個概念上；汪進一步將這些題材反映在現實和虛擬的多重層面，並體現在作品創作之上。

為了更深層地探討汪建偉的創作泉源和藝術生涯，我們必須提到「新刻度小組」，由顧德新、陳少平和王魯炎1988年在北京成立的「新刻度小組」，有效地建立觀念性的藝術語言。這些藝術家們會定期碰面，尋求從媒介到工作手法等在作品中各項層面的共通點，而後為中國創造藝術新的規則和基礎原理[4]。汪還提到美國觀念藝術家約瑟夫．克蘇斯（Joseph Kosuth）對他的影響，尤其是汪在90年代後期，曾在巴黎見過的《一把和三把椅子》（One and Three Chairs，1965年），這件作品以一個物件、一張影像和一段說明文字，三種方式來表現一張椅子的概念；汪表示：「知，也就是認知先於物質到達。」[5]這些概念啟發汪建立藝術形式，從根本上詰問意義、真理和語言在社會和政治上的結構。

今日，汪視他的作品是多媒體戲劇的一部分，劇場在此成為囊括繪畫、雕塑、裝置、影像、表演和攝影[6]在內，所有的藝術形式的基礎，是一種複雜的藝術形態；他的作品更甚至以偶然、過程和互動作為施行架構，完全再現生存經歷中的張力和環境的感知存在。他最近的作品移向通過排演的概念，和當代形式以及當代藝術的結構作直接的碰觸。汪在此書的藝術家自述中，分析排演與排演過程中的時間緊密地結合，是為特別具備當代性的實踐手段。在準備「何鴻毅家族基金中國當代藝術計劃」於紐約古根海姆美術館呈現的第一個委約項目《時間寺》時，他進一步強調：「我必須將我複雜的觀念思考不通過語言，必須要用形式來展示。」[7]這個形式部份體現於排演，連結他的實踐手法與劇場藝術。

戲劇與魔幻現實主義藝術

劇場為汪建偉提供一個舞台，就像透過一個萬花筒層疊感知，銜結每日現實中的推拉；汪經常將一個事件擺置在一個社會的、政治的、美學的、並且由他所建造的模型裡，創作闡述社會變遷的作品。劇場——是一個形式、一個結構、「一個交換信息的地方」，觀眾在這樣的設置之下，變成作品中積極的參與者[8]。

汪在2006年製作視頻《閃躲》（第25、27－28頁），演員們在卡拉OK、火車、中國證卷交易所和醫院等複合時空下，精心安排的演出交錯在博爾赫斯式夢境般的連續鏡頭中[9]。在《閃躲》中表現的政治範疇是社會的組織、混合的喜樂、疾病和經濟的建設，作品捕捉人民居住在中國城市中當下生活的時代精神，是由幻想與幻滅組成的混淆狀態。

汪的作品多數詳盡闡述社會現象，他在《人質》（2008年，第29－31頁）探討特別是在二十世紀期間，中國的人民如何被歷史和意識形態挾持；這件作品使用了一個裝置、視頻和八張照片，最早先的構想是在藝術家工作室內，經過縝密的佈置、編排和指導，一場在鏡頭前精密繁複的戲劇製作[10]。視頻以一個為人所知的畫面為起頭：一個農村女孩、一個牧羊人、一個軍人，這些都是毛主義革命力量的關鍵代表（第29頁）；影片場景設定在一個龐大的紅磚建築物裡，工人、農民和軍人們從事著根據中國改革文化規定下的休閒活動和運動；在最後，紅磚建築的倒塌（第30頁），象徵二十世紀的中國特別是歷史、工業、文化革命，還有其他在中國和在世界各地的社會革命活動的終結，同時，也包括了意識形態的崩解。對於作品之於革命思考間的關係，汪表示：「我的革命恰恰發生在社會的革命；我認為真正的革命是發生在對於現存所有的東西不信任，包括了你自己的事情。」[11]

《人質》用四個以玻璃纖維製成的大型雕塑體和機械所構成，環繞《普通報告》（第31頁，上圖）作延伸。《普通報告》是一個九尺長模擬工業化機器的物件，部分機身被稠密的白色液體或是自身噴發的白煙所吞噬，在它的後方，一個拉起紅色布簾的舞台，簾幕前，明亮的聚光燈照射另一件機械體——一個生鏽的發電機（第31頁，下圖）。這個部分藉由描寫工業化和現代化的失約，為《普通報告》和另一個主要展品《封閉系統》間提供重要的橋樑，《封閉系統》有著兩個宇航員在一個部分熔化的太空艙，標誌著中國踏入全球的太空競賽。當中國被這個懷抱著進步和創新的集體夢想所挾持時，他的人民受到新的、陌生的折磨。

爾後，汪在《歡迎來到真實的沙漠》（2010年，32－35頁）捕捉在中國社會遽變下，個人試圖追求自己的夢想，對日常生活帶來的真實後果視而無見的意象。在2008年北京夏季奧林匹克運動會結束的兩年後，汪創作《歡迎來到真實的沙漠》以回應中國作為「同一個世界，同一個夢想」[12]的理想展示品下「個體的喪失」，和在國家為了替自己在世界舞台上拿下一個位置，妥協國內的衝突與對立[13]所造成的「不確定感」。故事核心是一個和父母從鄉村搬到城市的十六歲男孩，儘管從小嚮往都市生活，他卻在那裡完全喪失自我，並開始沈迷於電玩（第32頁）；汪說：「唯一給予他真實位置的是虛擬世界，他竭力逃避現實，必須用虛擬來掌握自己真實的命運。」[14] 故事的最後，男孩在電玩的虛擬存在中，喪失了任何對現實的感知，並在大白天的街上，毫無理由的殺了一個人（第33－34頁）[15]。

《歡迎來到真實的沙漠》的作品標題，取自一篇斯洛維尼亞哲學暨文化批評家斯拉沃熱．齊澤克（Slavoj Žižek）2002年摘錄1999年《駭客任務》（The Matrix）一句電影台詞的同名文章；齊澤克的馬克思主義和從心理分析角度，檢視對911恐怖攻擊所做出的政治回應，批判全球資本主義與基本教義派、極權主義意識形態，皆同時製造了一個虛假的真實並作出對善與惡的辯述[16]。齊澤克「真實的沙漠」某些程度上還運用了尚．布希亞（Jean Baudrillard）的著作《擬像和仿真》（Simulacres et Simulation，1981年）。博爾赫斯天馬行空的描寫一個帝國貌似在爭奪中衰敗，在地圖上統治疆土的抽象表現，布希亞以驗證博爾赫斯的寫作為開端，他說：「今天，抽象概念都不再僅是地圖、替身、對照或觀念。」他進一步寫道：「這一個世代，是沒有了根源和真實的一個現實模型——是一個超現實。」[17] 汪將這個超現實，帶入同時是現實主義和抽象意念的一個反覆的表演彩排，並引領觀者更接近他們的自我詮釋。

在製作了視頻《歡迎來到真實的沙漠》之後，汪在北京雍和宮附近的方家胡同租了一間工作室，進行一個現場戲劇製作的縝密排演（第35頁）。五個當代舞者在演出中與物件互動，這些專門為表演所製作的木頭容器，像魔術師的口袋般，能被輕易地操作。背景無間隙的播放著視頻和額外的動畫，還有一個聲音裝置伴隨演出。舞者們接連的肢體活動其實是經過細心編排的舞蹈，從武術操練、京劇身段、和在商業廣告內被延伸使用的姿態，每一個動作都是在中國的身體運動歷史中，相當具備辨識度的姿勢；在表演者演出的部分，藝術家編導了一部中國的社會活動史。

劇場在汪的作品中建構政治範疇，強調政治是透過與人、和與個體及社會間平凡的往來。最近，他更在一系列的抽象作品中重現政治，將當代社會視作一個可以被實現於藝術創作中，交雜在現實與虛構多重層面間的灰色地帶。在2011年，這個居於兩者間的空間成為他在北京尤倫斯當代藝術中心的五部份個展根基。《黃燈》（2011年，第37－41頁），這個使用了劇場、視頻、和裝置精準排置的計劃，標誌著模糊的、過渡的狀態，強調互不為立的對峙空間——靜止和移動、對和錯、通行和禁令、主動和被動、參與和抗拒。黃燈同時是一個嚇阻和可行性，是一個屏障和緩衝，它就整體來說，是一個選擇的，一個行動和反應的符號。沒有黃燈，將失去預備停止或前進的瞬間。這個尷尬隱晦的臨界空間對汪而言非常具有感染力，他認為這是在日常經驗中賦予意義和命令行為的交換區[18]。

時間寺

作為「何鴻毅家族基金中國當代藝術計劃」的首位委約藝術家，汪建偉以具時效性的雕塑群打造一個迷宮，在空間中擺置形式和結構。《汪建偉：時間寺》（2014年）探討二十一世紀中國社會的變化和轉型。他將二十一世紀的中國「時間寺」與創立於二十世紀的古根海姆美術館「時間寺」接連在一起。作為古根海姆首位館長和協助創立館藏的策展人，希拉．蕾貝（Hilla Rebay）早期的書信中提到，她意圖建立一個「非具象並受推崇的殿堂」[19]。同樣被藝術作為自由的力量所啟發，汪的寺宇不只是一個博物館，它更是一個當代思維的蓄集地和圖書館；展覽的這三個元素：一系列的雕塑、電影和戲劇表演，每一個都考慮時間和空間，作為一種手段連接藝術家、作品、空間、和藝術製作所花費的時間。

在展覽的部分，觀者將面對五個巨大的物件，它們可以被理解為雕塑、建築形式、和將時間當作根基的事件的具體實踐，重申在製作過程裡流逝的時間，它們在本質上都是戲劇的展演，和藝術家長時間創作作品的實行結果；《時間寺》把古根海姆當成現場演出作品《螺旋坡道圖書館》[20]的標題，汪的圖書館是「受到法蘭克・洛伊・萊特（Frank Lloyd Wright）設計的古根海姆美術館所啟發。他更引用『宇宙』——是一個由模糊的、無限量的六角形空間（廳堂）所構成，被某些人稱之為圖書館。」[21]作品這部分揭示了博爾赫斯短篇故事《巴別塔圖書館》（La Biblioteca de Babel，1941年）的影響，在此書眾多探討的觀念裡，時間和空間象限在人的想像中變得相似，而創造出一個無法預知的新形態[22]；在被問到為什麼這意味著當代，汪緊接著指出「排演」和「當代事件」自然地連接著時間：作品為了被展示的時刻而進行製作、和觀者間的接觸、作為一個委託項目與古根海姆展覽計劃的終極存在。《時間寺》是不能從它作為一個委約計劃、展覽、觀眾的感知瞬間，和收藏地點，這樣的生命週期中被切割。作為何鴻毅家族基金系列的第一個計劃，它是一個開端，在一個全球化博物館及館藏中，重新思索中國的當代藝術。

汪選擇不考慮中國作為他當代實踐的基礎，但是我們可以看到作品在深究社會變革之時，帶出了「中國」的概念；這個國家在過去三十年間，經歷著快速的發展，這些時刻和活動都隨著藝術家強而有力的流動思維，匯入當前的事件，出現在政治和社會的改變。汪是這樣子談到這件裝置：「它是由這些（混合的）東西所構成，完全脫離了我們現在判斷事物的方法，也就包含了抵抗；任何包含抵抗的事物，就已經有了它的政治態度和形式。」[23]

汪在委約作品之一的電影《時間消失的早晨》（2014年）中，探討這個存在於感知與解讀方法間的隔閡，一部份也呼應著法蘭茲・卡夫卡（Franz Kafka）的《變形記》（Die Verwandlung，1915年）；並通過時間，表現了多種思考方法，思索自身的泯滅。在影片中，一個叫做徐的年輕人，像很多中國人一樣，抱持著對未來與擁有更美好的生活，如是的憧憬而搬到北京。套用汪的話：「有一天，當徐醒過來，發現在他的頭上有一個鰓，他的身體出現一連串的變形。」[24]如同卡夫卡的主角，徐的生活開始被困在虛擬和現實間，隱喻著今日在中國和在世界各地的生活。《時間消失的早晨》端詳日常生活和一個人的想像之間的邊界，如何變得模糊又抽象，在「魔幻現實主義的狀態」之中「產生新的生活形態」[25]。觀者可以通過影片體會中國將自己作為全球化經濟的奇幻境地，在這裡，想像參雜在真實生活中，漸成一個單一的虛幻建構。委約計劃的整體，這個中國的樣貌，不再是標記著既定的意識形態及其在歷史上的關鍵時刻，它透過一個新的時間曲折且持續的藝術，使觀者在劇場中同時成為接收者和協調人，宣告一個嶄新的抽象形式。

汪建偉的排演概念連結他所有的實踐手段，超越任何特定的藝術形式。而他以迭代、反覆的過程操弄時間，以之為作品媒材，精確且抽象、大膽無畏並難以預測。不管是通過多形態的雕塑、呈現相同架構在連環景象中的繪畫、或是錯綜複雜的影片與演出，汪彙集觀者和參與者，面對在時間的每一個點中潛在的潛能；在這個被懸置的時刻，歷史和意識形態的解放變得可能；《時間寺》是一個指定場域，在這裡，和無窮撞擊，在當代的條件下，開展綿延。

註釋

汪建偉，「排演：對尚未到來之物」於本書，第106頁。

1 關於文化革命時期的藝術，在由招穎思（Melissa Chiu）和鄭勝天共同策劃，舉辦於紐約亞洲藝術協會的《藝術與中國革命》（2008–2009年）文件記錄中可以找到更多相關介紹，詳情請見http://asiasociety.org/art-and-chinas-revolution（使用於2014年5月）。更多資訊請參考：招穎思編，《藝術與中國革命》，（紐約：亞洲藝術協會，2008年）。

2 《復活》寫於1899年，1936年才第一次被完整出版。

3 「上帝已死」（Gott ist tot）是弗里德里希・尼采廣為被引用的論點，在寫於1888年，1889年首度出版的《偶像的黃昏——或怎麼樣用鎚子從事哲學》（Die Götzendämmerung, oder Wie man mit dem Hammer philosophiert）一書中。

4 更多關於「新刻度小組」，請參考：侯瀚如，「走向一個非官方的藝術：中國當代藝術在1990年代的去意識形態化」，《Third Texts》10，第34刊（春季號，1996年），第37–52頁。

5 汪建偉與作者間的對談，北京，1月19日，2014年。

6 請見：黃專編，《劇場：汪建偉的藝術》，（廣州：嶺南美術出版社，2008年）。

7 汪建偉與作者間的對談，北京，1月20日，2014年。

8 汪建偉，與漢斯・奧瑞奇・奧柏里斯特（Hans-Ulrich Obrist）的對談（2001、2003、2006年）於《小漢斯：中國訪談集》，田霏宇、Angie Baecker編，（香港：話坊工作室，2009年），第277頁。

9 請見：湯偉峰，「我們之間的距離」於《他方的邊際》，Lisa Havilah編，展覽畫冊。（澳洲坎貝爾城：坎貝爾城藝術中心，2010年），第45–48頁。

10 《人質》剛開始在2008年是作為在上海證大美術館的個展，後來成為2010年澳洲坎貝爾城藝術中心《他方的邊際》中的第一部分。請見：沈其斌編，《人質：汪建偉個展》，展覽畫冊。（上海：上海證大美術館，2008年），以及湯偉峰，「我們之間的距離」。

11 汪，對談，1月19日，2014年。

12 「同一個世界，同一個夢想」是奧運官方精神口號。

13 請見：Michèle Vicat，「歡迎來到真實的沙漠」，《3 Dots Water: A Virtual Publication on Contemporary Chinese and Global Art》，http://www.3dotswater.com/pointerat-work006.html（使用於2014年3月）。

14 藝術家自述（時間未知），http://www.wangjianwei.com/hyldzssm.html（使用於2014年5月）。

15 《歡迎來到真實的沙漠》是為在瑞士巴塞爾的文化機構——文化風景線所製作，並在2010年巡迴至蘇黎世和日內瓦。

16 斯拉沃熱・齊澤克，「歡迎來到真實的沙漠」，《South Atlantic Quarterly》（德罕，北卡羅來納州）101，第2刊（春季號，2002年），第385–389頁。

17 尚・布希亞（Jean Baudrillard），《擬像與仿真》，Sheila Faria Glaser譯，（安娜堡，密西根州：密西根大學出版，1994年），第1頁。

18 請見：「無序紀事傑羅姆・桑斯對話汪建偉」於《汪建偉：黃燈》，展覽畫冊。 北京尤倫斯當代藝術中心，（上海：上海人民出版社，2012年），第15–25頁。

19 希拉・蕾貝給Rudolf Bauer，於4月16日，1930年，第84箱，希拉蕾貝基金會檔案庫，M0007，所羅門・R・古根海姆美術館檔案庫。引自Karole Vail，「一個建構中的博物館：兩個藝術家和他們的贊助人——希拉・蕾貝、Rudolf Bauer和所羅門・R・古根海姆」於《非具象的繪畫： 希拉・蕾貝和所羅門・R・古根海姆美術館的源頭》，Karole Vail編，（紐約：古根海姆美術館，2009年），第28頁。

20 汪建偉，《時間寺》展覽計劃，藝術家自述，12月28日，2013年。

21 同上。

22 豪爾赫・路易斯・博爾赫斯，《巴別塔圖書館》，Andrew Hurley譯，（波士頓：David R. Godine Publisher，2000年）。

23 汪，對談，1月19日，2014年。

24 汪，《時間寺》展覽計劃，藝術家自述。

25 同上。

時間寺

一條直線上的迷宮

高士明

「只有通過時間，時間才被征服。」——T・S・艾略特（T. S. Eliot）

時思寺

2011年夏日的某一天，我在浙江麗水的一個村落看到那座荒廢的古寺。寺的名字叫作「時思寺」。那是一座釋道合一的廟寺，初建於元至正十六年（西元1356年），這座寺廟中一半以上的建築是在後世續建。所以，我看到的這座元代的寺廟，其實是一個時間的綜合體。這些屋宇建於不同世代，在我到來的那個時刻，不同的時間被壓縮到一個平面上，通過這座寺廟不斷變遷的身體，那個歷代疊加、反覆累積的過程，我觸碰到許多的時間與不同世代的印記。在這塵界中所有的事物，實際上都是社會的檔案、歷史的索引，對汪建偉來說，它們都是時間寺中的祭品。

在中文世界裡，「時間寺」中的「寺」，並不必然是寺廟。「寺」是「行」與「止」的結合[1]。作為一個處所，它首先是一個通名，泛指議事、辦公的所在，以及招待賓客的場所。漢明帝永平十一年（西元68年），有白馬負經東來，初止於鴻臚寺[2]，「寺」遂由共名變成專名。

寺，是土和寸[3]的結合。「日」側加上「寺」，則是「時」，引申為空間與時間的丈量。在《爾雅》的第一個章節《釋詁》裡講「時，是也。」[4]而「是」通達於歐洲哲學史上的Sein[5]；在《說文解字》中：「時者從日，從之，從寸。」日是地球時間的坐標，之為往赴，日之行也，寸為度量。一寸光陰，光之陰，光的影子是測量時間的景象。此處，光陰或為可觀之象，無法測度者，是人的心靈對時間的感知與體悟。子在川上曰：「逝者如斯夫，不捨晝夜。」[6]而《論語》中又說：「雖百世可知也」[7]。前者感時而生悲，惆悵複曠達，後者因往推來，磊落而通透，都體現出中國人對於時間的複雜感受。

「光陰者，百代之過客。」[8]風雨江山，不過是過眼雲煙；人生百歲，也只如白駒過隙[9]。人的存在，恰似雪泥鴻爪[10]；天下滔滔，都只是這時間之河上的擺渡客。要超越此命運，需築就「時間之寺」。時間寺，以其古義，乃是一個時間凝結、駐留的場所。時間駐足之所，止於現在，在現在中成其所是，名曰「寺」。

一條直線上的迷宮

在牛頓（Isaac Newton）的世界中，時間是由無數均質瞬間連接而成，它不可分割，猶如一條有指向的直線。而對亨利・柏格森（Henri Bergson）來說，並無所謂外在的時間，把握世界的方式是「將自身置於對象之內」，「與其中獨特的，從而是無法表達的東西相合（coincide）」[11]。自我總是與世界在根源處相通的綿延，通過直覺，我們進入了整個世界的綿延，「我們自己特殊的綿延包含在世界活生生的、運動的永恒性中，如同振動包含在光中一樣。」[12]如果說，奧諾雷・德・巴爾札克（Honoré Balzac）的敘事隸屬於牛頓的時間，那麼，謝爾蓋・米哈伊洛維奇・愛森斯坦（Sergei Eisenstein）的蒙太奇則展示了牛頓時間的斷裂與破碎。詹姆斯・喬伊斯（James Joyce）在《尤利西斯》（Ulysses，1918－1920年）中所呈現的，是黏著、迂迴、纏繞在具體瑣碎事物中的時間，這仿佛印證了柏格森的綿延；然而，更廣泛時間的概念存在於博爾赫斯的寫作中，博爾赫斯是無始無終、循環回覆的，他說：「我常常永恒地回覆到永恒回覆之中」。在此，我並不是要進入關於時間無休止的形而上學辯論，也不是在重複德勒茲（Gilles Deleuze）在《時間影像》（Time Image）中，反覆糾結的命題，而是希望探討——「時間寺」的世界觀意義究竟如何成為藝術家工作的一種徵兆。

時間恒轉如流，在時間斷續之間現身的是最致命的東西。在斷續之間，存在著一個可能的時空，那是汪建偉名之為「時間寺」的場所，豪爾赫·路易斯·博爾赫斯（Jorge Luis Borges）稱作「一條直線上的迷宮」[13]。

在《去年在馬倫巴》（L'Année dernière à Marienbad，1961年）中，舞會上的時間突然凝駐。其實時間並沒有停止，影像依然在我們面前流逝，凝固下來的只是舞會上雕塑般的人群，攝像機依然如戀物癖般，在所有事物之間幽靈般地遊走。在更早的影像時刻，在《波坦金戰艦》（Bronenosets Po'tyomkin，1925年）那著名的「奧德賽臺階」上，愛森斯坦把時間切碎，再如立體派那般重新拼合起來，一百五十多個鏡頭反複交疊，層出不窮。這不只是安德烈·巴贊（André Bazin）所說的「時間空間化，空間時間化」[14]，這段被稱作「蒙太奇」經典的影像，還可以被視作「一條直線上的迷宮」的動態版本。另一個靜態的版本則出現在雷內·馬格利特（René Magritte）的畫中，窗戶被莫名的力量擊碎，但每一塊碎玻璃上都殘留著世界影像的碎片，世界被存儲在這堆破碎的鏡子裡。

時間的寺，指向一種獨特的世界觀。對汪建偉來說，這時間駐留的場域，即是影像的根本所在。一方面，觀影時光把人們從日常生活的沈悶單調中釋放出來，使之進入一種更為壓縮、凝聚的敘事時間；另一方面，影像是在時間上挖一個洞，在日常時間中構造出一種異軌的時間、「另類時間」（alternative time）。在這個意義上，攝影是對事件與時刻的命名。在現代性的經驗中，我們對事件、情境的感覺已經與照相機的干預緊密聯繫在一起。攝影的事件性和時間性已經被某種「瞬間」經驗抽空。藝術家們所要做的，很大程度上，正是對於這種由無數瞬間壘砌起的時間經驗的抵抗。

在汪建偉的影像中，「此刻」被無限放大，川流不息的時間影像分崩離析，下一刻被無限延遲。時間之軸同時也是意義之鏈，意義來自時間跨度，當下一刻被一再延遲，意義也就無限制地擱淺，永遠無法到達彼岸。影像之於汪建偉，是一條在時間之河上擱淺的船。而在時間的寺，「在開始之前和結束之後……」[15]，時間的河流已經凍結。

非解釋性的影像

「解釋性的意象統治了影像」，汪建偉說：「這是影像腐敗的明證」[16]。那麼，這個歷史的解釋性影像，那張時時潛在著的「有標題的照片」，同樣也是歷史學腐敗的證明，是否存在一種非解釋性的影像？汪建偉本人並沒有給出答案。

2011年夏天，青年藝術家劉國強發明了一臺「補幀相機」。他在眼鏡上裝了一架自動感應的微型照相機。戴著這副眼鏡，每次眨眼就會啓動相機拍照。身體的視覺輸送是一臺從不停歇的攝影機，日復一日地拍下我們冗長的生命影像，每當眨眼的時刻，生命影像就會失去一幀，「補幀相機」為我們補上生命影像中失去的那些瞬間。

在「日據時代」（1895－1945年）的臺灣，日本殖民者播放日語影片推行「皇民化」教育，而本地人大多不通日語，現場需要安排譯員進行及時翻譯，這種譯員當時被稱為「辯士」。許多辯士本身是抗日份子，翻譯字幕的時刻，往往就是他們對觀眾們做反日宣傳的時刻。於是，觀眾現場接受到的影像就形成了一個奇怪的結合體——皇民化的圖像，配上抗日的聲音。這個時刻，觀眾腦海中發生的，是一種悖反的影像、鬥爭的影像。

在解放戰爭（1927－1936年）早期的晉冀魯豫邊區，每當發起衝鋒之前，隨軍攝影師會給每位敢死隊的戰士拍照。這是生命中的莊嚴時刻，也許是最後時刻。戰士們隱約知道，由於物資匱乏，相機裡很可能並沒有膠片。但他們依然穿戴整齊，面對相機，擺好姿勢，完成生命中最後一次或許是唯一的拍照儀式後，衝向九死一生的戰場。

眨眼時「補幀」相機運作的時刻，日據時代的辯士們就著皇民化影片做抗日宣傳的時刻，戰壕中攝影師舉起空相機，為衝鋒前的戰士們拍照的時刻，是影像史上的重要時刻。那些一生中無數次錯過的瞬間影像，那段圖像與聲音悖反的影像，衝鋒之前那無膠卷的攝影儀式，讓我們從另一種角度思考影像的本質。這些影像在眾人的意念中傳遞、累積，漸而生產出一種生的意志、解放的能量。

近年來，從《人質》（2008年）中符號化的人民表徵，到《黃燈》（2011年）中反覆扮演的無名者的集合，汪建偉的影像逐漸從社會形式的視覺化表達，走向「群」與「眾」的集結與現身。他的影像成為拓印出現實肌理的拓片，不再是對某種現實的表述或某種意念的實現，而成為發生著的現實的一部分。汪建偉的影像是與戲劇同構的，在拍攝時刻，攝影棚、劇場疊合為一，通過劇場式表演與電影式表演的反覆交錯，現場的展演能量被轉譯為攝影機前的景觀。在攝影機前，生命影像總是一而再地被轉化為生命景觀。而如何通過景觀克服景觀？對汪建偉來說，這是一個巨大的難題。

「影像藝術家應該像卡夫卡（Franz Kafka）的信使，傳遞信件，卻不必知曉其中的內容。」[17]汪建偉如是說。影像從因果連續的時間軸上斷裂休止的時刻，恰恰就是它脫離解釋性意象，自身得以顯現的時刻。擺脫了解釋性意象的統治，影像刺破再現的舞臺，重返意義的未定狀態，影像在此是不知情的傳遞者而非意義的詮釋者。影像因而成為動詞，轉化為影像行動。影像由景觀轉化為行動的時刻，也是它重新成為生命影像的起始。

事件與排演

1929年9月，在馬爾馬拉海的一個小島上，五十歲的蘇聯革命家列夫·托洛斯基（Leon Trotsky）寫道：「我的前半生所經歷的是人類歷史上最波瀾壯闊的篇章。現在回想起來，在這段歷史的每一個切面上，都存在著許多不同的方向。遺憾的是，歷史只能一次性發生。所以，我們只能說——始料不及卻並非偶然。」[18]

托洛斯基所表達的，是一種建立在線性時間之假設上的歷史的鄉愁，時間之流的橫切面，是這種鄉愁所構造出來的歷史舞臺的幻象。在此，我們似乎可以站在舞臺之外，脫歷史地進行回顧往昔種種，如同孔夫子眺望時間的河流。然而，時間與我們的存在密不可分。正如博爾赫斯所說：「時間是構成我的東西。時間是裹挾我向前的河流，不過我就是那條河；時間是扭傷我的老虎，不過我就是那隻老虎；時間是燃燒我的火焰，不過我就是那場火焰。」[19]

對五十歲的托洛斯基來說，歷史如同一場賭局，由無數事件、無數決定性瞬間構成，而自我只是這場賭局的抵押物。即使作為歷史事件的重要參與者而進入那歷史影像的「決定性瞬間」，我們都只是一張照片標題的局部。在歷史學的景觀中，成為瑣碎的、不完整的局部，似乎已是現代人的命運。然而，歷史沒有終點線，一切尚未完結，照片的標題還可更換，事件尚是未定之局。只要一切尚未定局，就是我們行動的時刻。

行動影像，或者影像行動，把影像始終保持在尚未完成的狀態之中。在攝影現場，當「Action」被喊出的時候，就是我們行動／表演的時刻。更準確地說，是排演時刻。對汪建偉來說，排演不同於革命，如果說革命是反轉，是開端，排演則讓事物始終處於進程之中。排演朝向未來演進，那未來是尚未到來的和即將到來的，不是目的論意義上的終點或者結局，而是未定的、開放的，化入無始無終的進程。

德國哲學家馬丁 · 海德格爾（Martin Heidegger）在《關於人道主義的通信》（Brief ueber den Humanismus，1947年）的開篇[20]，這樣說道，行動的本質乃在於完成（Vollbringen），而完成意味著：把某種東西展開到它的本質的豐富性中，即生產出來。在這個意義上，「Vollbringen」也意味著「未完成」，生產不是製作出某種產品的過程，而是事件之發生與展開。此事件絕非歷史書寫中那些情節橋段，絕非那些每日現實因果鏈條上的決定性瞬間。事件本身越強大，每個局部碎片所被分配的意義就越小。然而，「事件」之為「事件」，在於它的上下文還沒有閉合，它依然是不可命名的「無題」，始終承載著歷史的勢能與潛能。

在排演中，事件之為事件，是歷史清場、所有潛在性噴湧而出的時刻。這個時刻，並不是紀實攝影家們意欲捕捉的「決定性瞬間」，恰恰相反，那是在「脫歷史」的時間，異軌的時間，額外的時間。在這額外的時間，那張有標題的歷史老照片幻化為灰飛煙滅的廢墟。這廢墟不是結局，我們的行動從廢墟上開始！

《黃燈》系列中，汪建偉的起點是大眾媒體所傳播的幾則社會新聞，那原本真實發生的、充滿張力的事件現場，在大眾媒體時代，淪為只是一次性消費的空洞軼聞和八卦。汪建偉從媒體報導中，打撈出來的這些社會事件，其原初意義已經失卻，剩餘的只是模糊、曖昧的形式。現在，這些失去意義指向的情節被搬到舞臺上，在攝影機前反覆排演。排演不是為了意義的完成，而是為了意義的清空。事件的意義越模糊，就離成為情節越遠。剩下的只有人群——那不是媒體報導中的公眾，也不是政治宣傳中的人民，甚至也不是片廠中充當無名角色的群眾演員本身，而是尚未定義的「群」和「眾」。排演的目的，正是為了把人群從那張「有標題的照片」中釋放出來，成為尚未被定義的「無題」，在「無題」中發掘他們的內在之可能。在此，每一幀人群集結的影像都蘊含著一次失落的歷史可能，而排演就是把佚名人群從已成定局的歷史情節中剝離出來，在失落中把情節重新變為事件，重新凝聚起歷史的潛能與勢能。

時間恒轉入流，它並沒有留下任何遺產。排演就是要打斷歷史的因果鏈條，使事件重新發生。只有在事件之中，我們才能成為主體，排演就是要在對歷史關係和事件的再造中，建構出更激烈的現實和更強大的主體。

排演是讓事物始終處於進程之中。在汪建偉的意念中，「時間寺」中的影像卻是發生在一個「失卻時間的早晨」[21]。失卻時間並不是生命經驗的遺忘，不是生命影像的「斷片」，也不是時間中的失重狀態。失卻時間的早晨，一切都共同在場且永恆在場。時間的寺，在進程之中，在歷史之外。

在排演之中，汪建偉不再糾結於詩人北島這代人所惦念的「結局或開始」。在開始之前和結束之後，在時間之寺，一切起點同時又是終點。

時間的寺，不是歷史之祭壇，歷史的意義已然清空，事件的潛能重新聚集，一切已幻滅、一切尚未完結、一切蓄勢待發。在時間寺中，有盛大的寂靜；在時間之寺，讓眾聲喧嘩！

註釋

請見:T·S·艾略特,《四個四重奏》,湯永寬譯,(上海:上海譯文出版社,1994年)。

1 請見:張文江,《古典學術講要》,(上海:上海古籍出版社,2010年)。

2 引用康熙字典,第293頁33行,由宋高承編著的《事物紀原》。

3 寸是傳統計量單位,約為一個拇指指節的寬度。

4 爾雅約出版於西元前221至西元9年,是中國最古老的字典,《釋詁》第一七二寫到「時,寔,是也。」

5 根據德國哲學家馬丁·海德格爾(Martin Heidegger)的論述,Sein是歐洲存在哲學的核心,請見:《存在與時間》,陳嘉映、王慶節譯,(北京:三聯書店,2000年)。

6 摘錄自《論語》子罕篇第十七。

7 摘錄自《論語》為政篇第二十三。

8 摘錄自唐代詩人李白《春夜宴桃李園序》。

9 引自《莊子一外篇一知北遊》:「人生天地之間,若白駒之過隙,忽然而已。」

10 引自宋朝詩人蘇軾《和子由澠池懷舊》:「人生到處知何似,應似飛鴻踏雪泥。泥上偶然留指爪,鴻飛那複計東西。」

11 請見:亨利·伯格森,《創造進化論》,肖聿譯,(北京:華夏出版社,2000年)。

12 請見:亨利·柏格森《創造進化論》,肖聿譯,(北京:華夏出版社,2000年),第21頁。

13 請見:豪爾赫·路易斯·博爾赫斯,「死亡與羅盤」於《博爾赫斯小說集》,王央樂譯,(上海:上海譯文出版社,1983年)。

14 請見:Erwin Panofsky,「Style and Medium in the Motion Picture」於《Three Essayson Style》,Irving Lavin譯,(麻州劍橋:MIT Press,1997年),第96頁。

15 請見:T·S·艾略特,「燃燒的諾頓」於《四個四重奏》,湯永寬譯,(上海:上海譯文出版社,1994年)。

16 汪建偉,與筆者在北京《太平廣記》上的對談,5月25日,2014年。

17 同上。

18 請見:列夫·托洛斯基,《我的生平:托洛斯基自傳》,(紐約:Pathfinder Press,1970年)。

19 請見:豪爾赫·路易斯·博爾赫斯,「對時間的新駁斥」於《探討別集》,王永年譯,(浙江:浙江文藝出版社,2008年)。

20 請見:馬丁·海德格爾,「關於人道主義的通信」於《基礎寫作》,(紐約:Harper Perennial Modern Though,2008年)。

21 引自汪建偉於《時間寺》(2014年)中展出作品標題《時間消失的早晨》。

排演：對尚未到來之物

汪建偉

潛能的時間：

對於一個尚未到來之物如何採取行動？我們面對這樣一個時間的困境，即我們如何用現在的經驗（源於過去）去完成一個對於未來的想像？

所謂困境，即潛能。潛能的時間將是這樣一個時間：任何一個物可以以一種方式行動，同時，它具有另一種方式行動的能力，並包含了不行動。即在同一個時間，對同一個物體來說，它具有兩種以上的能力，而相互依存彼此不相左。或者我們也可以說，任何一個物，或一個事件總是與開放性選擇有關，保持了它是或不是的整體性，而無論它是否一致，即一個矛盾體本身的真實性。它改變了一種這樣的對物的態度，即一個物只能處於被某一種必然或偶然捕獲的可能，而宣佈了物作為一個完整的共同體。

我們在馬拉美的《骰子一擲……》中看到了對於這個時間準確的描述，把偶然性的象徵與必然性的象徵結合起來，而成為了閃爍著一切思想的骰子一擲。

這個時間提供了一個關於想像未來的合理性。

排演：

這個時間與此相適應的工作可以被理解為一種排演。排演是一種無限的開啓，而不是方法，排演絕不是等待某種意外的驚喜，排演從一開始就宣佈了抵抗它的敵人——即興與隨機性。排演是對於潛在的、可能性的、持續性的行為，同時，這種可能性包含了與它一致的不可能，就像我擲出了一個骰子，它有可能到達那個位置，但我不知道它是否可能？排演同時展示了一種新的工作類型，無論它的功能與結構都不再被某種隨機控制，或者成為某一種可以被命名的方法（觀念藝術家、跨界藝術家、實驗藝術家……），而總是介於一種化學實驗室與傳統工藝的作坊，它們共同侷限在元素、材料、對比、量、比例、分配、密度以及不間斷的修正與調整的過程中。這個工作導致了不斷的偏離——失去了「正常的」時間，以及在「正常的」時間條件下對事物的判斷。正是這樣的工作引導出一種新的態勢，一種與過去慣性的斷裂，這種斷裂導致了對工作過程的命名性喪失，一種命名的匱乏。這種勞動用另一種方式呈現：質量、時間、參數。

形式：

排演也是形式真實反抗闡釋的行動。排演創造了一種條件，即將任何一個物處於不穩定，同時，使某種「超越自身」的行動得以綿延與繼續，在一個具體的勞動過程中，某物保持了對於偶然性和必然性的生成和運動，這個物在無限量的勞動和無時間限定的行為過程中，具有了某種形式——一種時間的形式，使這個物在保持了自身的屬性的同時，生產了一個「溢出」，物具有了它的複數，並超越了自身重複的原始價值，這個物的形式在它自身的行動中，轉化為可見性，這個形式保證了這個物「具體化的真實」。而形式化成為了一個物非解釋性的唯一存在方式。所以，形式就是一種單一的思想生產，它不需要與「其它」內容的知識解釋而成為它自己。

普遍性：

它必須為所有人提供一個匿名的和完整的普通性（阿蘭・巴丟）。這種普遍性始終保持了它自身單義性的力量，而恰恰是這種形式化的力量使它具有了普遍性，而普遍性得以使藝術保持了它自身的可識別和連貫性。

一個沒有殘留物的普遍性的形式，而成為它自身可以「存在」的正式闡明，它的任務包括不被現有的政治秩序所接納，因為它本身無法被這個秩序所命名，相反，它總是被這個秩序宣布為一種「例外」，被排除在這個正常秩序之外。同時我們應該承認當代藝術不是一種「人本主義」的藝術，它應該避免被新的浪漫主義（泛政治社會化）所劫持，當代藝術也不是人道主義的急救箱，這個任務是被篡改的、偽的，真正的人道主義沒有拯救，只有普遍意義上的平等，而這種平等是透明的，非解釋性的，也是超越人性的那部分。

去特殊性：

普遍性保持了對各種特殊性的警惕，以清除這些特殊性殘留在物的解釋，一種非透明的、被特殊性遮蔽的、解釋性的沉餘，因為真正的透明性拒絕任何方式的縫合。

特殊性由於附帶了無限的條件（地區、民族、宗教、文化……），它無法具有普遍性，它只能被封閉在通過交換條件、互相解釋才能產生意義的系統，而被納入了各種流通領域，成為一種物流，無限度的消失在娛樂新聞、政治事件、社會輿論的供求關係中。特殊性只是對風格和景觀的統治。

限制：

藝術家的工作必須每天面對困難的「環境」——他昨天未曾碰面，同時，未來不可能預測的狀況，它在最大程度上抑制了藝術家僅僅對於未來景觀（意外）的想像，它必須給出真實的思想與行動的限定。（而只在觀念上思考的概念正是由於失去了一個可參考的「環境」，使其自身只限於處理信息量的工作，而在毫無約束的狀態下失去了思想對象），對於任何限定性不再是假裝知道，或者總是處於製訂藍圖為假定性的未來提供服務。這個「環境」給予了藝術家在行動中所觸及的自身的邊界與壁壘。我無法想像被這種勞動排除在外的「非限制的工作」，也無法理解「只有自由」的勞動是什麼？是恐怖？

圖版圖說

第25頁
《閃躲》，2006年
HD彩色有聲視頻，8分23秒

第27－28頁
《閃躲》，2006年
HD彩色有聲視頻，8分23秒

停格影像

第29－30頁
《人質》，2008年
玻璃纖維、噴漆、金屬管、發電機、簾幕、八張全彩照片印刷；HD彩色有聲視頻，32分鐘；裝置尺寸可變

停格影像

第31頁
《人質》，2008年
玻璃纖維、噴漆、金屬管、發電機、簾幕、八張全彩照片印刷；HD彩色有聲視頻，32分鐘；裝置尺寸可變

《他方的邊際》於澳洲坎貝爾城藝術中心展覽裝置一景，2010年1月16日－3月14日

上圖：《普通報告》（前景）
下圖：《封閉系統》（後景）

第32－34頁
《歡迎來到真實的沙漠》，2010年
現場演出；五頻HD彩色有聲視頻；木箱與更動過的傢俱，90分鐘

停格影像

第35頁
《歡迎來到真實的沙漠》，2010年
現場演出；五頻HD彩色有聲視頻；木箱與更動過的傢俱，90分鐘

於蘇黎世 Zürcher Theater Spektakel演出一景，2010年9月3日－5日

第37－38頁
《黃燈》，2011年
第一章節《用贗品等待》
八頻HD彩色有聲視頻；分別為：6分33秒、7分7秒、6分59秒、10分24秒、6分59秒、6分14秒、5分54秒、6分6秒，循環播放

劇照

第39頁
《黃燈》，2011年
第一章節《用贗品等待》
八頻HD彩色有聲視頻；分別為：6分33秒、7分7秒、6分59秒、10分24秒、6分59秒、6分14秒、5分54秒、6分6秒，循環播放

於北京尤倫斯當代藝術中心展覽裝置一景，2011年4月1－24日

第40頁
《黃燈》，2011年
第二章節《我知道我們在做什麼……》
籃球框板、籃圈、籃網、籃球；壓克力、油彩、帆布；八個青銅籃球雕塑；兩個洗手盆與微型籃球場；法庭模型；裝置尺寸可變

於北京尤倫斯當代藝術中心展覽裝置一景，2011年4月26－5月15日

第41頁
《黃燈》，2011年

上圖：第三章節《內戰》
壓克力、油彩、帆布；木柴；壓克力、傢俱；塑料交通錐、玻璃纖維；壓克力、木板；裝置尺寸可變

於北京尤倫斯當代藝術中心展覽裝置一景，2011年5月17－6月5日

下圖：《返場》
現場演出；HD彩色有聲視頻；壓克力、木箱、更動過的傢俱

於北京尤倫斯當代藝術中心演出一景，2011年6月26日

《汪建偉：時間寺》展品清單

所有展出作品皆由古根海姆「何鴻毅家族基金中國當代藝術計劃」委約製作於2014年，如有不同者，將另付註記。

在此畫冊中，並非所有在展覽內的作品都依照藝術家的理念被呈現；個別作品與其部分皆能以多重迭代與組合的方式，被分開或是一起作陳列。依照現場裝置，雕塑作品尺寸不定。

1 《時間寺》
壓克力、油彩、帆布
四聯屏，整體為：258.5 x 822公分，每屏為 ： 258.5 x 205.5公分
紐約所羅門．R．古根海姆美術館
何鴻毅家族基金藏品

此四聯屏展覽用畫框並無在此加以示意。畫框高度分別為35、40、45到50公分不等，創造圖像的前後起伏，暗示著時間與流動。

第54 – 55頁

2 《時間寺》
壓克力、油彩、帆布
210 x 301公分
紐約所羅門．R．古根海姆美術館
何鴻毅家族基金藏品

第56 – 57頁

3 《時間寺一》
木柴、橡膠
共七部分，分別為：87 x 110 x 70公分；82 x 145 x 59公分；88.5 x 159 x 38公分；60 x 57 x 39公分；18 x 150 x 92公分；200 x 98 x 2公分；90 x 76 x 2公分
紐約所羅門．R．古根海姆美術館
何鴻毅家族基金藏品

第58 – 59頁

4 《時間寺二》
木柴、橡膠、鋼
共五部分，分別為：196 x 152.5 x 123公分；150 x 220 x 117公分；147 x 97 x 102公分；35 x 60 x 35公分；35 x 60 x 35公分
紐約所羅門．R．古根海姆美術館
何鴻毅家族基金藏品

第60 – 61頁

5 《時間寺三》
木柴、黃銅、橡膠
共二部分，分別為：87.5 x 205 x 124公分；92 x 188 x 91公分
紐約所羅門．R．古根海姆美術館
何鴻毅家族基金藏品

第62 – 63頁

6 《時間寺四》
木柴、顏料
共二部分，分別為：340 x 124 x 58公分；90 x 211.5 x 101.5公分
紐約所羅門．R．古根海姆美術館
何鴻毅家族基金藏品

第64 – 67頁

7 《時間寺五》
木柴、鋼
共三部分，分別為：274 x 83.5 x 23公分；35 x 60 x 35公分；35 x 60 x 35公分
紐約所羅門．R．古根海姆美術館
何鴻毅家族基金藏品

第68 – 69頁

8 《時間消失的早晨》
影片，1／5版
紐約所羅門．R．古根海姆美術館
何鴻毅家族基金藏品
於2014年盛暑於北京製作，這部實驗電影探索現代中國的變形，和體驗時間與其消逝的多重方法。

在此畫冊出版之時，這件作品仍在製作當中，欲見更完整的影像記錄，請造訪guggenheim.org/timetemple

第70 – 73頁

9 《螺旋坡道圖書館》
兩部分表演
紐約所羅門．R．古根海姆美術館
何鴻毅家族基金藏品

《螺旋坡道圖書館》在2014至2015年間於古根海姆進行兩階段的戲劇演出。它著重在人群與思考在美術館空間內的集聚與循環。在此畫冊出版之時，這個表演尚未發生，欲見更完整的影像記錄，請造訪guggenheim.org/timetemple

第74 – 77頁

專文選集
桂嘉慧整理編寫

中文
請諒解在部分來源的年代久遠與出處不可考的狀況下，即便我們盡了最大的努力，還是無法提供所有出版物的相關頁數。

藝術家表述與寫作
以下來源或許會出現在其他部分的專文選集。

2005年
「汪建偉：對於一個過程的多樣解釋」於《飛鳥不動》，第6–9頁。展覽畫冊。紐約：前波畫廊，2005年。中文、英文。

「關於『間隔』」於《間隔：試驗攝影》。展覽畫冊。上海：海上海創意LOFT，2005年。中文、英文。

2007年
「給『不明確』一個位置」於《方振寧：界面》。展覽畫冊。北京：牆美術館，2007年。中文、英文。

2008年
「關於『屏風』」於《劇場：汪建偉的藝術》，第64–98頁。展覽畫冊。深圳：OCT當代藝術中心， 2008年。

「關於『儀式』」於《劇場：汪建偉的藝術》，第130–174頁。展覽畫冊。深圳：OCT當代藝術中心， 2008年。

「關於『徵兆』」於《劇場：汪建偉的藝術》，第350–397頁。展覽畫冊。深圳：OCT當代藝術中心， 2008年。

2010年
高士明、汪建偉。「汪建偉：時間·劇場·展覽」。《當代藝術與投資》（北京）1（2010年）。

2011年
「在其他之中」。《今日先鋒》（天津）10（2011年）。

「是什麼讓我理解我的知道？」於《我是好奇之黃，我是好奇之藍——何岸個展》。展覽畫冊。北京：唐人當代藝術中心，2011年。中文、英文。

2012年
「關於『黃燈』」於《汪建偉：黃燈》，第6–7頁。展覽畫冊。北京：尤倫斯當代藝術中心，2012年。中文、英文。

董冰峰、汪建偉、姚嘉善、朱青生。「一個當代藝術空間？」。《當代藝術與投資》（北京）10（2011年）。

2013年
「反抗的褶子」。《藝術界》（北京）22（八月號，2013年），第26頁。中文、英文。

「去特殊性？」。《藝術界》（北京）24（十二月號，2013年），第22頁。中文、英文。

「汪建偉：我們的戰鬥」。《藝術界》（北京）22（八月號，2013年），第84–85頁。中文、英文。

「作為事件的徵兆」。《藝術界》（北京）19（二月號，2013年），第100–101頁。中文、英文。

「保衛當代藝術的主體」。《藝術界》（北京）21（六月號，2013年），第25頁。中文、英文。

「無法躲閃」。《藝術界》（北京）20（四月號，2013年），第41頁。中文、英文。

「擰乾態度的水份」。《藝術界》（北京）23（十月號，2013年），第28頁。中文、英文。

訪談
以下來源或許會出現在其他部分的專文選集。

2005年
Napack，Jonathan。「汪建偉」於《飛鳥不動》。展覽畫冊。紐約：前波畫廊，2005年。中文、英文。

朱其，「汪建偉」於《超越界限》。展覽畫冊。上海：上海滬申畫廊，2005年。

2008年
皇甫秉惠，「汪建偉訪談」於《人質：汪建偉個展》，第26–48頁，展覽畫冊。上海：證大美術館，2008年。中文、英文。

李振華，「汪建偉：一個質疑知識的知識份子」於《趣味的共同體：伊比利亞當代藝術中心開幕展》，第207–215頁，展覽畫冊。北京：伊比利亞當代藝術中心，2008年。中文、英文。

2009年
王家浩，「跨學科的可能性」。《東方藝術》（鄭州）14（七月號，2009年），第54–59頁。

梁爽，「質疑是一種思維方式」。《東方藝術》（鄭州）14（七月號，2009年），第88–91頁。

奧柏里斯特，漢斯·奧瑞奇。田霏宇、Angie Baecker。「汪建偉」於《小漢斯：中國訪談集》，第274–285。香港：話坊工作室，2009年。中文、英文。

2012年
高宇倩，「汪建偉」於《中國藝術面孔》，第225–252頁。上海：三聯書店，2012年。中文、英文。

桑斯，杰羅姆。「無序紀事杰羅姆·桑斯對話汪建偉」於《汪建偉：黃燈》，第15–22頁，展覽畫冊。北京：尤倫斯當代藝術中心，2012年。中文、英文。

鄭勝天，「黃燈的糾結」。《典藏國際版》（臺北）11，第3刊（五月號，2012年），第30–41頁。

關於藝術家

個展畫冊
以下來源或許會出現在其他部分的專文選集。

2005年
《飛鳥不動》。紐約：前波畫廊，2005年。收錄藝術家自述，以及Jonathan Napack和茅為清的文章。中文、英文。

2006年
《躲閃》。上海：滬申畫廊，2006年。中文、英文。

2007年
《三岔口》。北京：前波畫廊，2007年。收錄Anselm Franke和茅為清的文章。中文、英文。

2008年
沈其斌編。《人質：汪建偉個展》。上海：證大美術館，2008年。收錄藝術家訪談，以及皇甫秉惠、沈其斌和Marianne Brouwer的文章。中文、英文。

黃專編。《劇場：汪建偉的藝術》。廣州：嶺南美術出版社，2008年。

2012年
《汪建偉：黃燈》。北京：尤倫斯當代藝術中心，2012年。收錄藝術家自述，以及盧傑、朱文、蔡秉橋和杰羅姆·桑斯的文章。中文、英文。

群展畫冊
以下來源或許會出現在其他部分的專文選集。

1993年
《後八九中國新藝術》，第40–41頁。香港：Hanart TZ畫廊，1993年。中文、英文。

1997年
《中國旅程97：兩岸三地的裝置藝術展》。香港：香港藝術中心和香港當代文化中心，1997年。中文、英文。

1998年
《生存痕跡：'98中國當代藝術內部觀摩展》，第10–11、14、134–137頁。北京：現實藝術工作室，1998年。

1999年
《快鏡：中港台錄像新藝術》，第34頁。澳門：澳門當代藝術中心，1999年。中文、英文、葡萄牙文。

2000年
《進與出：中澳華人當代藝術交流展》，第52–55、78頁。新加坡：拉薩爾–新航藝術學院，2000年。中文、英文。

《後物質：中國當代藝術家解讀日常生活》。北京：紅門畫廊，2000年。中文、英文。

2001年
《被移植的現場》。深圳：何香凝美術館，2001年。

《跑跳爬走》。北京：東方現代藝術中心，2001年。

2002年
《合成現實：中國錄像藝術》，第66–73頁。北京：遠洋藝術中心，2002年。中文、英文。

《複眼：中國錄像藝術》，第64–71、91–92頁。新加坡：拉薩爾–新航藝術學院，2002年。中文、英文。

2003年
《ControlZ》。北京：泰康空間，2003年。中文、英文。

《二手現實——前現實》。北京：今日美術館，2003年。中文、英文。

2004年
《十八個個展》。台灣金門：金門碉堡藝術館，2004年。中文、英文。

2005年
《仙那度變奏曲》。台北：當代藝術館，2005年。中文、英文。

《超越界限》，第124–129頁。上海：滬申畫廊，2005年。收錄朱其與藝術家的訪談。中文、英文。

2006年
《江湖》，第5、58–59頁。紐約：丟頓畫廊，2006年。中文、英文。

《柏拉圖和他的七種精靈》。深圳：OCT當代藝術中心，2006年。

高士明、吳方洲編。《顯微鏡：一種現實主義的政治——中國當代藝術展》，第120–124頁。澳門：澳門當代美術館，2006年。中文、英文。

2007年
《可持續幻象：中國媒體藝術系列展覽之1999–2007》。北京：阿拉里奧畫廊，2007年。

《能量、精神、身體、物質》。北京：今日美術館，2007年。中文、英文。

《網：再現空間、時間與文化》。北京：前波畫廊，2007年。

2008年
《以身觀身：亞洲行為藝術邀請展2008專輯》，第58–59、91頁。澳門：澳門當代美術館，2008年。中文、英文、葡萄牙文。

《地圖遊戲：變化動力》。北京：今日美術館，2008年。中文、英文。

《我們的未來：尤倫斯基金會收藏展》。北京：尤倫斯藝術中心，2008年。中文、英文。

《趣味的共同體——伊比利亞當代藝術中心開幕展》，第207–219頁。北京：伊比利亞當代藝術中心，2008年。收錄李振華的文章。中文、英文。

2009年
《山水——綜合藝術世界中的自然生態》。北京：天安時間當代藝術中心，2009年。中文、英文。

《資產階級化了的無產階級》，第13、53、64–65、78、96、112、128、142、158頁。上海：上海松江創意工坊，2009年。中文、英文。

黃專編。《國家遺產：一項關於視覺政治的研究》。英國曼徹斯特：Righton Press，2009年。中文、英文。

2010年
《改造歷史：2000–2009年中國新藝術》。北京：中國國家會議中心，2010年。中文、英文。

《長徵計劃：胡志明小道》。北京：長征空間，2010年。中文、英文。

《紙上美術館：12位華人藝術家》，第171–177、287–288頁。北京：伊比利亞當代藝術中心，2010年。中文、英文。

2011年
《出格：中國錄像藝術的開端（1984–1998）》。廣州：時代美術館，2011年。中文、英文。

2012年
《開放的肖像》，第80–84頁。上海：民生現代美術館，2012年。中文、英文。

《偶然的信息：藝術不是一個體系，也不是一個世界——第七屆深圳雕塑雙年展》。深圳：OCT當代藝術中心，2012年。中文、英文。

書籍
此部分集選包含了與展覽不直接相關的書籍、章節，及部分節錄。

1994年
《中國當代藝術家工作計劃（1994）》。四川：國際文化發展公司，1994年。

2010年
黃專，「破執：汪建偉的歷史和政治敘事」於《藝術世界中的思想與行動》。北京：北京大學出版社，2010年。

2012年
高宇倩，「異類思想家——汪建偉」於《中國藝術面孔》，第225–252頁。上海：三聯書店，2012年。中文、英文。

相關專文
此部分選錄文章包含了期刊、文章專輯、個展或群展畫冊。某些來源或許會出現在其他部分的專文選集。

2000年
李櫻子，「汪建偉：我的工作就是不斷地犯錯」。《中國新聞周刊》（北京）16（2000年），第18–21頁。

2007年
Franke，Anselm。「穿越迷霧的幽靈——論汪建偉作品在一場新起的爭論中的處境」於《三岔口》，第10–13頁。展覽畫冊。北京：前波畫廊，2007年。中文、英文。

2008年
Brouwer，Marianne。「製造真實」於《人質：汪建偉個展》，第18–25頁，展覽畫冊。上海：證大美術館，2008年。中文、英文。

沈其斌，「不確定性、可能性、灰色地帶」於《人質：汪建偉個展》，第4–7頁，展覽畫冊。上海：證大美術館，2008年。中文、英文。

皇甫秉惠，「意料之中的意外」於《人質：汪建偉個展》，第10–17頁，展覽畫冊。上海：證大美術館，2008年。中文、英文。

2010年
王家浩，「汪建偉：時間–劇場–展覽」。《藝術界》（北京）1（二月號，2010年），第190–193頁。中文、英文。

2011年
李笑南，「紙上美術館：12位華人藝術家」。《藝術界》（北京）8（四月號，2011年），第198–201頁。中文、英文。

李乃清，「汪建偉：不告訴你哪兒有危險」。《南方人物周刊》（廣州）33（2011年），第47頁。

愛阿安，「汪建偉：中間人」。《藝術界》（北京）9（六月號，2011年），第99–105頁。中文、英文。

鄭鈺垚，「汪建偉：質疑的力量」。《東方藝術》（鄭州）5（三月，2011年），第80–81頁。

2012年
朱文，「黃燈——最漫長的一次閃爍」於《汪建偉：黃燈》，第4–5頁，展覽畫冊。北京：尤倫斯當代藝術中心，2011年。中文、英文。

郝科，「汪建偉工作室質疑『集體』的孤獨現場」。《東方藝術》（鄭州）1（一月號，2012年），第146–147頁。

唐凌潔，「開放的肖像」。《藝術界》（北京）15（七月號，2012年）。中文、英文。

郭娟，「理論熱」。《藝術界》（北京）14（五月號，2012年）。英文，中文。

賈徐美，「農民工」。《浙江畫報》（杭州）（十一月號，2012年），第38–43頁。

蔡秉橋。「遊走黃燈」於《汪建偉：黃燈》，第230–233頁。展覽畫冊。北京：尤倫斯當代藝術中心，2012年。中文、英文。

盧傑，「遭遇黃燈」於《汪建偉：黃燈》，第23–24頁，展覽畫冊。北京：尤倫斯當代藝術中心，2012年。中文、英文。

謝一，「汪建偉：多媒體的社會觀察家」。《大美術》（上海）4（七月號，2012年），第28–29頁。

2013年
郝科，「汪建偉『當代』即是與今天的『不共識』」。《東方藝術》（鄭州）18（九月號，2013年），第46頁。

郝科，「汪建偉：沒有結局的劇場」。《東方藝術》（鄭州）22（十一月號，2013年），第72–77頁。

範南萌，「汪建偉：跳出棋盤的棋子」。《東方藝術》（鄭州）22（十一月號，2013年），第88–91頁。

網路來源
此部分來源皆來自發表於網站上的文章。

藝術家表述與寫作
2013年
「《歡迎來到真實的沙漠》」。《99藝術網》，2013年8月2日。http://news.99ys.com/20130802/article--130802--137302_1.shtml。

「不確定性是最吸引人的」。《99藝術網》，2013年8月1日。http://news.99ys.com/20130801/article--130801--137182_1.shtml。

「王廣義——個非線型者」。《99藝術網》，2013年8月2日。http://news.99ys.com/20130802/article--130802--137314_1.shtml。

「另一種……？」。《99藝術網》，2013年8月1日。http://news.99ys.com/20130801/article--130801--137179_1.shtml。

「另一種表－關於何多苓」。《99藝術網》，2013年8月2日。http://news.99ys.com/20130802/article--130802--137307_1.shtml。

「死已經死了一關於秦思源」。《99藝術網》，2013年8月2日。http://news.99ys.com/20130802/article--130802--137322_1.shtml。

「吳文光的『眼睛』」。《99藝術網》，2013年8月2日。http://news.99ys.com/20130802/article--130802--137316_1.shtml。

「是否有一種『中間地帶』的描述」。《99藝術網》，2013年8月1日。http://news.99ys.com/20130801/article--130801--137174_1.shtml。

「為什麼要談中國，現在？」。《99藝術網》，2013年8月2日。http://news.99ys.com/20130802/article--130802--137213_1.shtml。

「建築成為話語」。《99藝術網》，2013年8月1日。http://news.99ys.com/20130801/article--130801--137178_1.shtml。

「徵兆與轉譯一關於沈瑋」。《99藝術網》，2013年8月2日。http://news.99ys.com/20130802/article--130802--137319_1.shtml。

年份未知
「中國的當代藝術是物，不是精神交流」。《中國當代藝術數據庫》，時間未知。http://www.artlinkart.com/cn/artist/txt_ab/584ayu/415cuvok。

訪談
2009年
盛葳、劉倩，「汪建偉訪談：『正確』的錯誤」。《CAFA》，2009年3月5日。http://www.cafa.com.cn/c/?t=5454。

2010年
徐金龍，「汪建偉訪談：觀禮台」。《CAFA》，2010年1月25日。http://www.cafa.com.cn/c/?t=541197。
張長城，「歡迎來到真實的沙漠」。《搜狐文化》，16分45秒，2010年8月17

日。http://arts.cul.sohu.com/20100817/n274266723.shtml。

2011年

段子迎，「汪建偉專訪：當代·當代藝術·共同體」。《CAFA》，2011年11月10日。http://www.cafa.com.cn/c/?t=543104。

2013年

李健亞，「汪建偉：先鋒是一種本性」。《99藝術網》，2013年8月2日。http://news.99ys.com/20130802/article--130802--137289_1.shtml。

杜曦雲，「用實踐去重建無法被規定的新的主體」。《99藝術網》，2013年8月2日。http://news.99ys.com/20130802/article--130802--137320_1.shtml。

張凡，「『時尚』，是拒絕平庸的一劑藥」。《99藝術網》，2013年8月2日。http://news.99ys.com/20130802/article--130802--137317_1.shtml。

張嘉格，「汪建偉：『黃燈現象』涉及廣泛的社會行為和政治太平」。《99藝術網》，2013年8月2日。http://news.99ys.com/20130802/article--130802--137284_1.shtml。

舒可文，「『黃燈共同體』——汪建偉與舒可文的對話」。《99藝術網》，2013年8月2日。http://news.99ys.com/20130802/article--130802--137293_1.shtml。

關於藝術家

相關專文

2012年

許彤，「暗示與幻覺——以《黃燈》為例試論汪建偉藝術語言中的借用與含混」。《CAFA》，2012年3月9日。中文、英文。http://en.cafa.com.cn/intimation-and-illusion-taking-yellow-signal-for-instance-to-comment-on-the-artistic-language-of-borrowing-and-ambiguity-of-wang-jianwei.html。

2013年

王棟棟，「『回顧』與『權力』——以汪建偉的卡塞爾文獻展經歷為例」。《99藝術網》，2013年8月2日。http://news.99ys.com/20130802/article--130802--137336_1.shtml。

薛蓮，「躲閃——一種中間狀態」。《99藝術網》，2013年8月1日。http://news.99ys.com/20130801/article--130801--137183_1.shtml。

2014年

沈寅、吳佳霖，「汪建偉：當代藝術的『三個無關』」。《外灘畫報》，2014年1月1日。http://www.bundpic.com/2013/12/24791.shtml。

由呂斯喬、朱曉瑞、朱穎協助整理。

展覽經歷

桂嘉慧整理編寫

在部分展覽正確展期無從考證的狀況下，僅提供展覽開幕日期或是月份，若是這些資料都無法被確認，則不提供該展相關展出日期。

個展

1991年

北京民族文化宮，《汪建偉》。

1992年

香港藝術中心，《汪健偉》。

1993年

香港藝術中心，《事件－過程·狀態》。

2003年

倫敦當代藝術學會，《儀式》，10月23－26日。

2004年

雪梨4A亞洲當代藝術中心，《汪建偉－大躍進》，3月11日－5月15日。展覽巡迴至澳洲阿得雷德實驗藝術基金會，2004年2月25日－2005年4月2日。展覽畫冊。

2005年

紐約前波畫廊，《飛鳥不動：汪建偉的個展》，2005年10月27日－2006年12月22日。展覽巡迴至北京阿拉里奧畫廊，2006年4月1日－5月14日。展覽畫冊。

2006年

上海外灘三號滬申畫廊，《閃躲》，5月20日－7月9日。

2007年

柏林Hebbel am Ufer劇院，《交叉感染》，6月1－10日。

紐約前波畫廊，《三岔口》，10月4日－11月3日。展覽畫冊。

2008年

上海證大現代美術館，《人質》，4月19日－5月18日。展覽畫冊。

深圳OCT當代藝術中心，《徵兆：汪健偉大型劇場作品展》，6月28日－7月28日。展覽畫冊。

2009年

北京今日美術館，《時間·劇場·展覽》，11月22日。

2011年

北京尤倫斯藝術中心，《汪建偉：黃燈》，4月1日－6月26日。展覽畫冊。

2013年

北京長征空間，《…或者事件導致了每一個無效的結果。》，9月14日－10月13日。

群展

1984年

北京中國美術館，《第六屆全國美術作品展覽》，10月1－7日。展覽畫冊。

1987年

加州帕薩迪納亞太博物館，《門戶開放之外：中國當代繪畫》。展覽畫冊。

1993年

香港藝術中心（香港漢雅軒畫廊策劃），《後八九中國新藝術》，1月1日—2月1日。展覽巡迴至倫敦馬博羅畫廊，1993年12月7日－1994年2月12日。展覽畫冊。

澳洲雪梨當代藝術館，《毛進到普普：中國後八九》，6月2日－8月15日。展覽畫冊。

1995年

光洲雙年展展展覽中心，南韓光州雙年展：《超越界限》，9月20日－11月20日。展覽畫冊。

大阪Kilin Plaza，《新亞洲藝術展——1995年：中國、韓國、日本》。展覽畫冊。

1996年

澳洲布里斯本昆士蘭美術館，亞太地區當代藝術三年展，1996年9月27日－1997年1月19日。展覽畫冊。

1997 年

新加坡拉薩爾－新航藝術學院，《進與出：中澳華人當代藝術交流展》，5月14日－6月21日。展覽巡迴至澳洲墨爾本皇家理工大學RMIT畫廊，7月18日－8月30日；雪梨大學SCA畫廊，9月4－28日；澳洲荷巴特塔斯馬尼亞大學Plimsoll畫廊，1998年3月；坎培拉澳洲國立大學，1998年8月。展覽畫冊。

荷蘭布雷達Chassékazerne，《又一次長征：90年代中國觀念和裝置藝術》，5月31日－8月3日。展覽畫冊。

卡塞爾第十屆文獻展，6月21日－9月28日。展覽畫冊。

日本山形美術館，山形國際紀錄片影展，10月6－13日。展覽畫冊。

維也納分離派美術館，《移動的城市》，1997年11月26日－1998年1月18日。展覽巡迴至博爾多當代視覺藝術中心，1997年6年5日－1998年8月30日；紐約PS1當代藝術中心（現當代美術館PS1），1998月10年18日－1999年1月10日；丹麥Humlebæk路易西安那現代美術館，1999年1月29日－4月21日；倫敦海沃美術館，1999年5月13日－6月27日；赫爾辛基Kiasma當代藝術館，1999年11月5日－12月19日。展覽畫冊。

1998年

北京現在畫廊，《生存痕跡：'98中國當代藝術內部觀摩展》，1月2日開幕。展覽畫冊。

香港當代文化中心及香港科技大學藝術中心，《中國旅程'97：兩岸三地的裝置藝術展》，1月22－24日。展覽畫冊。

1999年

澳門當代藝術中心，《快鏡：中港台錄像新藝術》，3月19日－5月30日。展覽畫冊。

墨爾本中國館，墨爾本國際雙年展：《生存痕跡》，5月14日－6月27日。展覽畫冊。

安特衛普省立攝影博物館，《Laboratorium》，6月27日－10月3日。展覽畫冊。

日本山形美術館，山形國際紀錄片影展，10月19－25日。展覽畫冊。

倫敦當代藝術學會，《北京——倫敦》。

2000年

法國比亞里茲，《國際音像節》，1月18－23日。展覽畫冊。

英國布萊頓巨蛋，布萊頓藝術節，5月3－25日。

布魯賽爾M.A.P.，布魯賽爾藝術節，5月5－27日。

阿姆斯特丹Melkweg，世界錄像節，9月16日。

北京紅門畫廊，《後物質：中國當代藝術家解讀日常生活》，10月21日－11月30日。展覽畫冊。

上海美術館，上海雙年展：《海上·上海》，2000年11月6日－2001年1月6日。展覽畫冊。

2001年

柏林世界文化中心，《行為的傳譯：東亞表演及身體藝術》，3月8日－5月27日。展覽巡迴至紐約皇后美術館，2001年10月28日－2002年2月17日。

新加坡拉薩爾－新航藝術學院，《複眼：中國錄像藝術》，6月8－7月18日。展覽巡迴至深圳何香凝美術館，10月。澳洲新南威爾斯大學Ivan Dougherty畫廊，2002年7月4日－8月10日。展覽畫冊。

東京歌劇城畫廊，《我家是你家，你家即我家》，7月1日－9月16日。

杭州中國美術學院，《非線性敘事：新媒體藝術節》，9月。

柏林Hamburger Bahnhof，《生活在此刻：29位來自中國的當代藝術家》，2001年9月19日－2002年1月6日。

柏林KW當代藝術學會，《事物狀態：中比當代藝術交流展》。

2002年

聖保羅Pavilhão Ciccillo Matarazzo，伊比拉布埃拉公園，聖保羅雙年展，3月23日－6月2日。

布魯賽爾M.A.P.，布魯賽爾藝術節，5月3－25日。

四川瀘定橋，《長征——一個行走中的視覺展示》，6月5日－10月25日。

新加坡Earl Lu畫廊，《場域與視覺：文化轉譯》，6月7日－7月26日。

廣州廣東美術館，廣州三年展，2002年11月18日－2003年1月19日。展覽畫冊。

北京遠洋藝術中心，《合成現實》，12月14－30日。展覽畫冊。

2003年

明尼阿波里斯市沃克藝術中心《緯度如何變為形式：藝術在全球化的時代》，2月3日－5月4日。展覽巡迴至都靈Fondazione Sandretto Re Rebaudengo，2003年6月1日－9月14日；休斯頓當代藝術館，2004年7月17日－9月19日。展覽畫冊。

巴黎現代藝術博物館，《影室：張永和、汪建偉、楊福東》，2月7日－3月23日。展覽巡迴至羅馬尼亞布加勒斯特國立當代藝術館，2014年10月29日開幕。展覽畫冊。

威尼斯軍械庫，威尼斯雙年展，6月15日－11月2日。

巴黎龐畢度藝術中心，《那麼．中國？》，6月25日－10月13日。展覽畫冊。

北京泰康空間，《Control Z》，9月16－20日。展覽畫冊。

北京今日美術館，《二手現實——前現實》，9月17日－10月16日。展覽畫冊。

雅加達Edwin畫廊，《相互作用：中國當代藝術》，10月2－21日。展覽畫冊。

巴黎龐畢度藝術中心，《巴黎秋季藝術節》，10月8－11日。

華沙Zachęta國家畫廊，《新區域－中國藝術》，2003年12月1日－2004年2月1日。展覽畫冊。

2004年

紐約現代美術館，《此刻的中國》，2月12－16日。

布魯賽爾M.A.P.，布魯賽爾藝術節，5月5－27日。

紐約國際攝影中心，《在過去與未來之間：中國的新攝影與錄像》，6月11日－9月5日。展覽巡迴至芝加哥Smart美術館、芝加哥大學及芝加哥當代藝術館，2004年10月2日－2005年1月16日；西雅圖美術館，2005年2月10日－5月1日；倫敦維多利亞與阿伯特博物館，2005年9月15日－2006年1月15日；聖塔芭芭拉美術館，2006年7月1日－9月17日；北卡羅來納州德罕杜克大學Nasher美術館，2006年10月26日－2007年2月18日。展覽畫冊。

上海外灘三號滬申畫廊，《全新空間》，6月26日－7月11日。

立陶宛維爾紐斯當代藝術中心，《慢速衝擊：亞太地區動態影像紀實展》，9月10日－10月31日。展覽畫冊。

台灣金門碉堡藝術館，《十八個個展》，2004年9月11日－2005年2月10日。展覽畫冊。

巴黎龐畢度藝術中心，《巴黎秋季藝術節》，9月13－12月19日。

上海美術館，上海雙年展：《影像生存》，9月28日－11月27日。

聖地亞哥美術館，《翻轉過往：東亞當代藝術》，2004年11月6日－2005年3月6日。展覽巡迴至密蘇里州堪薩斯城Kemper當代藝術館，2005年6月3日－9月4日；新罕布夏州漢諾瓦Hood美術館，2006年1月15－3月12日。展覽畫冊。

首爾美術館，首爾國際媒體藝術雙年展，2004年12月15日－2005年2月6日。

2005年

澳洲阿得雷德大聯盟市電影院，阿得雷德電影節：《影像是一切》，2月18日－3月3日。

臺北當代藝術館，《先那度變奏曲》，8月6日－9月25日。展覽畫冊。

北京OCT當代藝術中心，《柏拉圖和他的七種精靈》，9月23日－11月7日。展覽巡迴至深圳OCT當代藝術中心，2006年3月3－30日。展覽畫冊。

紐約布法羅Albright-Knox美術館，《牆：中國當代藝術的歷史與邊界》，2005年10月21日－2006年1月29日。展覽畫冊。

廣州廣東美術館，廣州三年展：《別樣——一個特殊的現代化實驗空間》，2005年11月18日－2006年1月15日。

深圳OCT當代藝術中心，深圳城市＼建築雙年展，2005年12月10日－2006年3月10日。

2006年

澳門藝術博物館，《顯微境．觀》，3月18日－6月18日。展覽畫冊。

紐約丟頓畫廊，《江湖》，5月24日－6月30日。展覽畫冊。

鹿特丹Boijmans Van Beuningen博物館，《當代中國：建築、藝術與視覺文化》，6月10日－8月13日。

2007年

愛爾蘭考克大學Lewis Glucksman畫廊，《金豬年——中國當代藝術Sigg收藏展》，3月13日－6月17日。

北京阿拉里奧畫廊，《可持續幻象：中國媒體藝術系列展覽之1999－2007》，4月29日－6月10日。展覽畫冊。

柏林Hebbel am Ufer劇院，《中國迴路》，6月1－6日。

奧地利Kunsthaus Graz，《中國歡迎你》，6月6日－9月7日。展覽畫冊。

荷蘭席塔德Het Domein博物館，《Chinergie：夏季中國展》，8月11日－9月2日。展覽畫冊。

澳洲達爾文24小時藝術／北領地當代藝術中心，《改變：中國錄像藝術》，9月14日－10月20日。

耶路撒冷以色列博物館，《中國製造：仕丹萊收藏展》，2007年9月18日－2008年3月1日。展覽巡迴至丹麥Humlebæk路易西安那現代美術館，2008年3月16日－8月5日。展覽畫冊。

北京前波畫廊，《網：再現空間、時間與文化》，9月20日－11月3日。展覽畫冊。

北京今日美術館，《能量、精神、身體、物質》，10月17日－11月13日。展覽畫冊。

維也納Ludwig Wien現代美術館，《面對現實》，2007年10月25日－2008年2月10日。展覽畫冊。

邁阿密海灘巴塞爾藝術展紐頓大樓，《超越偶像：中國當代藝術在邁阿密》，12月6－9日。展覽畫冊。

2008年

荷蘭阿姆斯特爾分Canvas國際藝術，《光明與黑暗：在華人的邊境上》，2月16日－3月22日。展覽畫冊。

盧森堡Mudam，《中國發電站，第三站》，4月26日－9月15日。展覽畫冊。

北京伊比利亞當代藝術中心，《趣味的共同體——伊比利亞當代藝術中心開幕展》，4月29日－6月9日。展覽畫冊。

北京阿拉里奧畫廊，《在光明與黑暗之間》，6月10日－7月26日。

北京今日美術館，《地圖遊戲：變化動力》，6月18－28日。展覽巡迴至英國伯明罕博物館及畫廊，2008年10月18日－2009

年1月4日；義大利特爾尼Siri工廠藝術中心及Palazzo Primavera，2009年3月28日－5月10日。展覽畫冊。

北京尤倫斯藝術中心，《我們的未來：尤倫斯基金會收藏展》，7月19日－8月10日。展覽畫冊。

北京天安時間當代藝術中心，《山水——綜合藝術世界中的自然生態》，9月19日－10月31日。展覽畫冊。

澳門藝術博物館，《以身觀身：亞洲行為藝術邀請展2008專輯》，2008年11月18日－2009年2月15日。展覽畫冊。

2009年

英國曼徹斯特Holden畫廊，《國家遺產：一項關於視覺政治的研究》，4月2日－5月24日。展覽巡迴至深圳OCT當代藝術中心，10月17日－11月30日。展覽畫冊。

深圳美術館，《歷史的圖像：2009中國當代藝術邀請展》，4月24日－5月24日。展覽巡迴至中國湖北美術館，6月12日－7月12日。

上海松江創意工坊，《資產階級化了的無產階級》，9月10－14日。展覽畫冊。

澳洲布里斯本昆士蘭美術館，《別岸的審視》，10月7日－11月15日。展覽畫冊。

北京中央美術學院美術館，《碰撞——關於中國當代藝術試驗的案例》，10月10－16日。

哈瓦那古巴國家美術館，《北京－哈瓦那：新中國當代藝術革命》，2009年10月30日－2010年1月15日。

橫濱新港展覽廳，《奶油：橫濱國際媒體與藝術節》，10月31日－11月29日。展覽畫冊。

北京阿拉里奧畫廊，《喜馬拉雅計劃——汪建偉&娜里尼·瑪拉尼》，2009年11月21日－2010年1月24日。

馬德里Matadero，《北京時間》，2009年12月17日－2010年3月21日。展覽畫冊。

2010年

北京伊比利亞當代藝術中心，《紙上美術館：12位華人藝術家》，1月6日－3月6日。展覽畫冊。

澳洲坎貝爾藝術中心，《他方的邊際》，1月16日－3月14日。展覽畫冊。

廣東時代美術館，《出格：中國錄像藝術的開端(1984－1998)》，3月26日－5月4日。

北京國家會議中心，《改造歷史：2000－2009年的中國新藝術》，5月4日－21日。展覽畫冊。

天安阿拉里奧畫廊，《懸浮的時間重量》，6月29日－8月15日。

北京方家胡同四十六號劇場黑方空間，《歡迎來到真實的沙漠》，8月17－19日。

蘇黎世Zürcher Theater Spektake，《歡迎來到真實的沙漠》，9月3－5日。

北京長征空間，《長征計劃——胡志明小道》，9月4日－11月14日。展覽畫冊。

日內瓦La Bâtie藝術節，《歡迎來到真實的沙漠》，9月7－8日。

巴塞爾Kaserne，《歡迎來到真實的沙漠》，9月15日。

上海美術館，上海雙年展：《巡迴排演》，2010年10月24日－2011年1月23日。

北京博而勵畫廊，《Out of Box》，2010年12月16日－2011年1月31日。展覽畫冊。

2011年

北京長征空間，《長征空間春季綜合展》，2月18日－4月7日。

首爾Artsonje藝術中心，《H BOX：一個游牧藝術影像放映室》，2月25日－5月1日。展覽巡迴至北京今日美術館，6月11日－7月11日。

北京長征空間，《ACT▶TION影像展》，6月25日－8月21日。

成都當代美術館，《典藏歷史——中國新藝術》，7月1日－8月31日。

上海民生現代美術館，《中國當代藝術三十年之——中國影像藝術》，9月7日－11月27日。

北京伊比利亞當代藝術中心，《時間的形狀——當代中國藝術中的多重歷史》，9月17－20日。

莫斯科Artplay設計中心，莫斯科當代藝術雙年展：《改寫世界》，9月22日－10月30日。

香港奧沙畫廊，《平行世界》，2011年12月10日－2012年1月8日。

2012年

上海民生現代美術館，《開放的肖像》，3月11日－5月20日。展覽畫冊。

中心A（溫哥華亞洲當代藝術國際中心），《黃燈：中國新媒體》，3月17日－4月28日。

義大利普拉多Luigi Pecci當代藝術中心，《1988－2011年，中國移動影像》，4月22日－8月9日。

深圳OCT當代藝術中心，深圳雕塑雙年展：《偶然的信息：藝術不是一個體系，也不是一個世界》，5月12日－8月31日。展覽畫冊。

首爾國家現代與當代美術館，《動：1960年迄今的藝術與舞蹈》，6月6日－8月12日。

倫敦海沃美術館，南堤藝術中心，《藝術的改變：來自中國的新方向》，9月7日－12月9日。展覽畫冊。

澳洲坎培拉國家肖像館，《人！中國當代藝術的肖像畫》，2012年9月13日－2013年2月17日。展覽畫冊。

上海美術館，《景像2012——中國新藝術》，9月15－25日。

廣州廣東美術館，廣州三年展：《見所未見》，9月28日－12月16日。

布宜諾思聖·馬丁文化中心，移動音像雙年展，10月29日－11月4日。

2013年

沙迦藝術基金會，沙迦雙年展：《重現：繪製新文化地圖》，3月13日－5月13日。

慕尼黑電視電影大學，Kino der Kunst，4月24－28日。

威尼斯軍械庫（由成都當代美術館策劃），《歷史之路——威尼斯雙年展與中國當代藝術二十年》，6月1日－11月24日。

北京今日美術館，《「2013馬爹利非凡藝術人物」獲獎藝術家作品展覽》，6月16－30日。

澳洲霍巴特古今藝術博物館，《紅皇后》，2013年6月18日－2014年9月15日。

上海當代藝術博物館，《時代肖像——當代藝術三十年》，8月18日－11月10日。

獎項

1984年

《親愛的媽媽》於《第六屆全國美術作品展覽》獲得金獎，北京中國美術館（現中國國家美術館）。

2008年2月

紐約當代藝術基金會年度藝術家獎。

2011年12月

北京今日美術館，瑞信·2011今日藝術獎。

2013年6月

北京今日美術館，馬爹利非凡藝術人物。

展覽策劃

2009年

北京尤倫斯藝術中心，《何岸：是什麼讓我理解我的知道？》，2月7日－3月22日。展覽畫冊。

由呂斯喬協助整理。

大事紀

桂嘉慧彙整編撰

1958年

10月28日，汪建偉出生於中華人民共和國南方的四川省遂寧市。

1958—1966年

汪建偉的父母親都是軍人，他生長在一個典型的軍人家庭，並在軍營裡渡過他的整個童年。通常將之稱爲「部隊大院」。

1966—1976年

包含主席毛澤東在內的中國共產黨（簡稱中共）領導人在1966年發起無產階級文化大革命（簡稱文革），標榜「破四舊」（破除舊思想、舊文化、舊風俗、舊習慣）。文革目的旨在意識形態上，為中共把所謂的資產主義和反動份子從中國清除乾淨，在政治意義上，肅清毛在中共黨內的政敵，將其定位為「資產階級反動路線」的代表。文革大規模造成加諸於數以百萬計人民身上的政治迫害，文物古蹟更遭到狂熱的高校及大學學生組成的造反團體「紅衛兵」所破壞。全國的學校和大學在大量號召青年批鬥傳統的、資產階級的、缺乏革命精神的價值觀動員中，進行停課。其中汪建偉的家庭也受到強烈的衝擊，他的父親受到暴力批鬥，並被送往農村接受改造。

1968年

著名的「上山下鄉，接受貧下中農再教育」運動，將成千上萬的學生送到鄉間接受農民的改造。

1974年

汪建偉的父親解禁後，從農場返回家園，與家人團圓，重新恢復工作。

1975年

汪建偉高中畢業後，被送到農村接受貧下中農再教育，他在閒暇之餘會從鄉間騎腳踏車到城裡，私下向一位在當地川劇工作的舞臺設計師學習繪畫，開始了寫實繪畫的基本訓練。在此同時，他通過被禁止的書籍接觸到俄羅斯的文學和繪畫。

1976年

9月9日，毛澤東卒。一個月後，常被描述為「十年浩劫」的文革，隨著同為中共中央政治局委員的張春橋、江青、姚文元及王洪文等四人所組成的「四人幫」，以企圖分裂且推翻黨中央的罪名羈押後，宣告終結。毛死後，華國鋒被指派為中共國家主席。

1977—1983年

經過兩年的再教育，汪建偉被送往部隊，作為解放軍的工程兵和作戰參謀，駐軍在北京南邊的河北省清河縣營區。汪在部隊的工作是負責繪製軍事地圖，在從軍期間，他沒有從事任何創作。

1978年

鄧小平被復職為中共副主席，正式開除四人幫黨籍，並引進改革政策。

在1978到1992年間，鄧小平作為一個國家的最高領導人，他進一步推動他的開放政策，鼓勵直接外資以促進中國經濟，並提供更多自由的國際文化交流。

1978—1979年

「西單民主牆」在北京展開，接近天安門市中心的西單街磚牆上，貼著中國人民宣洩著不滿，且公開表述批評政府的民運海報，在此，數以百計的海報，也就是大字報被張貼。這項運動在輿論轉向批判鄧小平後，急遽地來到尾聲，鄧小平隨後將西安牆的活動領袖以反革命罪逮捕。

1983年

汪建偉從軍隊退伍後，經介紹認識了作為軍隊護士的朱光燕（1956年生於北京），相識不到一年後，汪娶了朱，但由於嚴格的居住地管理政策，也就是戶口登記制度，將近七年的時間，他們分居兩地。當汪的戶口簿將他與他雙親在成都（四川首都）的居住處綁在一起時，朱的登記地卻是在北京。

1983—1985年

汪建偉由部隊轉業，被分發到隸屬成都市美術館的成都畫院，作爲一位保管兼資料員。在此，他大量地接觸到西方藝術畫冊，並開始臨摹國外藝術家的作品。他企盼受到其他藝術家作品的薰陶，找到作畫的時間。在這之前，汪建偉僅接受過很少的正式繪畫訓練，作為畫院的職員，他找到學習藝術和檢視他在成都的生活的時機，這段期間，他創作了一系列描繪當地茶館老主顧們的素描和速寫，這些作品將在五年後的1988年，成為奠定他一系列畫作的根基——也就是《茶館》系列（1988—1990年）。

1983年

汪建偉在1983年創作了《親愛的媽媽》，這件作品革新了四川畫派學院式的寫實風格，這是一種由四川美術學院學生發展而成的畫風，著重日常生活的細節，描繪帶著抑鬱及詩意的自然景觀。《親愛的媽媽》表現一個解放軍軍人在戰壕裡，起草著給他母親的書信。這是藝術家根據1979年中越戰爭期間，親身體驗的一場軍事演習來進行創作。《親愛的媽媽》獨特地記錄在中國疾速變化的時空背景下，藝術家的情感經歷。在當時，汪建偉深受俄羅斯「巡迴畫派」的影響，這個由俄羅斯寫實畫家組成的藝術運動誕生於帝國藝術學院，他們以富人文主義敘事風格的繪畫聞名，將個人獨特的感受和記憶，與重大的歷史和社會事件相互結合。汪建偉在這件畫作中，關注包含包括了瓦西里·伊萬諾維奇·蘇里科夫（Vasily Ivanovic Surikov，1848—1916年）與伊利亞·葉非莫維奇·列賓（Ilya Yefimovich Repin，1844—1930年）在內的俄羅斯歷史油畫家，他們以相似的戲劇化寫實風格，捕捉在十九世紀晚期俄羅斯的人民生活和歷史。

1984年

汪建偉的作品《親愛的媽媽》在舉辦於中國美術館（現中國國家美術館）的《第六屆全國美術作品展覽》上，獲得油畫組金獎，這個展覽囊括來自中國年輕的畢業生及有地位的藝術家的作品。對汪來說，這個經驗讓他對「藝術家」這個稱號的代表意義產生了質疑。

汪建偉在中國北方的城市–瀋陽，第一次遇見了他後來的老師鄭勝天。當時，鄭剛從美國回到中國，帶回大量關於西方現代藝術的資訊，這是汪第一次經過記錄圖像認識了裝置藝術和環境藝術，這對他產生了極為深遠的影響。

1985—1989年

隨著與當代國際藝術界的接觸和交流的提升，刺激「85新潮美術運動」這個全國性前衛藝術運動的生成。相較於現行狹隘、由黨所認可的官方藝術與文化政策，它追求實驗藝術和人文主義，倡導個人色彩和非官方藝術。這個自發性的前衛藝術團體和個人組織展覽開枝散葉，舉辦研討會，並為中國藝術寫下具國際視野的新觀念和方向。

1985年

汪建偉在國家美術館觀看了由羅森伯格海外文化交流處（Rauschenberg Overseas Culture Interchange, ROCI）舉辦的展覽，接觸了羅伯·羅森伯格（Robert Rauschenberg）的作品。此展吸引超過三十萬人前來參觀，展品有在中國前所未見的大型平面壁畫《中國夏宮》（1982—1983年）和代表裝置藝術、平面藝術、綜合繪畫和實驗劇場的作品，這個展對催生中國前衛藝術，特別對裝置藝術的培養起了顯著的作用。

1985—1987年

汪建偉在位於浙江省杭州市的浙江美術學院（現中國美術學院）油畫系攻讀研究所，汪在學院就讀期間，多數時間都在圖書館內，閱讀在他成長過程中長期被中國學術教育摒除的西方文學與哲學。存在主義哲學家如尚·保羅·沙特（Jean Paul Sartre）、阿爾貝·卡繆（Albert Camus）與豪爾赫·路易斯·博爾赫斯（Jorge Luis Borges）對他產生巨大的影響。

1987年

汪建偉畢業於位在杭州市的浙江美術學院（現中國美院）。

1988—1990年

汪建偉製作了《茶館》系列（1988—1990年），畫作中描繪年長的居民們在當地茶館內品茶及消磨時間的景況，他採用研究、觀察、寫生並與其互動的記錄式手段，創造了一種成為他標誌性的作品風格，本質上，他是對由成都茶館內個體所形成的微型社會進行文化研究。雖然汪一直到1999年才接觸法蘭西斯·培根（Francis Bacon）的作品，他們對時間的消逝與物體的運動，在視覺上的處理手法卻是相似的。

1989年

85美術新潮運動啟發重要的中國新藝術展——1989年於北京中國美術館舉辦的《中國現代藝術展》，這是第一個由國家級機構全國性地審視非官方的中國藝術，也是中國第一個不是博物館或學術官員，而是由藝評家所策劃的展覽。這個展覽建立在現代藝術中以裝置藝術和觀念藝術的形式在內的實驗性手段，是為其在中國文化中的新發展。在兩星期的展期間，該展曾兩次在預定閉展日前被強制關閉。當局官員譴責它是「資產階級自由主義」的典型案例。

同年，中共改革派胡耀邦於四月的辭世為民主示威活動凝聚動力，三個月中，示威行列橫越中國的多個城市，提出包括民主和自由的幾點要求。這項運動在北京的發展最為極端，城市宣布部分戒嚴。6月3日，中國人民解放軍和中國人民武裝警察部隊進入天安門廣場清除示威者，直到6月4日，他們主要針對學生抗議者的武力鎮壓，是在中國近代史上最為殘酷和血腥的，這個事件是中國政治的一個轉捩點，中共有效地清除改革派，並且重新將焦點轉向於中國的經濟繁榮而非政治改革。

1990年

更嚴格且保守的管制是作為回應1989年事件的結果，在中國的前衛藝術活動銷聲匿跡。與此同時，中國當代藝術也得到了更多來自國際的注目。

汪建偉與一個位於北京的藝術小組（新刻度小組，其成員包括陳少平、顧德新和王魯炎）相識，該觀念藝術組織的實驗手段，在眾多領域與汪建偉的知識整合方法產生了共識，並在實踐藝術的手段和作品製作的方法上受到彼此的影響。

1991年

在北京民族文化宮，汪建偉舉辦了他的第一次個人展覽，展出他的《茶館》系列，在這個系列中，汪探索對捕捉時間的興趣，並對中國傳統文化、社會關係、行為和社群進行解構，反映他在藝術上作為一個社會分析者的興趣。此後，汪建偉考慮將他實踐藝術的手段拓展至裝置藝術與觀念藝術，他更大量地接觸藝術、科學和哲學以作為他的方法論，藉此重新思索研究中國未來的新方法與策略。

1992年

汪建偉開始對灰色系統，也就是所謂的灰色系統理論產生興趣，這套理論是由中國數學家鄧聚龍於1982年所提出，是一個利用不確定及少量的信息研究問題的方法，因為這樣不確定的系統共存於自然中，灰色分析理論運用於監測自然科學領域中的變化，在中國和國際學者之間蔚為風行。到了90年代，中國開始從區域經濟規劃到農業、水利和氣象預測上，廣泛地使用灰色系統。

汪建偉在他自已的家裡，製作了第一個觀念作品《文件》（1992年），汪意圖用《文件》啓動那些被他定為「灰色地帶」或是「夾雜、過渡」的空間，結合藝術和科學的實驗過程產生預測信號。

1993年

汪建偉在使用視頻、文字和裝置的裝置作品《事件、過程、狀態》持續討論「灰色系統」，這件作品在香港藝術中心展出。同時，他開始閱讀科學巨匠尼爾斯·波爾（NielsHenrik David Bohr）和阿爾伯特·愛因斯坦（Albert Einstein）所撰寫的科學文章，這轉變了他對藝術的思考和實踐藝術的手段。他用新的實驗模型，試圖模糊藝術、科學和哲學，個人和社會之間的界限，並喚起複雜的社會實驗與經驗。

1993—1994年

受到一本由生物學家編寫，關於作物生長的書籍所啟發，汪建偉回到他曾「上山下鄉」的農村，與當地農夫在一塊農業用地上進行爲期一年的行為藝術，在《循環·種植》（1993—1994年）中，汪建偉和農民通過持續性的勞動，他們準備、種植並收割新品種的小麥，經歷整個耕作週期。這件作品說明汪建偉關注藝術作為生物研究和社會活動的實驗室，與他不停地探索用「過程」作為他作品不可或缺的要素。

1995年

汪建偉參加了南韓第一屆光州雙年展，這是一個以《超越界限》作為主題的第一個亞洲當代藝術雙年展，參展裝置作品《再生產》（1995年）中，結合了視頻和裝置。

1997年

汪建偉對空間和語言的興趣驅使他製作了錄像作品《生產》（1997年），這件作品是他早期的代表作，將日常生活與文化生產空間並置。作品記錄在四川省七個城市選定的公共空間內的社會互動。用和社會學調查相似的製作手法，汪研究在公共空間裡的私人對談如何衍生出個人空間，以及這樣複雜的關係如何重疊到日常生活的空間裡。

汪建偉參加舉辦在荷蘭布雷達的《又一次長征》群展，這是第一個在西方，將焦點著重在90年代中國觀念和裝置藝術的展覽，在展上，他遇見擔任第十屆卡塞爾文獻展的策展人凱瑟琳·大衛（Catherine David），此當代藝術展每五年在德國卡塞爾舉辦一次。

該年六月，汪建偉和馮夢波是中國第一個受邀參加卡賽爾文獻展的藝術家，汪建偉展出了錄像作品《生產》（1997年）。

由侯瀚如及漢斯·奧瑞奇·奧柏里斯特（Hans-Ulrich Obrist）共同策劃的《移動的城市》十一月在奧地利維也納分離派美術館（Wiener Secession）揭開序幕，該展主題為「二十一世紀轉向之際的亞洲當代藝術」，展覽在世界各地巡迴，中國參展藝術家包含蔡國強、黃永砯、汪建偉和張培力等人。

1998–1999年

汪建偉製作紀錄影片《生活在別處》，檢視中國城市在農村地區侵占土地的問題。影片跟隨一群居住在成都市郊的農民們，把他們的土地賣給了計劃在當地開發豪華別墅的建商，在建案失敗後，回到荒廢未完成的豪宅內的生活。

2000年

汪建偉參加在上海美術館舉辦，主題為《海上·上海》的第三屆上海雙年展，由侯瀚如領軍，包含清水敏男、張晴、李旭、和方增先在內的策展團隊，除了傳統的藝術媒材之外，《海上·上海》是第一個有新媒體藝術家和國際藝術家參與的中國雙年展。

汪建偉從他記錄式的作品形態出發，創造結合視覺藝術和新形態實驗劇場的作品。參加比利時布魯塞爾藝術節（Kunstenfestivaldesarts），和英國布萊頓藝術節（Brighton Festival）的作品《屏風》（2000年）視藝術與社會、責任與自由思考間沒有區隔，呈現一個非線性敘事的劇場表演和反思歷史的錄像作品，這是他第一個多媒體表演藝術作品，也是他第一次在作品中雇用演員。場景、影像裝置、聲音裝置與文字及演員們的演出，皆根據現代與傳統的中國與西方戲劇、西方當代舞蹈和多媒體藝術實踐。

2002年
汪建偉參加第二十五屆聖保羅雙年展。

2003年
汪建偉在明尼阿波里斯市沃克藝術中心擔任駐村藝術家，他結合多媒體裝置與當地的工人共同完成了現場行為表演作品《移動的味道》。此外，汪參與了在沃克藝術中心舉辦的《緯度如何變為形式：藝術在全球化的時代》國際群展，展出《生活在別處》。這個展覽透徹地檢視空間感知的轉換如何影響當代藝術的製作，及其吸收文化的過程。

2004年
汪建偉參加第五十屆威尼斯雙年展。
中國和法國文化部共同在巴黎龐畢度藝術中心舉辦《那麼，中國？》（Alors, la Chine?），其中展出了汪建偉的作品《我的視覺檔案》（2003年）。
同年，汪建偉參加了法國秋季國際戲劇節，在龐畢度藝術中心呈現《儀式》，這是一件使用劇場、表演和新媒體的大型多媒體作品。《儀式》探索特別是在中國對歷史的解讀與其對理解今日現實的關係。在這件作品中，舞臺成為一個過去和當下的交匯點，每一個人（從演員到觀眾）都被給予表演或是演說的角色。

2005年
汪建偉製作了他第一部著重探討時間的影像裝置作品《飛鳥不動》。

2006年
汪建偉創作《閃躲》，作品由兩部分在滬申畫廊呈現，阿根廷作家豪爾赫·路易斯·波赫士（Jorge Luis Borges）將現實和日常生活理解為一系列未知的連結，《閃躲》這件作品源自他的著作《幻想動物學教科書》（The Book of Imaginary Beings）。《閃躲》通過由建築碎片和抽象的人體外形，與一件充斥從卡拉OK到火車站再到醫院，空間和活動重複交疊的視頻所組合而成的大型雕塑體，探索時間和空間重組的觀念。這件作品展現了汪建偉持續對戲劇空間的探索，他用環境與行動間複雜的互動，以反映中國當今生活中的歡愉、經濟建設和疾病。

2007年
汪建偉在德國柏林Hebbel am Ufer劇院和中國深圳OCT當代藝術中心，呈現多媒體劇場作品《徵兆》，他並在德國柏林Hebbel am Ufer劇院舉辦個展《交叉感染》。

2008年
作為第二十九屆夏季奧林匹克運動會主辦國，中國邀請國際團體造訪北京。
汪建偉在上海證大美術館展出作品《人質》，這是一件因地制宜的大型裝置，組合一系列大型機械化的雕塑，和顯然要噴發、熔化、並且（或者）自我吞噬的科技，表現工業衰竭，與認為中國變成世界舞臺重要成員的想法；還有一件伴隨裝置的錄像，重現在文革時期群居的日常生活。《人質》討論多層面的社會現象，思索夢想和野心在中國快速經濟繁榮、工業化及現代化的當下，是如何被知識、歷史和意識形態，這樣既有的體制和權力所挾持。

2010年
以「城市，讓生活更美好」做為口號的上海世博會，共計有192個國家參與，是至今最大型、最昂貴，也是最多參加國的世界博覽會。
汪建偉在《歡迎來到真實的沙漠》（2010年）作品中，使用了表演、動畫、戲劇影片製作和五頻道的視頻影像，作品是架構在一個青春期男孩和父母從中國鄉村搬到城市後，沈迷於電玩的故事，男孩逐漸在線上虛擬的真實中滯留，現實生活和想像的邊界變得模糊不清，並導致他在商店街上殺人致死。《歡迎來到真實的沙漠》原先的構想是一齣在鏡頭前表演的劇，而這些影片和動畫，後來都成為現場彩排演出的佈景。從北京到蘇黎世年度的國際戲劇與表演藝術節－蘇黎世戲劇節（Zürcher Theater Spektakel）、日內瓦年度的跨界表演藝術節－日內瓦藝術節（La Bâtie Festival de Genève），及以巴塞爾作根據地，致力推動國際文化交流，並在2010年呈現中國的年度瑞士藝術節－文化風景線（Culturescapes），進行了為期近一個月共八場的巡迴演出。這件作品對汪建偉作為一位藝術家來說是非常重要的，在事件成為表演的前提下，強調藝術製作是一場不歇息的排演，持續的練習過程變成主軸的哲學。

2011年
北京尤倫斯當代藝術中心（Ullens Center for Contemporary Art）舉辦了汪建偉迄今最大型的個人計劃和展覽《黃燈》。這個浸濡式的裝置作品包含了影片、劇場、表演、裝置、雕塑、繪畫和攝影。不像他早先的作品僅在表演、錄像和影片中運用戲劇、過程和排演，《黃燈》橫越這個框架，重申在汪的作品中過程和排演的概念，在裝置和繪畫也都佔有不可或缺的地位。這個作品以四個章節在四個月內呈現，並以第四章（最終章）作為閉幕表演的形式，邀請觀眾重複地回到這個場域內體驗作品。《黃燈》的目的、形式和觀者如何參與並與當代藝術間的互動，改變了當代藝術的傳統架構。

2013年
《歡迎來到真實的沙漠》內使用的五頻影像，在第十一屆夏爾迦雙年展中展出。
汪建偉在北京長征空間的個展《……或者事件導致了每一個無效的結果》（2013年），展題引自一行1897年的詩句《骰子一擲不會改變偶然》（Un Coup de dés jamais n'abolira le hasard），這首詩是法國詩人暨評論家斯凡特·馬拉美對解構與隱喻的實驗。展覽作品有繪畫、雕塑、和不使用在現場表演或錄像播放的裝置作品。汪專注在展內個別作品彼此間的連結和互動關係上，展覽裝置被視為一個整體，但是每一個作品也可以個別獨立。在一幅抽象畫作銅色背景前的黃色正方體，放大再現一個微型物處在培養皿的咖啡色液體內，揭示了抽象的科學形式。三聯屏的寫實繪畫裝載了抽象交疊的瞬間。他們共同被認為是從寫實主義到抽象主義、抽象主義再到寫實主義的反覆翻載。汪用木柴、金屬和橡膠以裁切、接合、層疊和塑形的方式，推疊出紮實的架構，這樣勞力密集的生產過程被視為一場排演。在形式上，不論結合或分開，展覽的構成品探討了未知和潛能的概念，表現時間和運動。在此同時，作品通過實質的形體，和真實體現一個具時效性的反覆過程和藝術的持續製作，被認為是排演的一部份。

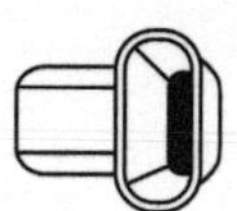

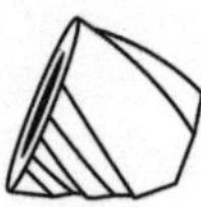

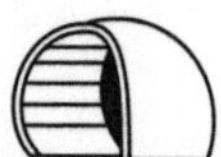